To my honored friend
Jacob Davis on his
83rd birthday שלי לכבוד ביאור
שלי לכבוד ביאור ז״ל

Jacob Davis
4 Oct 1950

from Dr. Freehof

PREACHING
THE BIBLE

Sermons for Sabbaths
and
High Holy Days

PREACHING THE BIBLE

Sermons for Sabbaths
and
High Holy Days

◈

Solomon B. Freehof

KTAV PUBLISHING HOUSE, INC.

NEW YORK

Library of Congress Cataloging in Publication Data

Freehof, Solomon Bennett, 1892-
    Preaching the Bible.

    1. Sermons, American--Jewish authors. 2. Sermons,
Jewish--United States. 3. High Holy Day sermons.
I. Title.
BM740.2.F64   296.4'2   74-889
ISBN 0-87068-244-X

© COPYRIGHT 1974

SOLOMON FREEHOF

MANUFACTURED IN THE UNITED STATES OF AMERICA

TABLE OF CONTENTS

BIBLE SERMONS

HIGH HOLYDAY SERMONS

BIBLE SERMONS

I

ON BROTHERHOOD

The best known Bible verse on brotherhood is from the Prophet Malachi. It is in the form of a question: "Have we not all one Father? Has not one God created us all?" The verse is often quoted but, actually, almost always misunderstood. The famous verse from Malachi, "Have we not one Father," does not quite say what the average person thinks it says. The words themselves are clear enough, but the mood of the statement is far different from what it is usually taken to mean. The words, "Have we not all one Father? Has not one God created us all?" are generally understood to be a triumphant declaration of human kinship.

But the average person does not quote the second half of the statement. The full statement is as follows: "Have we not all one Father? Has not one God created us all? Then why do we deal treacherously, one man against his neighbor?" The emphasis, the weight of the statement, is on this second half. This passage, therefore, is not a joyous assertion, but is a cry of anguish. Actually, the first half of the statement is conditional. What the prophet meant was this: Since we have all one Father, how comes it that we are so mean and harsh and brutal to each other? The passage is a protest against man's ignoring of what all men should have understood. The

Sermon delivered February 21, 1960

1

verse is an outcry at the bitter fact that we, by our own willfulness and blindness, have turned this world of ours which could be so beautiful and brotherly into an abode of treachery and hate. So the verse is the prophetic cry of anguish: Why, if we have one Father, do we deal so treacherously, one with the other?

This gloom, born of the prophet's disappointment, has a general psychological reality. The fact is that it is the same question which we ask ourselves constantly. It is the question that almost breaks the heart of a child when he first meets hate. It is the question that shocks an adult. When we meet someone who despises a whole section of humanity and who reveals it in an unguarded sentence, we ask Malachi's question: Why do we deal treacherously, one with another?

Why, indeed? For many deep reasons; for reasons that are hard to eradicate. For historical reasons, first of all, because we remember the wrong things out of the past. For sociological reasons, too. One group in society hates another group and ascribes its own miseries to someone else's sin. For psychological reasons, because we are so often thwarted in life; so often frustrated, the only relief we have is to have somebody to hate. There are historical, sociological, psychological reasons, all deep-rooted, for human treachery, one man against another.

If that is the case, the Bible seems to be too idealistic when it brings us so many grand assertions on human unity and human brotherhood. The Bible is indeed idealistic; but it is also, in considerable measure, realistic. Not only does it point the distant goal, but marks out the road; a rocky road, of course, but at least a road towards the goal. And the great verses in Scripture, besides that tragic outcry of the Prophet Malachi, may be looked upon as guidance verses on the difficult path to human rediscovery that we really belong together.

2

When we discuss fundamental Biblical ideas, it must always be understood that the task is difficult because the Bible is not philosophical; that it to say, it is not philosophical in the same way that Plato or Aristotle are philosophical. Those great Greeks would pick a theme, God, nature, matter or thought. They would discuss it theoretically, analyze its implications, and fit it into the broad context of human thought. Such is the theoretical, philosophical analysis of an idea.

Philosophy of this type does not exist in the Bible. The Bible is not theoretical. The Bible is not verbally analytical. The Bible, even though it is not philosophical, has a philosophy, but its philosophy is always implicit; it is hidden in a story, it is implied in a sentence from a prophet. We must look for the philosophy beneath the surface whenever we want to study the Bible analytically.

Let us note an implicit philosophy hidden in a story: The Bible has selected as the very beginning of the Sacred Scripture, the story of Creation, which culminates in the creation of man, of Adam. The first man is given the name of Adam because Adam means man or humanity. What is the implication of the story? Be sure that the rabbis of the Mishnah who lived at the beginning of the era were closer to the authors of the Bible than we, and they understood its implied philosophical intents better than we do.

The rabbis in the Mishnah discuss the question of the Creation of Adam, Man, and ask the question: Why did God create man as an individual? That is not a trivial question. He created all the other species as whole species. He did not create one lion. He created the lions. He did not create one bird. He created all the birds. He could have created all of mankind. Why did He create only one person? That is the rabbinical question. When they ask, they always have their answer ready.

The answer they give is that God's purpose was that no one shall ever say, "My blood is better than yours. I descend from a nobler descent." So God created mankind in one person, Adam, which means Man. This is the philosophy implicit behind the Creation story selected for the very beginning of Scripture.

If that is the case, why do we speak of "the chosen people"? Jews are constantly accused of believing that they are the choice of mankind, God's "chosen people." But it cannot possibly be that "the chosen people" means what people say it means. It cannot be a boast. Ask yourself, how does Scripture deal with the Jews? Does it flatter them and thus encourage them to racial or national pride? On the contrary, Scripture is always denouncing them, giving them no rest, harrying them. It would seem that these are not the superior people. They are the *victim* people of Scripture.

Chosen people means that we are people appointed to a task, a task which we never asked for, a burden placed upon us to represent the pure, ethical, monotheistic faith in the world. We did not ask for this. We do not boast of it. But that is what it means, and the proof is the way the prophets deal with it.

The prophets understand the universal implication of Genesis, and they are aware that sometimes the people will think "the chosen people" means that they are choice people. The prophet is always careful to dispel this illusion. The Prophet Amos says: "You think you are superior because I brought you out of the land of Egypt? But I also brought the Philistines out of Crete and the Aramaeans out of Kir." Then the prophet brings up the sharpest contrast one can imagine, the black Ethiopians. He says: "You are like the Ethiopians to me, O House of Israel, no better, no worse." The Prophet Amos is simply repeating the philosophy implied in the story of Genesis.

4

The Prophet Isaiah expresses the thought in another way. He does not discuss racial difference. He discusses political and historical differences. Let us imagine the prophet asking himself, "Who was the greatest historical enemy of the people of Israel, even before it ever got to the Promised Land?" Obviously, the Egyptians who enslaved them for four hundred years. Furthermore, the Egyptians constantly invaded Palestine and allowed it no peace. Possibly a rival to the Egyptians for Israel's most hated enemy would be the Assyrians, the ferocious Nazis of the ancient day; the tiger-people, the Assyrians who knew no mercy; the Assyrians who came down "like a wolf on the fold." The Prophet Isaiah says, at the end of the twentieth chapter as he addresses Egypt, the hated Egypt, and as he addressed Assyria, the hated Assyria: "O blessed be Egypt, My people. Blessed be Assyria, the work of My hands, as Israel is My possession." All three people are mentioned as one. This mood is basic Scripture.

If that is basic to Scripture, then we would think that an increase of Bible reading would bring an increase of brotherhood. Not necessarily. People get from the Bible what they bring to the Bible. The "Bible Belt" is not the most liberal part of the United States. Much depends on *how* you read the Bible. If you read it for fanatical purposes to find verses that your sect is right and all other sects are wrong, the Bible can only increase the fanaticism that you bring to it. Or if you read the Bible in order to attempt to predict "the second coming," the Bible adds to the madness that you bring to it.

It is not merely *reading* the Bible that would help our embittered age. It is discovering the depths of the Bible. There is an obligation upon liberal ministers who are not worshippers of every Bible verse. Let them not waste their time commenting on the headlines or getting into the

5

headlines. Let them not waste their time reviewing dramas from the pulpit, or novels. If they want to discuss literary matters, let them set aside another day for it.

The main duty of a liberal minister from the pulpit is to explain and to preach the *liberal* meaning of Scripture. It is the liberal understanding of Scripture that the world needs. Once you get below the verses to their sub-strata, once you get to the bottom of the Bible, you find that the foundation of Scripture is fraternity. Basic Bible is brotherhood. Let the eloquent, liberal preachers of every group devote their time to preaching basic Bible. This is the need of the age, not shouting twisted verses that twisted minds twist still further. Once we get into people's hearts the basic meaning of Scripture, what is behind Genesis, the Creation story, what Amos said, what Isaiah said, then we increase what we need most today: the conviction of human kinship.

In the old West there were pitched battles between sheep herders and cattlemen. They used to fight over whose flocks or herds should graze on certain sections of the range. Such disputes over pasturage have been going on since the beginning of time. It is older even than the building of cities. Nomads fought with each other over pasturage. There is no doubt that such disputes over pasturage have had an effect on world law. But it has never had an effect on the world's literature or philosophy. These millions of disputes over pasturage seem never to have left any cultural deposit, with the exception of one such dispute.

One battle over pasturage has given us one of the greatest verses on brotherhood. It was an old fight, thirty-five hundred years old. Father Abraham was a shepherd. Lot, his nephew, was a shepherd. They each had flocks, and their herdsmen happened to bring both flocks to the same place, and there was a battle over pasturage. Then Abraham said these grand words to Lot: "Let there not be strife between you and me for we men are brothers." This is not a cry of anguish, as were Malachi's tragic words. This is a plea, a frank proposal. "Let there not be any strife" means, "Make an effort to achieve a change. Conduct yourself so as to avoid strife." This applies to inter-religious discussions. Avoid debates on religious matters because it is almost impossible to have a debate on religious matters which remains calm and brotherly. Sometimes we think we can debate logically, but we discover that behind the mask of logic there is a face twisted full of emotion. When two religious doctrines confront each other in dispute, it is not logic dealing with logic; that is to say, it is that only superficially. It is emotion against emotion. Then, "Let there be no strife." Let us not debate each other's theology.

Would there be any sense in a Jew discussing with a Christian the matter of the Trinity, and asking how there can be three Gods that are yet not three? It seems illogical to a Jew and he thinks he is arguing on the basis of logic, but actually he is touching the deepest sentiment and stirring up the most bitter indignation. Or suppose a Christian says to us, "What is the sense of your Jewish refusal to send out missionaries? Why are you so clannish? If you have something to teach, do as we do. We spend millions of dollars sending missionaries to China, to India, to Africa, and you do not send anyone." How can we explain it to them? We do have some logic on the matter.

We do not missionize because we believe that Christians are "saved" without having their Christianity destroyed. We do not need to convert anybody. People do not need to be converted. But it is hard to explain that. Our habit of not converting is also rooted in our family past. We were a beleaguered clan, and that fact helped create our attitude. If somebody wants to discuss that subject with us, it starts with logic and ends with quarrels.

This emotionalism in inter-religious debate suggests, perhaps, that the verse of Abraham, "Let there be no strife between us, for we are brothers," can be interpreted somewhat differently. He may mean to say that in spite of the fact that we are brothers, or because of the fact that we *are* brothers, there is a greater likelihood of there being strife, since brothers often quarrel more hotly than strangers. So let us be doubly careful to avoid strife because, you see, we are brothers and being brothers makes us touchy when we argue.

Let me illustrate: Last week I was interviewed for the radio by a young Christian minister in behalf of the Council of Churches. Among various questions on brotherhood, he asked me this: Is there any anti-Semitism in other lands besides Christendom? That question was disturbing because the fact of the matter is that the Jews lived in India, the Malabar Coast, for centuries and never had any religious trouble. There were Jewish settlements in China, in Kaifeng-fu, for centuries and they never had any trouble with the Taoists. They lived in the Mohammedan world with comparatively little trouble.

The real anti-Semitism was always in the Christian world. What should I have said over the radio about it? Should I have explained that most of the hideous accusations against Jews could only have arisen in the poisoned folk consciousness of the Christian world? It is a painful fact. Jews were killed by the tens of thousands on the charge that they needed the blood of Christian children to bake into the matzoh. How did the populace get such an idea? Ask yourself, where did such an idea come from? It could not have occurred to a Mohammedan. It is only because the Christians believed that the wafer and the wine of the host was converted by the miracle of the Mass

8

into the body and the blood of Jesus; therefore they think of matzoh as turning into blood and wine into blood and flesh. This notion could only have come from the folk consciousness of ignorant Christians. So my answer to this minister might well have been, "There has been almost no anti-Semitism anywhere in the world, compared to Christian anti-Semitism. The ugliest anti-Semitic accusations could only have come out of the Christian consciousness."

Suppose I had answered that way? I am not asking whether the answer would have been politic; of course, it would not have been. But what is logically wrong with the answer? After all, it *is* a fact that the bulk of anti-Semitism could only have arisen in the Christian world. If it is a fact, why should not the truth be stated? The answer is that it *is* the truth, but it is not the *deep* truth, it is not the signicant truth.

The significant truth is this: The strife has been bitter precisely because we are brothers; precisely because we and the Christians share the Bible. We can have no disputes with the Confucianists in China; we have nothing in common. And we can have very little dispute with the Mohammedans because they have the Koran, an entirely different book.

But we and the Christians share the Old Testament and fight over every important verse. It is our kinship that is the source of our quarrel. That, in effect, was my answer to him. I said that Judaism and Christianity are brother religions, and brothers fight more bitterly than strangers. That is the basic truth and, therefore, what Abraham meant in that pasturage quarrel was, "See, we are brothers. Let us be extra careful with each other." "Let there be no strife among us." So must all of us conduct ourselves. Avoid such disputes, generally religious disputes; they can never be peaceable.

9

The Bible is especially realistic when it deals with family matters. In no ancient literature is the family described in more actual life colors than in the Bible. It is true the Bible describes the ideal of the family in the Psalms: "Behold, how good and how beautiful it is that brothers dwell together in amity." It has the ideal, but when it needs to describe the reality, it does so frankly.

The most famous family in Scripture is that family from which we are descended, the three generations, Abraham, Isaac, and Jacob. The most important generation is Jacob's twelve children, the twelve tribes. Jacob's other name was Israel. This is truly our family. In describing this family, the Bible tells how the older brothers were murderously jealous of the young Joseph, their father's favorite, and how brutally they treated him. But the full story of the family, then, ensues. The conclusion is typical of all families. The family often begins with quarrelsomeness in its early years, but ends up in reconciliation at the end. The most beautiful thing about a family story is that it usually finds itself in the sunset years, when people need each other most. In the early years there are rivalries, misunderstandings. Brothers and sisters quarrel. So the Bible gives the realistic description: quarrelsomeness at the beginning, reconciliation at the end.

In the beginning, in the quarrelsome, jealous, bitter, violent beginning, young Joseph walks to join his brothers where they are pasturing the flock. A stranger meets him on the way. He asks Joseph: "Where are you going?" And Joseph uttered what has become one of the great verses on human brotherhod. He said, "I am seeking my brothers." He spoke words which describe what ultimately unites a family, namely, that beneath the surface of discontent and anger, we are seeking each other. "I seek my brothers."

10

Beneath all the quarrels and disagreements in the world, we believe that the people of the earth are seeking each other. That, I believe, describes what America has meant to the world. People here have had a chance to seek and find each other. Only strangers can really hate each other permanently. People who live near each other may dislike each other at first, but as they get to know each other, they find each other human. They used to tell that in the Middle Ages, when the German Jews, as a result of the Black Death persecutions emigrated into the Slavic lands, every Polish duke had his personal Jewish agent. The Poles were generally anti-Semitic and harsh. When a group of Polish lordlings would get together and get deep into drink, they would talk of all sorts of things and express their hatred of the Jews, of all the Jews, of all the Jews except one. Each lord would defend *his* Jew, and would not allow a single word to be said against him. The one that he knew, he knew to be human and knew to be noble. It is about the unknown people that we say things we ought not to say.

America, then, means that people who for centuries in Europe were kept apart by frontiers, here have met each other as individuals. In Europe, Catholics were in Bavaria, Lutherans in Prussia. Austria was Catholic, Prussia was Lutheran. The Catholics were in Belgium, the Protestants in Holland. The different races lived in different places. But here they came together as individuals. That meant, of course, that old hatreds were brought over too, but it also meant that individuals could meet and each one of us could "seek his brother."

This should be a consolation to all who, like the Prophet Malachi, are anguished about human hatred: The individual contacts are still in the power of every person to make and still are meaningful. Every human being who personally finds another human being of another origin and sees brotherliness in him, has created a nucleus for the future human unity.

This, at least, is one world problem in which our personal life is not shriveled into nothingness. Every human being of every human faith and every type has some friend of another affiliation or origin. This one friendship may seem to be minor compared to the world problem, but it is not minor. Every such personal friendship is an integration nucleus for future decency of humanity.

The Biblical doctrine of brotherhood begins, one might say, with a sigh and ends with a hope. It asks the bitter, living question, why do we deal treacherously with each other. Alas, we know that the roots of human bitterness are deep and the weed is not easily destroyed. But Scripture says to us, that while history justifies our anguish, faith prohibits our despair. Why despair? In the first place, there is the basic teaching of Scripture that will some day find its way into the hearts of men, the grand conviction of human kinship. Then there is always the courtesy of concord, to avoid the bitter, insoluble disputes. "Let there be no strife, we are brothers." And finally there is the quiet, unpretentious quest for friendship: "I seek my brethren."

These are not solutions, but they are steps on a road along which, as our faith persuades us, we can continue to walk towards the clearer light and the greater happiness of mankind.

II
ON FAITH

There is no difficulty in locating any verse in the Bible. The Bible is well indexed. There is a Hebrew index for the Hebrew Bible, of course, and then there are English and German and French indices for Old and New Testament together. These indices are called "Concordances." They are rather remarkable. If you only vaguely remember a verse, if you remember only one word of the verse, you can easily find it. If you are looking for the verse, "A little child shall lead them," then under the word "little," you will find all the sentences in the Old and New Testament that have the word "little." All the sentences that have the word "child" are recorded. All the sentences that have the word "lead" and even "them" are recorded. The verse you seek has six different places in the Concordance. Thus the Concordance will help you find quickly, any verse in Scripture. But the index is also useful for something much deeper, more important, namely, to analyze certain Biblical concepts and to evaluate certain Biblical ideas.

Let me illustrate this with today's theme: We are discussing Faith. You want to know where the word "faith" is used in Scripture, and you turn to the word "faith" in the Concordance and you discover that the word "faith" is used twice in the Old Testament. Then your eye looks down the rest of the column and you discover that in the New Testament it is used about a hundred and fifty times.

Sermon delivered February 28, 1960

13

Immediately, you are confronted with a problem that is more than merely statistical: Does this disproportion in the use of the word "faith" mean that the New Testament, the Christian religion, is much more deeply concerned with the idea of faith than the Old Testament, the Hebrew, the Jewish religion? Why is it that the word "faith" is used only twice in the Old Testament and a hundred and fifty times in the New? As the French say, "It makes one furiously to think." It certainly means something.

Then you look further: Perhaps the Old Testament preferred another word to "faith." You confirm your suspicion when you look up the word "trust." Here you find that with the word "trust" the situation is the reverse. It is used in various forms hundreds of times in the Hebrew Bible but is comparatively rare in the New Testament. Then you realize that you are on the threshold of something important.

Evidently "faith" and "trust," two ideas close to each other are, nevertheless, separate enough to indicate a preference and, perhaps, a significantly revealing preference. Let us see if we can get to it. Why does the New Testament prefer the word "faith," and the Old Testament prefer the word "trust"? The statistics are too heavy to be accidental. We can perhaps approach the thought by another contrast: It is frequently said that Christianity is a religion of creed and Judaism, a religion of deed. The statement, epigrammatic, can be justified to a considerable extent. We find that in every state of Christian development in the long history of Christianity, there is always an attempt to clarify the creed. A Christian is always confronted with a creed which says to him: This you must believe, to be a Christian. There is the Apostle's Creed, the Westminster Confession for Presbyterians, the Augsburg Confession for Lutherans, and so on. All the way through history, it is part of the mood of Christianity to be absolutely clear about what a Christian must believe. Christianity *is* a religion of creed.

14

But, contrariwise, in the Bible there is hardly a clear statement of what you are in duty bound to believe, and in the whole Talmud, which is as big as the Encyclopaedia Britannica, there is very little discussion of what a Jew must believe. But there are endless discussions of what he must *do*, what the commandments are, what the "mitzvos," the duties are. So Judaism is definitely a religion of deed.

Yet that distinction is *too* epigramatic. It is an exaggeration and, therefore, unjust. It is true that Christianity is a religion of creed. Nevertheless, it would be unjust to say that Christianity does not care about your deeds in the life that you live on earth. Judaism is indeed a religion of deed, but it would be incorrect to say that Judaism does not care about your beliefs, the beliefs back of your deeds.

Perhaps the difference between "creed" and "deed" will lead us to the difference between "faith" and "trust." The difference between emphasis on creed or deed is a psychological one, a difference of approach. Christianity believes that if you begin with the right belief, you will come to the right action. Judaism believes that if you begin with the right kind of life, you will arrive at the right belief. In other words, the correct distinction would be that Christianity tends to move from the creed to the deed, and Judaism, from the deed to the creed. That is to say, Christianity prefers to begin the process of human growth by a system of belief, and Judaism tends to start the process with a practical way of life.

This points to the difference that hides behind those statistical facts with which we began. To Christianity, faith means belief. A man who does not believe is called an infidel, a man without faith. So, when asked, what is your faith, the Christian answers: I believe this, that, and that. To Judaism faith is not so much belief as it is a way of life: I build my life, I put my trust in this. Of course, that involves belief, and the Christian belief also involves personal commitment and trust, but it is mainly a question of emphasis. We might say that Christianity emphasizes faith as a grand assertion of what your belief is. Judaism emphasizes faith as a grand assertion of what are your personal commitments, how you live, what does faith lead you to say and to do that, otherwise, you would not say or do. The way to look at "faith" as "trust" in the Bible is, really, to ask the life-question: What does my life demand that trust can help? What part does trust, and trust in what, play in the development of my person as an individual and in the world, and an individual in history?

Abraham Lincoln is said to have made a distinction between character and reputation, and with his usual power to visualize, he said, "Character is the tree and your reputation is the shadow it casts." This is a good metaphor because our reputation can easily change. There are times when people think well of us and times when they think less of us. The shadow shifts, gets larger and smaller with the changing hours of the day. But the tree's roots are firm in the ground. If the tree grows, it grows so slowly that the eye does not see it. The characteristic of character is well-rootedness, firmness.

We might make another distinction, somewhat different from that made by Abraham Lincoln, namely, a distinction not so much between reputation and character as between goodness and character. A person may have goodness and yet have very little character. It depends on how he arrives at his goodness. He may tell the truth, but only after a struggle. He debates with himself, should I or should I not tell the truth this time? Or, he may be generous, but always after an inner battle: Should I give, how much should I give, perhaps I can get out of giving? He ends up generous, but he has a battle to get there. It is possible for a man to make all the good decisions all the

16

way through his life and not have character. Character is that stage of personality where decency is no longer a battle. It is the fixed habit of righteousness.

There is so much goodness and kindness and good intention around us, and so little absolutely trustworthy character. Why is character rare? The reason seems to be that our character develops as a reflection of our environment, and our environment is changeable. How we act depends upon the people we react to. If I deal with deceitful people, I am almost driven to deceive in self-protection. It is very heroic to be truthful in a company of liars. When we are with selfish people, they infect us. Our life mirrors the life around us.

How, then, can we ever get to the stage when we are sure of ourselves, when it is no longer a battle to be good, when we do our work without question, without looking for excuses, when we are decent without having to fight out the question of whether the recipient of our goodness deserves it or not. When are we going to be sure? When are we going to have character? *Only* when we pick the right light to reflect.

As long as we mirror our changeable, human environment, we are changeable and may attain a shaky goodness, but never attain character. When we seek to be the reflection of an *eternal* righteousness, an endless mercy, a ceaseless creativity, when we begin to reflect eternal things, we are under a nobler law than the law of social imitation. The Ten Commandments can build character only if you remember the prologue: "I am the Lord, thy God." If I contemplate an eternal law, an endless justice, then I am walking in another realm. Then people may be as false as they want to; they may not deserve my kindness, but I am not doing it *for them;* I am under another mandate. If I remember the preface of the Ten Commandments, I have the chance to develop an unshaken character that does not depend upon how people act to me.

The grand verse describing that ethical faith, the faith in answer to the human need for moral stability, is: "The righteous lives by his faith."

The classic landscape painters, particularly the dreamy landscape painters like Turner, could concentrate serenity within a small canvas. You look through such a canvas as if you were looking through a window into a peaceful, natural world. A poet, too, can sometimes achieve such a peaceful landscape. The Twenty-Third Psalm is headed, "A Psalm of David." It is a pastoral shepherd's psalm, which produces a landscape, a quiet landscape: "He leadeth me beside still waters. He causes me to lie down in green pastures." There is almost an hypnotic calm about the background scenery of the Twenty-third Psalm of David.

But it is a dream landscape. It does not represent the world as it is. It represents the world as we wish it were, green pastures, still waters. The world as it is, alas, is not lush, green grass. It is thorns and thistles and brambles, and the streams of life are dangerous, snagged, choked currents, not quiet waters. If life is so hostile, how do we find the peace of heart or the peace of soul, the serenity that we need as much as we need ethical stability?

The Buddhists have achieved it in an astounding way by what one might call an heroic reversal of human experience. They insist that all the brambles of life and all the torrential, destructive waters should never disturb the serenity of your soul because they are not real. This life which you think is so real is only a dream. You will wake up from it and you will know it had never existed. Then why be disturbed by sorrows or why, for that matter, be bribed by joy? It is all, as they call it, "Maya," the screen of illusion, and the man who emancipates himself from believing in this world which is only an illusion is the person whose soul is with Buddha, whose soul is at peace. It is

18

an astounding mental achievement to persuade millions of people over scores of generations that the pain that they feel does not really hurt them, and the sorrow that breaks their heart is all imaginary!

This denial of the world is not the way of Judaism, not of our realistic religion, our plain-spoken religion. No, life *is* bitter, full of pain and full of disappointments and full of unexpected shocks. If you ever find serenity, if you need peace of mind, you have to find it in this very world.

Judaism finds it by going behind the facts of nature which are real, to nature's Master. It does not ascribe a will and a malevolence to inanimate objects or to viruses. The only world will is the will of the Creator and, in spite of our experiences, we struggle to believe in His beneficence and we put ourselves in God's hands. There come times in human life and they come often, in which it is a blessing to arrive at the conclusion that you cannot do everything for yourself, and you do not need to. Things are put, also, in God's hands and you say, "Into Thy hand I commit my spirit."

Are we going to keep on worrying up to the very end and be afraid day after day and hour after hour? "Blessed be the man whose strength Thou art, in whose heart are Thy ways." We cannot easily achieve this trust and, indeed, we should not achieve it too completely. There is room for human effort; but we must learn to recognize the point where we put things into the hands of the Eternal. Job is able to say: "Yea, though He slay me, yet will I put my trust in Him." But he was a saint. It is a little too much to expect from us. We are not that exalted in spirit. But as much as we can, we do put ourselves in the hands of God and leave the decision to the Creator of the universe. "The heart that is stayed on Thee, Thou keepest in perfect peace." This is the path which our fathers followed and by which they endured troubles at least as great as ours.

19

The Soviet Union is one nation in this modern world that is completely dominated by the feeling of faith and trust. Its psychic strength is rooted in the fact that it has an unshakable faith in a noble future. It would, of course, disturb the Soviet Union to realize that the mood of faith which it cherishes is essentially Biblical, in a disguised form. But it is clearly faith that sustains the Soviets. It is a belief that all previous stages in history have already been lived through. Now comes the final stage of the working class to dominate the world. It is written, as it were, in the stars; the world dominance of Communism, they believe, is inescapable; it is part of nature. Thus taught Marx and thus taught Lenin. It is a faith in something that is essentially unprovable, but it is a faith in the future, held with strength, and it gives rise to dynamic energy that has made possible the resurrection of a powerful nation.

Now, it is clear that without some such faith, no country can endure. The Prophet Isaiah, who lived 800 before the Christian era, said it to the King of Judah. He was in the midst of a war period and his enemies were gathering around him. The king and his court were panicky, and the prophet said: "Unless you have faith, you will not endure." He meant, of course, "Unless you believe that the future is with you, you will not have the courage to endure the present." The belief in tomorrow is the source of your courage to live today. "Unless ye have faith, ye will not endure."

Thus, what life needs, besides moral stability and inner security, is a social hope for the world. That is an historic need of society. The social hope available to people in the western world is of much more august splendor than Marxist-Leninism. It is Biblical and it was the discovery of the Bible. It was the creativity of the prophets who first reversed the current of human history. People in the past believed that the golden age was of yesterday; the miseries are of today; and the tragedies, with the twilight of the gods, in the future. To this the prophets said that mankind is moving upward: "There shall come a day . . . swords wil be beaten into ploughshares . . ." There will be a world of brotherhood. This hope is supported by our faith and belief in an Eternal Justice.

As we lose this Biblical faith, we will become victims of those who possess faith. The Russians with their strong faith are wise enough to make their faith the theme of constant propaganda. It is taught to every child: This is the way history must develop, and we are the vanguard of the future.

It is clear that for our historical future we need to rebuild the Biblical belief that a just God has sent mankind on a mission for peace and justice. This is, indeed, "only" a faith. It is, perhaps, as unprovable as Marxism-Leninism, but the probability of it is greater because Marxist-Leninism is only a recent development of another philosopher, Hegel; but the belief in a just God with just intentions has accompanied man since the days of Judea and has been held as basic in the human heart.

To the extent that a nation attains faith in history, it grows strong and will outlive the storms of history. For that there is a great verse: "Trust in the Lord at all times, God is the Rock of Ages."

I had a professor at the Hebrew Union College who was a philosopher. He was dedicated to a very difficult quest in which he only partially succeeded because the facts were against him. He wanted to write a philosophy of the Bible, and the facts here were against him because the Bible is not philosophical, not in the sense that Plato or Aristotle are philosophical. If Plato and Aristotle had to discuss the question of God as they do, they would analyze the concept theoretically and test it against other human concepts and deal with it as an idea, as a modern scientist dissects something to see under the microscope.

21

Such philosophic dealing with an idea as an object is not found in Scripure.

As to *proving* the great ideas, the Bible does not bother. In discussing the reality of God, it merely says: "The fool says in his heart there is no God," as if the proving of it was not worth discussing. What matters is not whether you can build up a chain of syllogisms to prove to another philosopher the reality of a certain concept; the Biblical concern is what you are doing about it. How are you building your life on the assumption of the great concepts? What is the good of being able to prove it theoretically? The important thing is to be able to show in your life what it means.

So to the Bible, faith is not the assertion of beliefs. It is a commitment to a certain attitude in life. It asks: What does life need? Life needs character, moral firmness. "The righteous lives by his faith." What is it that a human being inwardly needs? Calmness and serenity: "The heart stayed on Thee, Thou keepest in perfect peace." And what does the world at all times, especially in troubled times, need? It needs faith in the direction of history. "If ye have faith, ye will endure." "God is the Rock of Ages."

This is the life commitment which the authors of the Bible chose. With it they created the world's spiritual literature, and with it we can follow them to worthy and creative life.

III

ON FINDING GOD

The Prophet Isaiah described the household of Israel as the "deathless people," "Am Olom," and in this case the "forthteller" Isaiah was a "foreteller." Now, three thousand years after he spoke those words, this household continues as a family, scattered over the world but aware of a unity which neither persecution nor dispersion nor the erosion of the centuries could destroy. The eternity of the people of Israel is a prime puzzle for the historian. It is contrary to all logic that such a fragment of humanity should outlast the erosion of the centuries. History as yet has no explanation adequate to the massiveness of the phenomenon. Why is this, as Isaiah said thirty centuries ago, an "Am Olom", an "indestructible people"?

Often, we give as a quick explanation that we live because our religion has sustained us. Our religion is the soul of which the people is the body. That is, of course, a correct answer; but like many a correct answer, it conceals a problem, since the persistence of the religion is just as confusing a puzzle as the persistence of the people. Let us stop to consider the chances, the odds, on this religion's surviving. Everything was against its living beyond a generation or two. Everything about the Biblical religion was contrary to the probability of its longevity.

In the first place, it was of an exceptional type. The whole world was pagan. Everybody's religion consisted

Sermon delivered March 6, 1960

23

of, or was aided by, the worship of idols. But this one small people had no idols, claimed to worship an omnipresent, invisible God. What odds would the historian give for this strange religious exception existing and enduring? History does not like exceptions. History swamps out exceptions. And yet a little religion, entirely different from all the paganisms of all the world, lived on.

One cannot explain it too easily. It is more than the fact that this religion was a social exception, a belief different from all others in the world. It was inherently a difficult religion. All the world was pagan because paganism is a natural development. What could be more normal than to try to explain the forces of the world by visible art, the power of the sky, the power of the mountains, the power of the streams? You make a statue which you can see and it embodies the idea for you. Paganism is in accordance with human nature.

But you tell this little people: No such helps for you; no statues to make God visible and believable to you. You must believe in One, invisible, and yet omnipresent, omnipotent, all-knowing. Now, who was asked to believe this complex thing? Philosophers? No. Farmers blacksmiths, carpenters, and petty merchants were asked to accept a refined and difficult and delicate concept of an invisible God, Who rules by justice and righteousness. This was so difficult that it is almost impossible to expect that it could continue. Yet this religion, socially exceptional and intellectually difficult, continued. Why it did is a more perplexing problem than the problem of why the people persisted.

Of course, we have a quick answer: We say that God so intended it. It is God's will. We believe that. But God's will works through human beings, and it is part of our duty to ask ourselves, how did God do it through us. "What hath God wrought?" In other words, we try to find out how human effort helped this difficult religion to persist. When we look at the Bible for explanation, we notice that actually the religion died a thousand deaths. The Bible is the story of the continual dying out of pure, ethical monotheism. As we read the Book of Judges, the constant plaint is that the people abandoned God, forgot God, turned to idolatry; and then, always through prophets, judges, psalmists, law givers, they came back. So evidently God works through human beings in a human way; and when we say, "It is God's will" that Judaism should live, we are indeed expressing a truth, but a stenographic truth, a shortened truth. The Bible, fortunately, reviving the faith in God scores of times, did it not only by eloquent exhortation but by devising of methods. We might say that the Bible is the record of methods for the recovery of the concept of God.

This aspect of the Bible, that it is the story of the recovery of the lost God, is of special interest to us in modern times, when people are again groping towards religion. They are not sure what they want, but they are groping. It should be of importance to modern people to know that the Bible itself was groping, that the Bible is the story of mankind losing God and finding Him again. This is perhaps the central theme of Scripture and one that has not been discussed frequently. What, then, is "The Best of the Bible," the best words of the Bible on this perennial, human quest now vaguely reawakening in our time, the attempt to find the lost God again?

The great philosopher, Baruch Spinoza, divided nature into two parts or, rather, he looked upon nature from two separate aspects. One was that nature was a collection of objects, already created, and the other is that nature is a creative force, always mysteriously working. Nature as a created object he called "Natura naturata," nature created. Nature as a living, creative force, as a dynamic, he called "Natura naturans," nature as active process.

25

The field for the scientist is "natura naturata," nature created, a group of existing objects. The scientist is not concerned in his science with the deeper, creative mystery. Why is it that this vast universe is orderly? Why is it that it follows laws? Why are we so confident as scientists that if we discover certain principles governing the relation of the moon to the earth, that exactly those same principles will govern the satellites around bodies in the furthest galaxies? Where do we get our faith that the whole infinite machine is law-abiding?

This mystery does not concern the scientist. He knows that the laws are there. He believes them and, therefore, he works with the facts as they are. That is what Laplace, the great French astronomer, said. He wrote a book on celestial mechanics, and Napoleon asked him, "Is God mentioned in your book?" and Laplace gave the famous answer, "I have no need for that hypothesis." In other words, to explain nature as object, what Spinoza called "natura naturata," you do not have to concern yourself with the hidden question of whence came this order and what does the order of the universe imply as to a creator.

But the other half of nature, natura naturans, nature as an active process, is the theme for philosophers and theologians. They ask whence comes this order. Can there be an intelligent universe without a self-aware intelligence having created it? And it is this study of nature as a force which led almost every philosopher of the world to believe in God. The atheistic philosophers are only a handful in the whole history of thought. The overwhelming majority of philosophers studying the remarkable order of the world, come to a conclusion that order implies intelligence. The most famous argument of this natural theology was that of the English philosopher-theologian, William Paley, of the eighteenth century. He was the one who, repeating the argument of the philosophers from the laws of the universe to a law-giver who ordained it, summed it up in what became the most quoted metaphor on the subject. He said that if you travel through a desert and you stop and pick up a perfect watch, it is reasonable to assume that **somewhere** there is a watch-maker; it is impossible to believe that so complicated and orderly a mechanism would exist without an intelligence. That famous argument of Paley was used by Voltaire. He used it with some embarrassment. He liked to be a skeptic, but he felt that the logic of the universe drove him from it, and so he said, "The universe embarrasses me. I cannot look at a watch without believing in a watch-maker."

At all events, this argument in various forms has been the argument of almost all the philosophers, based upon the orderliness of the creative power in the universe. If, then, most of us were philosophers, accustomed to the subtlety of dissecting thoughts into their components, we could study nature intellectually, and from nature arrive at nature's God, as most of the philosophers of the world have done. But since we are not philosophers, we need another approach to nature.

The Bible itself is full of nature. Its authors have a deep feeling for nature, for trees, forests, streams, stars, sun, moon. Yet, though the Bible is full of the influence of nature, strangely enough, this plain philosophic argument of creative nature to nature's creator never appears in the Bible, except perhaps where Isaiah uses a sort of an argument and says, "Lift up your eyes to the stars and see who created them." That is about as much philosophic argument as appears in Scripture.

But the Bible has a different relation to nature than the intellectual one of the philosophers. The Eighth Psalm says: "When I behold Thy heavens, the work of Thy hands, what is man, that Thou art mindful of him?" What does this say? It speaks of the **emotional** reaction to the universe. Seeing the stars in their majestic pageant over the sable path of the night humbles me, says the psalmist; I feel small and I realize that I need other powers to

27

sustain me. The Scriptural attitude to nature is not an intellectual one. It is, rather, a psychological one, an emotional one. It soon becomes clear that the Bible means to say that the way to God is by achieving an **emotional** attitude to nature, a receptive attitude to its splendors.

This emotionel response seems to be a natural tendency of the human race, namely, to react to nature with certain moods mirrored in the heart. In fact, the greatest flowering of human poetry in modern history was the romantic, emotional reaction to nature. All those English poets, all of them related to the mood of the German, Goethe, Wordsworth, Keats, Shelley the "Odes to a West Wind" "To a Passing Cloud," expressed the emotion that nature awakened in them and created the greatest efflorescence of English poetry.

One might think that this emotional response to nature is so natural that it will naturally and always exist. But it is not so. Sometimes the emotion dies away for generations. It is a noticeable fact that in the poetry of recent years the splendor of nature has almost completely disappeared. Now poetry no longer sings of the skylark and of the west wind, but of human agony, human misfortune, of the dump heaps, of the wastelands of life. Thus does the emotional reaction to the grandeur of nature come and go, and we are living in a period when man has closed his heart to that emotion. Nowadays, if he goes on a vacation, he goes to a resort, with the same night clubs that he could find at home.

Scripture says of the way to God: "To a high mountain go thou." Or stand beside the sea and react with feeling to it. Watch the waves and think that those waves have beaten on those shores when the land was untenanted, as long as the moon was, as long as it lifted the water in the middle of the Atlantic and let it go again twice a day; since the beginning of the earth, that ceaseless beat of nature's power has continued. Think in that mood and you will move, in all likelihood, from nature to nature's God.

So it was in Biblical times. They did not argue celestial mechanics. They reacted to natural emotion. It was not for them and it is not for us, the mathematics of the stars; it is the music of the spheres. The psalmist sums it all up: "The heavens declare the glory of God."

In the year 1908, Felix Adler founded the Ethical Culture Society. Felix Adler was the son of the rabbi of Temple Emanu-El in New York, and he was educated as a rabbi. When he came back from study in Europe he was to succeed his father. But he changed his mind and founded the Ethical Culture Society. It is a nobly-intended organization. It has done good work, particularly in the field of education. It never spread, having only about fifteen societies in the United States and five or six in England.

Felix Adler, with his intention of having a system of ethics without religion, of goodness without God, was not really an innovator. His innovation consisted in forming a society for the purpose, but he was preceded by at least a century of philosophers. Hitherto, ethical theory was related to religion, except for Aristotle's Ethics. But for the last century or so, climaxing in the foundation of the Ethical Society, there was an arduous effort on the part of many philosophers to establish an ethical system that did not need to depend upon religion.

Now, why did they do it? What drove them to it? Certainly all of them would acknowledge that the Bible was the fountainhead of modern ethical idealism. The few customs of the pagan tribe, the few parochial, mutual acts of considerations which people of the same clan had for each other, were extended in Scripture to include the world. The Bible gave breadth and sensitiveness and dynamics to ethics. The philosophers would all acknowledge

29

the unique ethical contribution of the Bible. But they must have felt that since mankind in the last century was losing God, it would be a pity if he would also lose decency. The whole effort towards secular ethics may be described as a century-long salvage operation; to save ethics, when faith was dying.

But what these ethical philosophers did not think about (perhaps it did not concern them) was that the ethics of our ethical world is so permeated with the water of its source that it has in itself a power to draw back to the original fountainhead. In other words, the ethical life is spiritually pedagogic and Scripture so considered it.

There is a remarkable phrase of the Prophet Jeremiah and, in this case, a still more remarkable comment in the ancient book of sermons, the Midrash. Jeremiah said (it is in the sixteenth chapter; the prophet is speaking in God's name of the people): "Me they have forsaken and My law have they abandoned." And the Midrash, commenting, says in God's name: "I would forgive them if they have forsaken Me, if only they held on to My law because," continues the Midrash, still speaking in God's name, "if they only held on to the moral law, the radiance in it would lead them back to Me."

In other words, the ethical life is a process in which certain hidden pedagogic forces work. If you are a decent person and, as far as you know, you are irreligious, your decency teaches you, at least, the value of the preciousness of other people. You consider them. In your decency you discover how good you feel when you perform a considerate act, and you may find something of the belief that the ethical law is, as the prophet said, "written on your heart," and you might discover what Emanuel Kant discovered, the majesty of "the starry heavens above" and of "the moral law within."

Live the ethical life. It will lead you, perhaps, even

30

all the way. So the Prophet Amos said: "Avoid evil; learn to do good; so will the Lord of Hosts be with you." The road to the Deity is, according to Scripture, the path of decency.

When the Roman General Pompey captured Jerusalem, just about the turn of the era, he penetrated the Temple and marched with proud Roman strides to the curtain that marked off the Holy of Holies. He pulled the curtain roughly aside and fell back dumbfounded. He was dumbfounded at what he saw. And what did he see that shook his Roman confidence? He saw nothing! That is what astonished him. A shrine without a god was dumbfounding to the pagan intelligence. As a matter of fact, it should be a problem, theoretically, to a non-pagan intelligence. Why have a shrine altogether? If God is omnipresent, why have a particular place that is called holy? We notice that in the famous vision of the Prophet Isaiah, when it seemed to him that in the Temple he saw God seated on the throne, immediately the seraphim said: "The whole earth is full of His glory."

Nevertheless, in spite of God's being accessible everywhere, in spite of the Scriptural statement, "Wherever My name is called I will come and bless thee," nevertheless the people were urged to come to the Temple, especially on the three great pilgrimage festivals. They could worship anywhere. But that place had its psychological worth. It was associated with acts and words dedicated to God. Memory made it sacred. That is why the Prophet Habakkuk said: "God is in His holy Temple. Earthly thoughts be silent now." Our association with God, our sense of His accessibility, is in this place of memory.

Thus, besides emotional response to nature, besides the patience of the ethical life, the direct search for God is in God's house, in the house in which we associate thoughts for God. We pray. We read great words given

31

by tradition. These are merely words uttered, formed by our vocal cords. But we never know when we will uncover depths. We will talk to God and talk to Him, time and time again, and one day our heart will reverse the dialogue and we will say: "Speak, Lord, Thy servant heareth."

The Irish poet, Thomas Moore, saw clearly what these associations of worship can mean. He, naturally, used Christian terminology, but he expressed the Biblical idea of coming to God's house and seeking Him in prayer:

"Come ye disconsolate, where'er ye languish,
Come to God's altar, fervently kneel;
Here bring your wounded hearts, here tell your
    anguish,
Earth has no sorrow that Heaven cannot heal."

The great words of the psalm are: "God is near to all who call upon Him, who call upon Him in truth."

If our religion were simpler, if the Bible religion were more "folkish," or more tolerant of the little familiar idols and pretty little amulets which mankind has loved since time immemorial, it would have been easy to maintain it. After all, paganism continued for millenia and in many countries still continues. Or, if contrariwise, we were all sages and could live permanently in a world of profound thoughts, we could maintain the pure Biblical religion without interruption.

But the religion is profound and we are human. So it is natural to lose our awareness of God. The Prophet Isaiah said: "Thou, O God, dost ever hide Thyself." God hides Himself, but we are mandated all our life to seek Him. In some ages the quest is intense and eager. In some ages it is an unconscious drive toward the light. But in our own way and in our own generation, we search

32

for God. Scripture which has had much experience with this theme, tells us the way: Learn to respond to the grandeur of nature, "The Heavens declare the glory of God." Practice, even if automatically, deeds of righteousness; the hand will some day reach the soul; the Lord of Hosts will be with you, if you learn to do good and to avoid evil. Seek Him in His house and call upon Him in truth. The quest of Scripture can be summed up in these words: "Seek ye the Lord. He may be found."

IV

ON PERSONAL SUCCESS

This is Brotherhood Week, and we are eager to emphasize those ideals which are the common treasure of Judaism and Christianity. We are grateful that we have outlived the miserable and murderous Middle Ages, when Jews were libeled and their religion was slandered. In those dark days, persecution was directed against the Jews and propaganda against their faith. Most of the propaganda was in the form of contrast between the New Testament and the Old, always, of course, in favor of the New. The general argument was, first of all, that the New Testament teaches a religion of tenderness and love; that the Old Testament worships a God of harsh justice and even of cruelty. Another supposed difference between the two in the Middle Ages was with regard to the achievements of personal success and the acquiring of earthly possessions. The New Testament was described as spiritual, the Old Testament as material. Now, of course, this whole type of argument, of proving the superiority of one religion over another, is usually unreliable. It is nearly always based upon an unfair selection of individual texts and suppression of other texts that would prove the opposite.

Sermon delivered February 5, 1961

Nevertheless, even in Brotherhood Week, it is well to realize that there was value in the rather ugly debate and disputatiousness of the Middle Ages. It pointed out (in exaggerated and unfair form) the differences between the two religions. We ought to learn, and the sooner the better, that if we are to appreciate each other deeply, we have not only to feel fellowship on the basis of our common ground, the beliefs which we hold together, but we must learn to appreciate and respect the differences which exist between us. It is so in personal friendship. We are attracted by the fact that a certain person has much in common with us; but we are not true friends until we have learned to honor each other's temperamental differences.

So it is valuable, even in this month of good will, to go back to the alleged differences, try to take away a little bit of the medieval poison from them, the exaggerated disputatiousness, and see what there is of reality in the difference which we all should appreciate.

It is the second of the supposed superiorities of the New Testament which concerns us, namely, that difference between the spirituality of the New and the materiality of the Old. It is easy to make what lawyers would call a prima facie case in favor of the New Testament.

In the Gospel of Saint Matthew, in the Sermon on the Mount, the founder of Christianity says to his disciples: "Lay not treasures on earth, where the moth can destroy and robbers break in and take it away. But lay up only treasures in heaven, where nothing can destroy what you have. Man's heart is where his treasure is." This is a grand statement: Do not accumulate property. Your heart is where your property is. Accumulate only spiritual goods.

Now, by contrast, in the Old Testament, also in an especially eloquent section in the Book of Deuteronomy, Moses, in his last speech, says to the people about to enter the new land: If you obey my commandments and listen to my ordinances and practice justice, I will send you blessings. The land will be fertile, the crops will increase. Your herds will multiply and you will live a comfortable life. Thus the reward for virtue in the Old Testament is material blessing, while the New Testament advises that we should pay no attention to any earthly treasure. It is an interesting contrast and one which we ought to analyze if Jews and Christians are to understand and respect each other's faith.

There is manifestly a basic, temperamental difference here between the two ancient faiths with regard to the question of personal success, whether it is in money or in power or in fame. The New Testament, the Gospel, takes the stand that the whole process of acquiring success is corrupting, that the soul will be safer without success. The Old Testament seems to take another point of view. It faces the fact that whatever will be said by any Scriptures, people **will** seek, success, success in money, success in power, success in fame. It is quite aware of the fact that in the attaining of success there will be moral dangers. Then let these moral dangers be faced! Perhaps they can be overcome. Perhaps they can even be converted to virtues. If we study the attitude of Scripture to the question of personal success, we may get close to the heart of Judaism.

When we borrow words from another language, it is because we lack those words in our own. There is a group of words we have borrowed from the French. They all mean about the same thing: the word, "parvenu," sometimes the parallel word, "arriviste," and the phrase, "nouveau riche." There was a special reason why these words were developed in France. In the time of the Bourbons, the nobles were entrenched in their privilege, living a life of beautiful formality, a life of satin and lace. Then in the "minuet" of their daily life, there suddenly burst into their society some men who made, unexpectedly, a hundred million francs. They came from nowhere but wanted to be recognized because they have money. For these social invaders, the French language developed terms of contempt: parvenu, nouveau riche.

Of course, such terms do not have the same emotional power when used in English, because in America, at least, our society is not quite so stratified and, fortunately, our old families, after a few generations, lose their wealth. Thus there is no permanent aristocracy. We are accustomed to new people coming up. Nevertheless, the phrase has some residual meaning with us. We recognize that the man who has newly acquired success is likely to be a vulgarian. He has to display what he has. He never had millions before, and so he has to have a magnificent house, furnished by the best and most expensive furniture maker; and he has to have the finest jewels and the finest furs. He feels impelled toward what Thorstein Veblen called "conspicuous spending." This vulgar self-display seems to be a psychological necessity for those who are newly successful.

This self-display is not only a fault in manners, it is a fault in morals, because it indicates an inner pride, a powerful conviction of sudden self importance: I am somebody now! I am going to show it. Scripture faces this danger of new-found pride. In the Book of Deuteronomy, Moses says to the people: "Listen, O Israel. You are about to cross the Jordan. You are going to a wonderful land, a

37

fertile land. You will have flocks and herds. Even from its hills, you will dig copper and iron. Now I warn you: Be careful lest your heart grow lofty and you say, 'My strength and the power of my hand have gotten me all this.' Remember, it is God who giveth the power to acquire substance."

Thus Scripture warns the successful against developing the lofty heart. "Beware lest your hearts be lifted up." It leads the successful in another direction. This other and opposite direction is indicated in the story of our Father Jacob. What a newly rich man he was, a real success! He left home as a fugitive, as many immigrants do. He had nothing but the clothes on his back and, as he said, "staff in hand." The first night on the road, this poor, humble fugitive, penniless, dreamed. In his dream he says, "O God, if you will only give me bread to eat and a garment to wear." His demands were simple. He was a poor man. Then he came to the home of his former kinsman, Laban. He worked there for twenty-one years and came back immensely rich. He had earned it too, by clever manipulation of the flock, devotion to business, as he says, "day and night." Now on the way back home he has three camps full, family, servants, flocks, herds. He is an immensely rich person. He prays, and he says, "O God, I have three camps full of possessions. I am just too small to be worth all that. I do not merit it. I am not big enough to have all this power."

It is the modesty in Jacob's statement, "Too small am I for all these blessings," which is the first moral achievement of the successful, if they can attain it. It is a simple matter for a poor man to be humble. He wants something. He has to plead. But when a rich man is modest, it is a psychological and a moral triumph. It wins the admiration of all. It was because our Father Jacob in his great wealth

38

could say, "I am too small for all these possessions," that we proudly carry his name as the head of the family of Israel. We bear the name of a successful and a modest man.

The Pittsburgh novelist, Gladys Schmitt, wrote perhaps her best book when she produced **David the King.** Yet, although she did a great deal of preparatory research and meditated long over the personality of her hero, she would surely admit that David remains a puzzling personality. Here he is, the author of the Book of Psalms, which is perhaps the greatest outpouring of mystic, poetic faith in the history of human writing. Yet what makes him puzzling is that he was also a newly successful person, also one of those "arrivistes" who arrived from a comparatively humble home. He was a shepherd of his father's flocks in Bethlehem. He got to the army camp as a boy in order to bring food to his soldier brothers. He got into the king's tent because he could play the harp and charm the king. He worked his way into friendship with the king's son Jonathan, and he married the king's daughter. He went through a period of exile and finally became the great King of Israel and the founder of the Davidic dynasty.

How can we explain the co-existence in one person of the noble, mystic spirituality which created the Psalms, with the drive and the alertness and the iron strength which brought him up from Bethlehem to the throne? This combination of opposite qualities makes David an interesting subject for analysis and the theme of many a novel. The explanation is, in a way, given in Scripture itself, at the end of the First Book of Chronicles. A passage that appears there in reference to David is put into the daily Prayerbook. It begins: "And David blessed the Lord." He said, "O Lord, who am I, what is my father's house, what do I amount to?" After he expresses humility, he says, "Riches and honor and power come from Thee and therefore I give thanks and praise to Thy holy name."

Because of David's humility, or because he could finally attain humility, he was impelled to express his thanks and his praises to God. Now it is just here that agnostics or atheists feel superior to religious people. They say: You are always praising God, always giving thanks to Him. Is your God not satisfied by now with all the millions of thanks He has received? Is He so insatiable? Do you imagine your God sitting in heaven and just lapping up all your gratitude?

It is, of course, an ignorant comment. Judaism never said that God needs our thanks. On the contrary, in the daily prayer, in the Kaddish that we recite, we are reminded that God is high above all praises and thanks that are uttered on earth. It is not that God needs our thanks. It is that we need to utter them. The mood of gratitude is the outer expression of the inner attitude of modesty. Modest within, grateful outwardly, is the true religious type. This ideal is more than Biblical. It was Seneca, the Roman philosopher, who said that he who receives a benefit with gratitude has already paid the first installment on his debt.

In other words, when the mood of thankfulness is found in a person of great possessions, he is beginning to rise morally even if he is pagan. Let him be grateful that his grandfather brought him to this land and not to Patagonia; to a land rich in resources. If he is a man who has made his success in the city, let him then be grateful to the long-dead Jefferson and Washington and Franklin and Madison, who built a nation on such principles

40

that even in these days of dominant government there is still enough room for an individual to pursue his career and carry out his hopes with confidence and with strength. Whomever he thanks, whether he thanks God, Who does not need it, or his grandfather or his great-grandfather for bringing him here, though they do not need it, being long since dead, or the founders of this republic, the man who attains to the inner attitude of being grateful is now a gentleman, and whether he is religious or not, is a true child of God.

Cleveland Amory has recently written a book called **Who Killed Society?** By "society," the author does not mean the larger organization of humanity; he refers to "The Four Hundred," the Belmonts, the Astors, the Vanderbilts, etc. He seems to be bemoaning the fact that the old, formal, exclusive society of "The Four Hundred" has given way to the present, nondescript mixture called "Cafe Society."

There is, of course, something to bemoan about "Cafe Society." I do not know too much about it; I have not been privileged to be in more than one or two night clubs in my life. I have seen, however, as you have, many pictures of the night club habitues. Except, perhaps, for some young woman who can still summon up at two o'clock in the morning the false look of happiness, all the faces are lined, weary, and bored. One wonders why they do it. We may suspect that the old society, also, was no better off than the Cafe Society. That, also, followed a series of formalities which they had to endure. People were just as bored then as now.

Perhaps the Cafe Society came into existence because the old "Four Hundred" society was too dull. If so, they have found this round of regular attendance in night clubs just as dull and just as boring. There is no basic difference between Salon Society and Saloon Society. Both are clearly "a weariness to the flesh." Why should they endure it? Sometimes we give a too-easy explanation: These people have no inner, intellectual resources. They have to depend, pathetically, upon an equally weary comedian's turning out a new variation of the few ancient jokes, and they laugh wearily in response, if they laugh at all.

But this is not a sufficient explanation. King Solomon was known as "the wisest of all men." He was broadly cultured. In the Book of Ecclesiastes, he describes his life. He says that he built palaces, filled them with dancing women and singers. He tasted every joy that money could buy. Then he says: "Vanity of vanities! I found it is a weariness to the flesh and a burden to the soul." He asks in worldweary despair, "Is this my reward for all my work? Is all this boredom and the sense of the vainness of life my sole reward for attaining this material and political power?"

What was the reason for his world-weariness? The same reason as that of "society's," of the rich people whom we envy that they can go night after night, to a cafe if they want to. What makes their life, as their faces testify, "vanity of vanities"? It is clear that King Solomon made the mistake, as he himself describes it, of doing everything for his own pleasure. When you use expanding resources for the sole purpose of your own pleasure, you find that all the joys you have bought have become repetitious; that one winter resort is like another, and one foreign country, if you go constantly, is like another. The reason that the self-indulgent are miserable is, as Walter Scott said in another connection, a man is always miserable and bored when he is "a wretch concentred all in self."

A poor man cannot afford to indulge himself to the point of utter boredom, and yet he is often bored too. But when you have almost unlimited resources and you can buy whatever you want to, as often as you want to, and your life is centered on your own pleasure, you discover as quickly and thoroughly as King Solomon discovered: "Vanity of vanities; it is a weariness to the flesh."

It is clear that the foolish sin of pride and the animal sin of ingratitude is matched by the self-destructive sin of world-weariness. The answer to that, clearly, is to be found in what God said to Abraham at the beginning of our history. God said to him: "I will give you success. I will make thy name great." That is a fine and simple way of promising fame and power. But the verse continues: "But be thou a blessing." This is the only way to cure the misery that comes from self-indulgence: "Be thou a blessing." Use your power which you now have for some social blessing.

This is not just a pious wish. It is a valuable discovery made by thousands of people who have attained and achieved. We think of all the thousands of noble people in our little Jewish communities in the Middle Ages, the men who made money suddenly and gave it away generously; who built synagogues and provided dowry for brides and increased the size of God's acre, the cemetery, and the ghettos. All these philanthropists found out how life can be interesting and meaningful. In our day, too, great foundations are bringing happiness to the donors and blessing to the world. It is only when a man discovers that his success can be a public benediction that he begins to fulfill the words which God said to Abraham:

43

"All the people of thy world will be blessed by thy presence."

A Christian businessman in church hears the verse: "It is easier for a camel to go through the eye of a needle than for a rich man to enter heaven." He does not feel uncomfortable any more. He is used to the words. He makes a distinction between practical life and the Bible. But even the Christian businessman must know that this New Testament aversion to material success was believed in with noble sincerity throughout Christian history. Hundreds of thousands of people followed the Gospel literally. They gave up everything which they had and the prospects of getting anything in the future, and took the vow of poverty. The Gospel was the motivation of all the monastic institutions of the Middle Ages. This New Testament contempt for material success is a genuine and even an admirable motif in Christianity.

In this regard, we must say simply that Judaism has a different psychology. We have never praised poverty. The poor should be shielded. The poor should be protected. The poor are an opportunity for other people's training in decent philanthropy. But the poor are not to be envied. Poverty is no blessing. Not to know where your food is coming from, where to provide shelter for your family — how can these worries bring you nearer to God?

We face the fact that human beings will seek, indeed, and should seek success in money, in power, and in fame. We know also that success, when attained, may bring us to the brink of moral pitfalls, and that it is better to know just what they are. It is better to be aware of the danger of your heart being "lifted up" and of your falling into the absurd "parvenu" pride. It is better to know that

44

you are in danger of becoming an ingrate and thanking nobody but yourself. It is important to know that if you buy all you can, just for yourself, you are buying misery and boredom and "vanity of vanities."

But those people who have learned to avoid the pitfalls, who have managed with all their achievements to attain a gracious modesty, who have risen to a true-hearted gratitude, and have managed to find a path toward social blessing, for them Judaism says, in the words of the Psalm: "May your like increase. Ride forth and prosper in the cause of justice and truth."

V
ON SOCIAL PROGRESS

There are always men who can write well enough to be worthy of being published. Men of literary skill are not too rare. But men of literary talent are less frequent; and men of literary genius are rare indeed. So it is strange, since literary genius is so rare, that there have come periods in literary history when in the same time and in the same place there arose a whole brotherhood of literary geniuses.

It happened almost within our lifetime in the nineteenth century in Czarist Russia. In the same place and in the same time, there were Leo Tolstoi, Dostoevski, Turgenev, and Chekhov. A similar constellation of literary talent and almost of genius appeared in Elizabethan times, in early Jacobean times: Shakespeare, of course, was of true genius; but around him there was a cluster of talent, Ben Jonson, Kit Marlowe, others. Why all together and all in one place? If we go back to ancient literary history, we find the cluster of Greek tragedians, Aeschylus, Sophocles, and others who wrote tragic dramas which the world has not equalled after two thousand years.

Whenever it happens that there are such galaxies of talent in one place and at one time, the historians of lit-

Sermon delivered February 12, 1961

erature naturally devote their attention to finding some explanation. Their usual explanations, of course, are what might be called sociological; that is to say, they study the era, the state of society, and the mood of men in order to explain this dazzling, literary phenomenon. Yet none of these sociological explanations can be more than contributory, because, in essence, there is a great unsolved mystery about the flame of talent. It appears in the skies of the world as a new star, a nova, flashes in the world.

Certainly the sociological explanations (we might call them the common-sense explanations) fail completely in an explanation of the appearance of Holy Scripture. The Bible represents one of the greatest galaxies of spiritual, literary talent which has ever been assembled within comparatively one period. When we start in the usual sociological manner to explain the ancient environment and try to give a common-sense reason why the great thoughts and the great writers of the Bible appeared in that particular place, in that particular time, we fail completely.

Let us consider the environment. The whole world, without any exception, was heathen. It worshiped idols. Yet this tiny little human segment living between Jordan's gorge and the Mediterranean came to believe in a pure monotheism, entirely different from the religion of the whole world environment. Why?

The whole world at that time always had narrow ethical ideals. Sometimes they had high artistic ideals or high literary ideals, but to the intelligent Greeks, every non-Greek was a barbarian. He had no rights. The whole world believed that one owed some duty to one's own folks. That is what ethics meant. It is derived from "ethos." meaning, "people," or "nation."

47

Why is it, then, when all the world, the entire environment, had a narrow concept of clan-ethics, that this tiny people said: "Thou shalt love the **stranger**, and care for the homeless and the stranger within thy gates"? How did they find a **universal** ethics? Do you wonder that our fathers simply took a pious shorthand in explaining the fact and said, "The Bible is inspired"? It was their way of saying that human explanations fail.

Now, the most remarkable contrast between the plain facts of the environment and the literary genius of Scripture is not confined to the field of monotheism or of world ethics; it also presents a new attitude toward the world's future. There was always a general human attitude with regard to what will happen in a hundred years or in a thousand years from now. Most of the pagan people of the world believed that the future of the world depends merely on chance. Thus, the only way to mold the future is by magic. The more intelligent, philosophic Greeks believed it was not chance which set the future, but inexorable fate. Therefore man's life is tragic. He cannot escape the destiny that the gods have planned for man. One might say that the whole world believed that the future is dark. But the people of Israel was the only one to believe that the world's future is bright; that there is social progress; that mankind moves upward from century to century. Here is a people which for some mysterious reason burst through the fog of the whole world's pessimism and declared that mankind has a noble future.

Now this exceptional confidence cannot be explained by any reference to the environment or any of the glib explanations available. We cannot explain it, and what is more, we can hardly share it, nowadays. Such a confident mood is far from us, when we look into the future and see how dark it is. Yet we know that this exceptional belief of Scripture, that society moves toward brotherhood, peace, and security, is a precious belief. If we could only grasp it and hold it, it would be a blessing to the soul of man.

Our own question is a psychological one. Is it possible for the modern man, constituted as he is, broken down in faith as he is, uncertain, insecure, and weak inwardly, can such a modern man take to his heart the Biblical belief in social progress? If he could, it would be a blessing. What, then, is the root of Biblical belief? On what specific grounds does it base its confidence that the future of society is greater than its past?

The good physician who meets the patient for the first time, studies him carefully. As a result of his observation and the answers to his questions, he makes his diagnosis, his explanation of the basic ailment of the patient. After the diagnosis, he begins his therapeutics. If his diagnosis is correct, his remedy is likely to be well chosen and his prognostication is generally optimistic. Things will turn out well.

It is remarkable how medical is the vocabulary of the prophetic literature. The first chapter of the first major prophet, Isaiah, reads like a medical encounter with the patient. The prophet begins to describe his people as "a sick nation," and gives in detail the outer evidences, the symptoms of the sickness. He says they are bruised, battered, full of sores, no soundness in their bodies from head to foot. Then he begins to diagnose the reasons which he finds to be all ethical. He says, "You are a sinful nation; you are heavily laden with sin."

Having given the diagnosis that there is corruption of character, which is the source of the symptoms of national

49

sickness, he suggests a remedy, namely, that with God's help, the patient must attain an ethical regeneration. There can come a character purification. So he says in various phrasing: "Behold, I will purify you. I will refine you as silver is refined in the furnace. I will put you through the furnace of suffering and you will come out free of dross."

This is the frequently reiterated doctrine in Scripture. Social progress comes through the character improvement of the individual. If that diagnosis is correct, that character corruption is the source of social evil, then the remedy will work.

But nowadays, many students of the Bible reject the prophetic diagnosis and say that the sickness of Judean society had little to do with moral degeneration. It was a sick society for realistic and objective reasons. To the north and east were the militaristic states of the Assyrians and the Babylonians. To the south and west was the imperialistic state of the Egyptians. These were the rival powers of antiquity; and the only way they could reach each other was to march through the land of Judea, through the coastal plain. So this little nation was the toy, the football kicked about by two powerful opponents. That is why it was hard to maintain stability and prosperity. The national suffering was due to an **outer** cause. That is the true diagnosis (they say) so that even if the people of Israel were all righteous, nothing could have saved their state from being ground together between the upper and the nether millstones.

Thus do realistic scholars throw doubt on the ethical diagnosis of the prophets about the ancient Judean society; and we have the same doubt about our own society. Can we realistically say that the progress of our society depends upon human character? It depends surely upon outer forces. The Egyptians are in the west (that is America) and the Assyrians are in the east (that is Russia). Each has atomic bombs at its command. Then what good will personal character do when these hydrogen bomb explode?

Yet we have not looked deeply enough into the prophetic message. They were not fools. They did not believe that if the people's character improved, Assyria would not attack Egypt and Egypt would not counterattack, and the land of a righteous Israel would not be devastated. It surely would be devastated anyhow. All the little nations in the path of the giants would be crushed. This is obviously true. Yet most of those little nations would die and only one of them would live. In fact, most of those ancient nations did die, and only one has lived. The only one that lived was the one which had accepted this strange and apparently unrealistic diagnosis that history depends upon character.

What actually depends on character is not whether the bomb will be dropped or not. What depends upon character is our power of endurance, our belief in the future, our confidence that we can find something to live for. Those with such moral character survive catastrophes and those without character are crushed. The catastrophes occur anyhow and the rain falls on the just and the unjust. But our ability to survive depends upon the inner defenses.

It ought to be clear today, in a time of world danger, that character is vital. We need people of certain moral strength, people who are not too easily excited to foolish action, people who have a decent amount of mutual respect and will not divide the nation by increasing religious or racial hate, people of reasonable confidence who are willing to undertake explorations toward peace. These moods are all elements of character which we are able to build up into national health. We have the psychological means today and the new powers of public persuasion with which to build public character more quickly than it ever could have been done in the past. If we pay attention to the mood of the average man, not only as a customer, but as a citizen, we can build or rebuild character and have a fair chance of a decent future. "Behold," said the prophet, "I will put into you a new heart and a new spirit."

Perhaps the most famous verse in all of Scripture is: "Hear, O Israel, the Lord our God, the Lord is One." We observe that it is in the plural; it is addressed not to an individual, but to the people. While the prophets are concerned wih individual character and its purification as a path to social progress, most of their message was to the whole people and not to the individual. Their concept of the future was, therefore, much more a social concept than an individual one. They believed that there can be no human future if there be social injustice. Perhaps the most vehement preachment of the prophets from the earliest to the very last of them were denunciations of oppression and injustice. The great social justice passages are beloved and familiar. They need not be repeated. What is relevant to our theme is that whenever the prophet visualizes, the future, he sees a world built upon justice; for he is convinced that only a just society can endure. The great power of Communism in the world comes because it borrows the prophetic ideal. Communists say, "We stand for justice and therefore we are the representatives of the future." That claim will continue to be persuasive as long as there is widespread injustice and oppression in the world. Whether they will cure it or not (or eventually substitute for the oppression a still greater oppression) the fact remains that the appeal for the future in the name of justice is one of the strongest appeals of the Communist world. It is tragic that we have left this optimism to them. We really believed it long before they did.

The United States believed in political injustice. When it was an infant nation, it proclaimed the rights of man, made them the foundation of democracy, and established the first modern republic. In our rough-and-ready way, we also believe in economic justice, it being the unacknowledged creed of America that every American shall have increasing material comfort. That is our practical type of social justice.

What we do not have yet is what goes deeper than political and economic justice, namely, personal justice, the sense of the dignity of the individual, regardless of race or the land in which he dwells. This is what hinders us from being the herald of the world's future.

America must again become the voice of true, personal justice, so that all peoples everywhere understand that we are working for a day when no one is disadvantaged for unfair reasons; that everybody is to us equally the child of God. We must believe in complete political, economic, and personal justice before we can begin leading the world toward its future. The prophet describes the future in the words: "They shall not hurt, they shall not wound, in My holy mountain."

The prophets were many-sided. They taught many things. But people who write about the prophets almost invariably paint an incomplete picture. They leave out part

53

of the essential preachment because it does not happen to interest them.

Now, the prophets, of course, believed in progress based upon personal character. They certainly insisted that society must be based on social justice. But there was a third preaching of the prophets, their attack on idolatry, the scornful, bitter denunciation of the heathen paganism around them. We understand why modern writers ignore this part of the prophetic message, because they consider that paganism is gone and the whole preachment against idolatry is now outdated and does not need to be discussed. But, surely, whether paganism has vanished or not, we cannot understand the prophets if we brush aside a great part of their message.

The preachment against paganism was vital to the prophets. They saw that with all the world pagan, and this tiny people alone preserving the pure, spiritual faith in God, that Israel dare not compromise with idolatry. If they do, then the light of truth will have completely vanished from the world. So they kept on fighting against idolatry and insisting upon this tiny people preserving this unique monotheism. It was natural, then, that when they thought of social progress, they included the concept of the one, spiritual God among the means for attaining it. So the Prophet Zachariah said in this picturesque language that there will come a day when people will grab hold of the cloak of a passing child of Israel and say, "Let me walk with thee. We hear that God is in your presence." Or less picturesquely but more poetically, Isaiah and Micah said: "Behold, there shall come a day when the mountains of the Lord's house shall be established as the top of all mountains, and nations shall flow unto it, and they shall say to each other, 'Come ye, let us go to the mountain of the Lord and He will teach us of His ways and we will walk in His path.'"

The climactic stage in social progress is seen as the time when all mankind will be inwardly united in the worship of one God. The Communists in their perverted way believe that too. In their atheistic way, they are the propagandists of one world religion. Their doctrine has all the elements of religion except the crucial one. First of all, it has a creed, an iron bound creed which must be studied and interpreted as no Talmudist ever interpreted Scripture. In addition, it is a missionary movement. Its believers are ordered to go forth and bring the truth to the benighted. In addition, those who are brought into the affirmed brotherhood must sacrifice everything, even their lives, if necessary, for the faith. World Communism is a world religion in all its social and psychological manifestations except, of course, in its basic philosophic one. It is a world religion without God.

Being without God, it is without the concept of the Universal Father; and therefore, it is without the concept of universal brotherhood and mutual responsibility. Therefore Communism can visualize the world as an eternal conflict with capitalists. All non-Communist nations are bitterly vilified and their destruction prepared for. That is because theirs is a religion without a Father to Whom all are equally children.

The idea of a truly world-wide religion, of course, was the one element in the Biblical concept of social progress which captured the heart of the Christian Church. The idea of a world-wide worship of God is the heart of that tremendous Christian effort, the Christian mission. It was the vision that brought young men and women from farms and from cities and sent them "from Greenland's icy mountain to India's coral strands."

55

This concept of one religion covering the earth, as the missionary hymn says, "from pole to pole," is inspiring but also impossible. There can never be one world religion. Religions are too deep-rooted to be swept away. They have too many elements of memory and psychology and national environment. What Judaism means about world-worship of God is not a world imperialism in the spiritual field, in sweeping all humanity into one religious organization. What the Bible means is something more practical than the dream of the missions to conquer the world. It is simply that all the great religions already possess in them the concept of the Universal Father and the implication of the universal world brotherhood. But, alas, they do not realize that they cherish the same spiritual essentials. What the prophet means is that once paganism vanishes, all people will realize that they are not as divided as they thought they were, and in that day, "the Lord shall be One and His name shall be One," because He is already worshiped, but worshiped under different names. When men know that their hearts are one, when troubles will drive them at last to that awareness, they will take the "giant step" toward the good society.

Obviously, all of this is what we might call "dream-talk." We know how mean and how selfish people can be. How, then, can we count on the improvement of human character? We find great idealistic revolutions becoming tyrannies. When idealists come into power, the power corrupts them. How, then, can we count on social justice? We see what fanaticism can do in the world. How do we expect people ever to acknowledge that they have been brethren all along? The whole prophetic vision is, alas, Utopian.

Yet, without such Utopian vision we could not endure the present. There is no doubt that for the future to be built, it must first be believed in. To believe in the future is not an obvious or even a natural human attitude. In early days mankind feared the future. World hope entered the world's mind through the Hebrew Scriptures. It became a strong faith only at certain periods. After the great explorations, the discovery of the Atlantic and the Pacific, man naturally began to look forward to the as yet undiscovered. The mind became future-directed. Then after the age of discovery came the beginning of scientific discovery. Every year brought a new insight into the truth. All this accumulated in men's minds and was built into the conviction that we are moving forward as the Bible had said.

But now the Biblical sense of progress has faded from the hearts of man again; and it is clear that we must recover it. Perhaps it is difficult for us to believe in one or the other of the Biblical reasons for its faith in the future, but we will hold on to what we can. This we know: Without some firm faith we will not endure. When we pass before us all the contributions of Scripture to the mind and soul of man, we can say that the faith in social progress is its greatest psychological gift. We hold on to the best of Scripture as long as we can, turn toward the future and say, as the prophet said: "Behold, there shall come a day."

VI

ON FRIENDSHIP

The modern republic of Egypt, under General Nasser, is beset with many problems. There is the basic problem of economic deterioration. Then there is the continued political tension. Now, added to those two problems, there is one that is agitating them and the world a good deal, a problem of ancient art, or archaeology and art; and that, too, is bound up with the economic problem.

Soviet Russia is helping modern Egypt to raise the height of the Aswan Dam on the Nile. Russian engineers and equipment are working very hard on that task. When that work is finished, the ancient, Egyptian temple of Abu Simbel, that tremendous excavation in the living rock, will be flooded and permanently under water. In front of the temple are the four megalithic statues of Pharaoh, enormous and unmovable. There is no practical way of saving this great structure which is expressive of the greatest period of Egyptian history, when Egypt under the autocratic Pharaohs was a monolithic state which organized the people to fight the power of the desert and the wildness of the Nile.

Nevertheless, even if this great temple with its mighty statues of the seated Pharaohs will be totally submerged,

Sermon delivered February 19, 1961

there will still be left other great monumental masses to express the monolithic power of ancient Egypt. There is the great colonnade of columns in Karnak and the indestructible masses of the Pyramids, which may be the last remnant of human handiwork at the very end of human civilization.

Thus the massive mood of ancient Egyptian life will nevertheless continue to be expressed. But there was found, a generation ago, a tiny statuette, a portrait bust of the queen of the Pharaoh Akhenaton. This portrait bust of the Queen Nefertiti is an exceptional type of art for Egypt. It is not a central theme which is voiced in the massive monuments. It is only a minor theme. Yet, precisely because it is a minor theme, it is precious. If that were destroyed, there would be almost nothing left to express the minor theme which it perpetuates. Under the massive integration, which is the essence of ancient Egypt which the great monuments voice, there was evidently a hunger and a quiet striving toward personality, toward being different as an individual. That was an unusual mood in Egypt and is expressed in this statuette of the Queen Nefertiti which is the picture of a recognized individuality.

This contrast between the great theme and a minor one gives us some insight into the literature produced by the important civilizations of the past. These great literatures all voice massive themes which truly express the essences of the civilizations. But sometimes there are also minor themes which point out a bypath which it would be interesting not to miss.

In Jewish literature, the massive things are well-known. They express the unique essence of Judaism. We have talked of them often: the great drive toward ethical development, the irrepressible optimism about the human future, a thought which Jewish literature introduced into the consciousness of the world. These are the massive, spiritual monuments which, we trust, will never be submerged.

But there are also minor themes in Scripture which, because they are minor, are not frequently discussed, and yet which point to special moods and sidelights. Personal friendship, the theme of today's discussion, is only a minor theme. The Jewish Encyclopedia, which contains long and learned articles on all the important themes of Scripture and post-Scriptural literature, devotes only a half of one column to the theme of "Friendship;" and even this little article uses only half of its little space for the Biblical idea of friendship. It is distinctly a minor theme. Yet, precisely because it is minor, it may open for us a little path into the forest of the creative Jewish consciousness of bygone days, and let us see something that the great massive themes may perhaps have overlooked. It is to explore this rather exceptional mood that we are speaking today of the Biblical theme of personal friendship.

Now, the word "friend" occurs in Scripture approximately about fifty times, which in this vast literature is almost close to nothing at all. These verses are fairly scattered. There is some sage advice about selecting friends in the Book of Proverbs. There are some bitter words about faithless friends in the Book of Job. But the majority of all references to friendship in Scripture surround the career of one man, David, either in his biography or in his self-expression in the Psalms. Once we observe that strange fact, we realize that there must be some special explanation. The reason seems to be because the biography of David is given in Scripture in somewhat different proportion than that of almost every other biography. Notice the biography of Esau and Jacob, the twin brothers. We are told of their infancy. Then the history skips all their teen-age life up to their young maturity. Consider the biography of Moses. We are told of his infancy, when he is found in a basket on the Nile. Then the whole teen-age period is omitted and skipped, to his adult life. David is one of the very few (another one is Joseph) of whom we are told something of his adolescence.

It is obvious that in our adolescense, friendship is a crucial experience. When we are in our teen-age, we are still fighting for self-realization. We are uncertain about the meaning of our own personality, and we need the reassurance of other people's affection. The great problem among young people is "being popular," or the fear of being unpopular. It means much to them, because their personality is just becoming self-aware and needs encouragement. So friendship is the basic factor in the adolescent years.

Therefore, since we are told of the adolescence of Joseph, we are also told how the lack of friendship and unpopularity ruined him. Since we are told of the adolescence of David, we are told of the beautiful, personal friendship of David and Jonathan. Their names became almost a term for youthful comradeship. It was in a dirge for Jonathan that David mourned: "Beloved in life and not to be parted by death."

Then David moves from his youth into his adult life, and through his adult life into the greatness of achievement, and he has hundreds of friends. The rather cynical judgments in the Book of Proverbs are suitable here: "A

61

king has many friends," and, "The man who gives gifts will not lack for friends." The cynicism was justified in the case of David, for towards the end of life, his friends began to leave him. His sons rebelled against him. The old hero was now an old fugitive, fleeing for his life across the Jordan. It is from those bitter days of disillusionment that come the most poignant words repeated many times in the Psalms: "O God, my friend has left me, he has turned against me. Had he always been an enemy of mine, I could have endured it, but he was my friend. He ate my bread and now he turns against me." The cry of David in his Psalms is: "O God, I am alone. My friends have left me."

It is one of the bitter experiences in life to discover that those whom we thought were friends were only hangers-on. As long as we could do something for them, they were friendly with us. But they left us for the next person who could help them. It is part of the strength required of us in our adult years to learn to endure such disappointments. We must discover that the loss of friends can somehow be endured. That is as it should be. A person in the midst of his active life, when decent achievement can give him a certain amount of self-respect, is not as dependent on the smiles and the quick approval of people around him. David's time of success ended. In the last of the many rebellions against him, he was almost all alone.

Fleeing across the Jordan, David found a number of old friends who still remained friends. They stood by his side and strengthened him. Then when he finally triumphed and wanted to bring his loyal friend Barzilai back with him to Jerusalem to reward him for his loyalty, Barzilai said, "You are old. I am old. I cannot taste life any more. I do not know the difference between the bitter and the sweet. Why should I be a burden to you? I shall stay here. Go on, my friend, back to your palace." In other words, David had discovered an old friend, a trustworthy friend, who wanted no reward. This was the blessing of his old age.

Scripture's description of friendship is broad and complete. It speaks of the necessity for friendship in our youth, the company of friends or half-friends in our middle life, and, finally, the friendship rediscovered as the consolation in our old age. To Scripture, the friendships of our lives are a dynamic and a changing fact. They begin in our youth as an indispensable necessity. In middle life they can be a joy, but are not indispensable. In old age friendship can be our final consolation. It is with regard to this blessing that the Book of Proverbs says: "Sometimes a friend can be even more loyal than a brother."

Rudyard Kipling, the poet of Empire, may some day come back to popular favor. Yet there will be one phrase for which he will never be forgiven in his otherwise great poem, the **Recessional**. He speaks of "the lesser breeds without the law." relegating perhaps the majority of mankind permanently outside of the law as "lesser breeds."

Kipling was a great reader of Scripture. But he never learned that contempt from Scripture. He got it, from his basic, non-Biblical, environmental influences. This scorn for aliens was the mood of all the peoples of the world. Those people who differ from us in skin or belief or national adherence were scorned as being "without the law." The Greeks called every non-Greek a barbarian. The contempt for strangers was so widespread and so universal that modern students of sociology had to coin a word for it, "zenophobia," which means hatred for all strangers. If Kipling had taken the Scriptural attitude to strangers, he would have expressed himself differently.

The word "friendship" is never used in all the many dicta in the Bible about strangers, but the idea of friendship is clearly meant in every reference to them. The attitude of Scripture to strangers, aliens, to people different from us, is unlike that of the rest of the world. Scripture always advised gentleness to strangers, and suggests that if we want to emulate God, we must remember that God loves the stranger. So, "Love thou the stranger because thou wast a stranger in the land of Egypt." Friendship to strangers is as natural as a little rivulet through the landscape of Jewish thought. That theme of friendship to strangers entered into the mind of the prophets; and they embodied it into their massive theme of the world future. When the prophets described that great future hope for mankind, they thought of all the world finding the true faith, saying: "Let us go up to the mountain of the Lord." To this the Prophet Isaiah added, addressing the stranger: "Let not the stranger who joins unto the Lord say, 'I am an alien and I am separated from God's people.' No, 'I will bring him, saith the Lord, 'to My holy mountain. I will give him joy in My house.'" Then comes that famous phrase: "For My house shall be a house of prayer for all people." The prophets, thinking of the dream of the future, thought of it in terms of friendly hospitality and kindly appreciation of the feeling of strangers.

Of course, this prophetic concept of the future was developed at a time when all the rest of the world was idolatrous and heathen. Therefore the unity of mankind was seen as the day when all paganism would be abandoned and the various peoples would come to the mountain of the Lord. But these days, when paganism has ceased

64

from most of the world, the unity between faiths does not depend upon their merging. Judaism considers Christianity an authentic faith. There is no reason why Christians should cease to be Christian.

God reveals Himself in many ways. That is a principle in Judaism. For what is the difficulty between the religions? The difficulty is not theology. That remains the business of each of the respective religions. The difference is psychology, something in the mood and in the attitude of people. It is because people have foolishly believed that if we are different, then if I am right, you must be wrong, or if you are right, then I am wrong. That is an incorrect conclusion.

The differences between religions are basic and important, and can well continue as God's intention. What we must change is our attitude to each other. Therefore the mood of friendship between "Israel and the stranger" in ancient Scripture is eternally relevant. When we know each other as persons and respect each other's right to differ, when each one learns "the heart of the stranger," then we learn the meaning of good will. Good will is based upon the theory that the theological differences are irrelevant to the hope for human unity. It is a mistake to believe that personal friendship is irrelevant to the grand questions of doctrinal differences. Doctrinal differences constitute a problem, but the building of human unity constitutes another. Blessed is America, which has brought us together under a great Constitution and just laws, and has given that dignity to every individual that he can seek another man's friendship without self-deprecation. We meet as equals. Every personal friendship in business, in profession, in neighborliness is one more strand in the rainbow bridge across the abyss. That is why we say in our prayers, "Bless our country, strengthen the bonds of friendship and fellowship."

65

In the prophecies of Isaiah, the word "friend" occurs only once, and that in a passage which is rather strange. It is not that the passage is difficult, either to translate or to interpret; it is simply that it is difficult to accept as real. The verse reads: "Hearken unto Me, Children of Israel, descendants of Abraham, My friend." God speaks of Abraham as "My friend," a very strange expression. How can a mortal man be a friend to the Infinite? How can this transient combination of dust rise to a level of comradeship with the All Eternal Spirit? Is this not a difficult idea? Even if it is, it is, nevertheless, repeated in the Book of Chronicles, where King Jehoshaphat speaks of "Abraham, the friend of God." As a matter of fact, it is mentioned once more by implication, of Moses, the greatest of the prophets. God says: "I speak to him as a man speaks to his friend."

What can these three passages mean, speaking of Abraham, of Moses, as "friend of God"? The easiest way to deal with these difficulties is to dismiss them as primitive. It was the custom of scholars a generation ago, when they came to something in the Bible which was difficult to explain to dismiss it as naive and primitive. Yet it is hard to feel so superior to old Jacob in Egypt, who, thinking of his father Isaac and his grandfather Abraham, said: "Father Isaac, my grandfather Abraham, they walked with God."

It is not primitive at all, no more primitive than Aristotle, who defined friendship as "one soul in two bodies." Scripture describes man as having been blessed with the Divine Spirit, meaning that there exists a spiritual kinship in Scripture between us and the Infinite. There is no infinite gulf between the finite and the Infinite. Scripture would mean that to the extent that we go deep into our own personality and discover the basic realities of our self, to that extent would we find the "one soul" which, according to Aristotle, is the basis of friendship. Friendship with God is mentioned only of Abraham and only of Moses. Therefore it is meant to be a climax of religion, the highest reach.

The concept is akin to the modern philosophic idea of the Jewish philosopher, Martin Buber, whom modern Christians revere so much. He tried to embody into theology the existentialist idea of personal involvement, and said that you cannot understand a human being when you consider him merely an object for you to observe, study, and use. You can really understand him only when you consider him a personality. Then between his personality and your personality there is a dialogue of equality. You will understand another person only on the basis of "I and thou." So, says Martin Buber, you cannot understand God merely by being a philosopher and analyzing the concepts of Infinity and of the Divine. Your relationship with God must be an involvement, your speaking to Him, and your feeling that He answers you. As with understanding human beings, it must be "I and thou." In other words, what Martin Buber has grafted onto the tree of the modern philosophy of existentialism is the Biblical ideal of Abraham and Moses, in which the highest religion is described as friendship with God. This is the direction of religious growth. We think and feel until the gulf between Infinity and finitude diminishes, until, let us say, this Temple building becomes a spiritual home and the nearness of God becomes, at least occasionally, a reality. Then we will know the highest reach of friendship in Judaism. We are not materialist nor doctrinaire. We are children of Jacob, who said of his father: "He walked with God Who was his friend."

Now, what we are discussing is not one of the massive concepts in Scripture. It is not the main highway through Scripture lands. Personal friendship is just a bypath, but a bypath which leads to certain views. First, the friendship between two human beings is a dynamic fact which changes often through life; from our youth, when it is indispensable, through our manhood, when we can often live without too much of it, to our old age, when what remains of friendship is a profound consolation. The relationship between different groups divides the world with bitterness. It may be cured by remembering what Scripture says of "the stranger within thy gates." Friendship, brotherliness, can cure a multitude of Doctrinal differences. The ultimate friendship, the unreachable but never-to-be-lost ideal is that religion shall not be something distant from us. The time may come, even if it comes only occasionally, when the deeds we do in life begin sometimes to feel like partnership action of men as co-workers with God, when the prayers we read cease to be a recitation and sometimes begin to feel like a conversation. Then we begin to know why Scripture said, "Abraham, My friend," and we understand that we need never, never be forlorn and alone in this world.

VII
WHEN SORROW COMES

When studying Scripture, it is well to remember that the Bible is not a book. It is a collection of books, a library of books, gathered over a period of perhaps fifteen hundred years. The importance of realizing this long time span from the earliest to the latest literature in the library of the Bible is that we can make a better judgment of the value of an idea when we consider its place in the total evolution of Biblical thought.

There is a very late booklet in Scripture which happens to be inserted into the earlier matrix of the works of Isaiah. It contains two chapters (25 and 26, as it is now numbered). In this late Biblical booklet there is a famous verse: "God will destroy death forever and wipe the tear from every cheek."

Found in this late part of Scripture, the verse represents historically the dawn of the idea of deathlessness, the beginning of the faith in immortality. "God will destroy death forever." About that time (it is difficult to date precisely) about four hundred years before the present era, the idea of immortality first arose among our fathers, and that was early enough still to find a place in Scripture.

Sermon delivered January 7, 1962

This hope found a permanent place in later Judaism. The Christian religion which began a few centuries later, had already found an atmosphere where that idea was regnant. Therefore the belief in immortality is dominant in Christianity, and dominant, of course, in the still later Biblical religion of Mohammedanism.

The idea of immortality has its strength. It can be defended philosophically. It has a high place among the elements of religious belief. It is firmly rooted in Judaism. We find indications of it in our prayerbook. The Union Prayerbook (especially in the prayers before the Kaddish) expresses the faith that there is a certain deathlessness, we cannot say when or where. The hope, though not specific, has a bearing on human life. To the extent that we believe firmly that those dear ones of ours and we ourselves, in our turn, are going, not into oblivion, but into deathlessness, then all human parting is temporary. Since, "He will destroy death forever," it follows that, "God will wipe the tear from every cheek."

The difficulty with the belief in immortality, which thus arose in Judaism and became a central part of Christianity and Mohammendanism, is not basically philosophical. The difficulty is primarily psychological. That is to say, the belief can be logically defended. The Greek philosopher, Plato, had a belief much like it. But the difficulty is psychological. It is a belief dependant upon the mind alone, since we have no human experience of it. We belong to this earth and none of us has touched eternity. Immortality cannot be bolstered by our daily experience and, therefore, since it is so delicate a belief, based upon refined logic and human hope, it is difficult to keep up a firm conviction of it. Although the average religious Jew and certainly the average religious Christian would say, "Yes, I believe believe in immortality of the soul," it is

70

not a belief which is present constantly and deeply and powerfully in the average man's heart. It does not touch our earthly experience which, ultimately, is all we know of our own knowledge.

Therefore, this belief, so noble and so consolatory, is never sufficient for us in time of crisis. It is not strong enough to help us. It ought to be, but it is not; and that, strangely enough, is why the Bible is an inestimable treasure to the human species. The Bible bases its consolations upon another foundation entirely. Except for one or two such late verses, the whole of the Bible, from the beginning to virtually the end, was written without any clear conviction of life after death. There is no definite belief in deathlessness. There is no belief in another super-mundane realm. Those theologians who say firmly that there can be no complete religion without a belief in immortality, have to face the fact that the greatest literature in human spiritual experience was written without such a belief. To the Bible, death is the end, and there is no easy consolation of later reunion. The Bible, because it believes solely in this world, is for that very reason precious to us. It corresponds to the realities of our daily state of mind and, therefore, also, human life is particularly precious to Scripture and human sorrow deeply understood. The consolations upon which it arrives are never easy consolations. They come out of the earthliness of human life. The Bible is a literature which speaks out of human experience and, therefore, speaks to human experience. This is its attitude from the beginning and almost to the end. In dealing with man's problem of how to face the sorrows of bereavement, the Bible speaks our daily language and reaches our heart.

It took a millennium and a half to write the Bible. Many tears were shed over that long period, and all sorts of bereavements were experienced. Therefore the Bible is so

71

full of the subject that it is surely worthwhile to systematize what the Bible, as human, says to human beings when sorrow comes.

Early in the Book of Job, Eliphaz, the more philosophical friend, speaks to Job and tries to console him in his sorrow. He tells Job that if he will live a life of righteousness, he will receive a certain earthly reward. The earthly reward for righteousness will be long life. The manner in which long life is described will give us an insight into some of the Bible imagery. He says to Job, "Live a good life. Your reward will be as that of the wheat which is ripened, and being ripened and complete, is cut down and brought to the barn. So will you, in ripe old age, be brought to your rest."

Now, this metaphor explains the phrase which is used frequently in the Bible of an old person dying, "gathered to his fathers." The "gathered" means, as the ripened crop in its time is gathered in. Also it explains the phrase we use with unconscious Biblicism when a person dies in good age. We say, "He died in a ripe old age." "Ripe" is the Biblical metaphor. It means that to the Bible and to us in our human experience, when a person dies in a ripe old age, this is not to be looked upon as a calamity. It is as natural as the ripe corn being brought into the barn.

That is correct, of course. When an old person dies, his death is natural. He died at a good age, a ripe old age. But we say it calmly about other people's parents, about old people in general. But about our parents, it is more than merely a natural event. It is a personal event. Their going makes us orphaned. It involves a deep emotion which needs some sort of Biblical answer.

72

A number of times, in Scripture, we find an analysis of the human sense of orphanhood. It is often described in verbal pictures. One of the most revelatory of the pictures of orphanhood is given in the death of Jacob. The old gentleman had been through much experience. Egypt was the third country in which he had lived, and now he is dying in his old age in this foreign land, and his children are gathered around his bed. The old man, according to Scripture, marshaled his strength and sat up in the bed, looked around at his sons and his grandsons, Ephraim and Manasseh. His mind cleared and he analyzed each one of the grown boys, describing each one's character and what each one should do and what each one can attain. Then he says, "Let my name be called upon them, and let the angel who protected me in all my journeys protect them, and may my blessing rest upon all of you." Then Scripture says, "And Jacob lifted up his feet into the bed and he expired and was gathered to his fathers."

Clearly, Scripture wants to say that the real consolation for the departure of **our** older generation, not **the** older generation, but **ours**, is their blessing. Therefore the Bible often says, "Forget not the teaching of your father," or the Book of Proverbs will say, "Remember the instruction of your mother." We often do not appreciate the influence which they shed over us until after they are gone; but when we realize what we have in us of them, what guidance we are carrying in their name and their life, then when a parent goes, the memory of the touch of the hand in blessing is the ultimate consolation. So it was in Biblical times and so it is always.

We can accept the natural departure of the older generation and compare it to the ripening of the crop as Scripture does. But when our own generation ages and its mem-

73

bers begin to fall away, then the suffering is a different one than that of the death of parents. With the death of parents we are orphaned. With the going of our contemporaries, we learn for the first time that we ourselves are mortal; that our life will not last permanently. That is another kind of sorrow which needs other types of consolation.

It is very strange how almost offhand the Bible is when it discusses widowers. Father Abraham is described when his beloved Sarah died, and his own grandson Jacob is discussed when his dear Rachel died. In both cases the men are described as weeping, but not for long. Abraham gets up from the presence of his dead wife and proceeds to arrange for the acquiring of a grave and doing whatever needs to be done. Jacob, too, tells (in that deathbed scene about which we spoke) how on his journey from Padan, his dear wife died, and he said, "I buried her by the roadside and put a monument on her grave."

Scripture seems to feel that men should be strong. After they have wept a little, they should attend to what needs to be attended to. So it does not spend too much emotion on them. But when it speaks of widows, one can say that its pages are stained with widow's tears. If a person took a Concordance, a list of the words in Scripture, and looked up the word "widow" and "widowhood" and ran down the enormous list, the very length of the list would be revealing. One would discover that much of the Biblical effort at ethical refinement of the human species is based upon the appreciation of the sorrow of widowhood.

After all, the practical problem in ethics is to break down the selfishness of the human heart, the natural callousness which a person has, always thinking of himself instead of strangers. In order to break down that natural callousness, Scripture says, hundreds of times, "Remember the widow, the widow and the orphan." It speaks of the agricultural charities, leaving a corner of the field to the poor, and says, "Leave it for the widow." Speaking of the courts and the duty of even-handed justice, it repeatedly says, "Do justice to the widow and the orphan."

The fact of widowhood served as the emotional motive for our ethical refinement. The very presence of widowhood awakens compassion. Yet it is more than that. When the prophets wanted to describe the people of Israel in exile, tragic, alone, and helpless, they could think of no other metaphor than that Israel is like a widow. The lamentations of Jeremiah begin, "How she sitteth desolate, the city that once was great, the city of Jerusalem. She has become a widow." The Prophet Isaiah, promising redemption and comfort to the people of Israel, says, "Thou wilt forget the sorrow of thy widowhood. God will have compassion upon thee." The Bible makes use of the natural fact that widowhood awakens compassion in the human heart and gives us a sense of God's compassion. The ultimate consolation of widowhood is the tenderness of friends and the renewed consciousness of the mercy of God.

The first bereavement in Scripture, the first of many, is not the death of a parent, which leaves us orphaned, nor the death of a husband or wife, which leaves us forlorn. Scripture begins with the death of a son, and that death by violence, Abel's death. It is rather touching that over this first bereavement not a tear is shed. Adam and Eve were too new to this world and its joys and sorrows. They had not yet learned how to weep.

But in the rest of Scripture, the loss of a child brings out the most passionate tears. The Bible mourns with dignity in all bereavements except in the bereavement of the loss of a child. There it weeps with a keening outcry beyond control. Perhaps the saddest example is that of old King David. His oldest son, Absalom, had rebelled against him and almost toppled his father from the throne; in fact, King David and the remnant of his loyal followers had to flee across the Jordan. But when, finally, Absalom was slain and all the friends of David rejoiced that this traitor had been killed, and they brought what they thought was the joyous tidings to the old king, he sat upon the floor and wept and said, "Oh Absalom, Absalom, my son, my son, would I had died for thee, my son, my son."

There is no other grief so deep, so uncontrolled in Scripture; and it would seem that Scripture, with all its human understanding would never find an answer to that sorrow. Yet it does. Its answer is found in the words it puts in the mouth of a great Gentile, Job. The whole Book of Job is represented as not occurring in a Jewish environment; and none of the historic names of God or Jewish history are mentioned in it. Job is described as a noble Gentile who is bereaved of all his children by one great natural calamity. His wife, furious and heartbroken, cries out to Job, "What is the use of holding to your religion? Curse God and die." Job answers: "Do not speak foolishly. Have we not received happiness from God's hands? Should we not accept sorrow?" This is a magnificent response. It declares that we get in life all sorts of joys that we do not in any sense merit. Then why should we complain if we get sorrows that we do not deserve? Job, keeping his life's balance in mind, remembering the unearned joys that he had received in his children's lives, can now accept the sorrow and say, "God has given (for which we are grateful). God has now taken away (which we now accept). Blessed be the name of the Lord."

Job means to say that the only possible consolation after a while when the tears begin to dry, is the memory of the happiness, of the joy of the infancy, of the young growth of the children, of their strength and their laughter. That joy cannot be taken away. Finally there is a stoic acceptance of what cannot be changed. "The Lord has given, the Lord has taken away."

The great leader Moses was married and had children. Yet when Moses dies, the great section at the end of Deuteronomy, in describing his death, makes no mention of his family. Did they not weep? According to the tradition, even his ancient mother Yochebed still lived. Why does Scripture omit mention of the tears of the family when Moses dies?

Scripture has here another sort of sorrow to discuss and to analyze and, if possible, to console. Besides the loss of the older generation and of our own and, occasionally, of the younger generation, there is the loss of a great leader. This is the bereavement of society. When Moses died and the people stayed there near the valley of Moab and wept for thirty days, it is said that there never arose again in the history of our people such a prophet and such a leader. He seemed so unique and irreplaceable. What consolation comes to a society when a great man goes and the whole society feels orphaned?

To this Scripture gives one of its great answers: After the people had stopped mourning for Moses, Scripture says that the voice of God came to Joshua and said to Joshua, "Moses, My servant, is dead. Therefore be thou strong and of good courage." And almost the exact words are repeated almost five hundred years later, when old David was dying and he called his son and successor, Solomon, before him. David said, "Behold I am going the way of all the earth," (a magnificent phrase). "Therefore be thou strong and be a man."

The only consolation which any society or any organization of human beings can possibly have when it is orphaned and its great leader dies is "to be strong" and take up the responsibility. When Joshua was strong enough to lead the people across the Jordan into the Promised Land, Moses lived in him. Society is continuous. It is never permanently orphaned. Its consolation for the loss of a leader is the courage and the responsibility of the successor.

Christian scholars have a great affection for the verse with which our discussion began this morning, "God will destroy death forever." They search around in the later parts of Scripture for other such ideas which they call "intimations of immortality." There is such a verse in Ecclesiastes, that "the dust returns to the earth as it was, the spirit to God, Who gave it." There is another such verse in Daniel. There are at least two or three such verses which Christian theologians cherish because to them it seems impossible that a religion as great as the Biblical religion should not have had a firm belief in immortality.

Precisely because we all cherish the belief in immortality, we must realize that it is remarkable that the Bible developed so great an approach to the problem of human sorrow without having this available and consolatory belief. Perhaps it is even a blessed factor in the evolution of religion that this belief was lacking in the earlier days of the evolution of our faith. Just because the Biblical authors did not have a sense of immortality, for that very reason, human life was doubly valuable. If this is all we have of

78

life, it is immeasurably precious. Life is a priceless and a rare treasure. So be careful what you say. Beware of what harm you may do. You may never have an opportunity to make up for it.

Therefore our Scriptures developed its ethical sensitivity, and therefore, too, its type of consolation fits the human heart, wherever people live and in whatever age. What the Bible tells us about sorrow and meeting sorrow could be spoken to any civilization and in any era. Has the older generation been "gathered in like a ripened crop"? Remember, it has left with you its blessing. Is it a dear life-comrade who has gone? Think of the tenderness and the goodness that was instilled in many hearts, making sorrow, ultimately, a benediction. Is it a child who is gone? Think of the joys that that child brought, and resolutely accept the fact of your bereavement. Is it a great leader? Our only consolation is to continue his life task and let him live in our courage. Because the Bible is so human, because the Bible is so earthy, it speaks to all of us and will remain the prayerbook and the hymnbook of the human race.

VIII
WHEN THINGS GO WELL

The discovery of the Dead Sea Scrolls created such world excitement that it aroused a frenzy of hunting and exploring in the barren Judean desert. By this time there has been accumulated a vast amount of material which has been found in about eight caves. The material is in varied states of preservation. There are one or two complete scrolls. The Book of Isaiah, for example, is almost complete. Then there are half-scrolls and fragments of scrolls; and just now they are discovering little, broken pieces, as if the parchment got dry and crumbled. But since one never knows when one little piece having a half dozen letters may throw crucial light on a difficult Biblical text, many of the scholars engaged in Dead-Sea-Scroll work are now working on the little fragments.

Now, let us imagine we have such a fragment before us: We want to identify whether that fragment is New or Old Testament. We cannot tell by the language because it is in Aramaic, and there is a lot of Aramaic in the Old Testament; and the New Testament was, very likely (at least the Gospels) originally written in the Aramaic language of the people. We have this little piece of parchment before us and we are going to try to identify it. It reads as follows:

Sermon delivered January 14, 1962

80

"Lay not up treasures on earth, where the rust and the moth can destroy, and thieves come in and steal. But lay ye up treasures in heaven, where moth and rust cannot destroy, and thieves cannot break in and steal. For where a man's treasure is, there also is his heart."

It is a beautiful statement. What part of the Bible does it belong to? You can sense at once that this injunction not to lay up treasures on earth does not sound like the Old Testament, the Hebrew Bible. The very first patriarch, the revered Abraham, and after him, his son Isaac, are described as having vast flocks and herds. So, too, Job, the greatest non-Jewish hero in the Hebrew Bible, is described as having accumulated "treasures on earth."

The Hebrew Bible does not urge people to avoid laying up "earthly treasures." In fact, such material chattels are offered as a reward for righteousness. Many times are we told in Deuteronomy and in the Prophets: "Obey God's commandments . . . Your flocks and herds will increase . . . Do justice and it will be well with thee." In the Old Testament there is a tendency to consider the accumulation of property as a blessing for goodness.

In the New Testament it is clearly the reverse. When the young potential disciple asked Jesus what he should do to prepare to follow him, Jesus said, "Sell all that thou hast or give it to the poor and follow me." So it is clear that the injunction, "Do not lay up earthly possessions," is not Old Testament. It must be New and, of course, so it is. It is a well known quotation from the Gospel of Saint Matthew.

There seems, therefore, to be a clear distinction. The Gospel's early Christianity advised against any interest in earthly possessions, and the Old Testament often speaks of earthly possessions as a reward by God for human

81

goodness. On the basis of that distinction, there has been a great deal of bitter controversy between the religions. Polemical theologians, speaking against Judaism, said, "The Old Testament, typically Jewish, is always materialistic. The New Testament is spiritual." Jewish controversialists, in answer would say, "The Old Testament, the Hebrew Bible, is human. It knows what people's life is really like. The New Testament speaks of unearthly things. Even Christians do not really accept it; you do not think that a Christian really believes what the Gospel says, that 'it is easier for a camel to go through the eye of the needle than for a rich man to enter heaven.' Do Christians not try to earn money on earth? The New Testament is not human; it does not touch life."

But such polemics are really more controversial than cogent. Not only do they not do any good, they are superficial. The difference between Judaism and Christianity, Biblical Judaism and Biblical Christianity, is not merely that one considers the possession of earthly goods as a proper reward for virtue, and the other looks upon it as a sort of sin. It is that, of course, but there is a deeper reason, which leads us to a fuller understanding of the moods of both religions.

Both religions are noble. Both have ethical and spiritual intent. But there is a difference of emphasis, and the difference is found in the second half of that verse from the Gospel. After saying, "Lay not up treasures on earth," it says. "Lay up treasures in heaven." The whole concept that heaven is a place where we will live forever, a place where we can build up spiritual treasures for a joyous eternity, is an impossible thought in the Old Testament. Of course the idea of immortality came into Judaism later. But in Biblical times, the heavens were merely where the stars were. The Bible says, "The heavens belong to God.

82

The earth is ours to live in." So the difference between New Testament and Old Testament is a deep difference of emphasis as to our earthly life.

The Christian religion is, one might say, centrally concerned with man's eternal salvation. The Jewish religion is centrally concerned with man's ethical progress. Both are interested in both, but the emphasis is distinctly different. Therefore in Christianity all earthly concerns, one's livelihood, one's poverty or one's emergence from poverty, are brushed aside; they are irrelevant in the light of eternity. And in Judaism these matters become crucial, because Judaism is mundane and Christianity is super-mundane. Judaism is earthly and Christianity is other-worldly.

Because Judaism thus emphasizes our life here and our problems here, it deals with ethical and spiritual problems which are never touched on in the New Testament, the New Testament being concerned with other things. There is no question as to which is better. We may say one of the two moods suits us, fits us better. Our psychology has grown out of it. But it is a simple fact that the Hebrew Bible is concerned with every phase of human experience, and is concerned with it from the ethical and spiritual point of view. Every human activity, therefore, comes under its judging eye. It therefore is concerned with a man fighting his way out of poverty, with things going better for him now than they went last year and the year before. All this is vital to Judaism because of the ethical problems involved. The activity of winning wealth is not wrong, but it may go wrong. Thus the Bible has much to say on our ethical and moral problems and our ethical and moral dangers when things begin to go well with us and life suddenly moves on to a more sunlit path.

In the history of Christianity, perhaps the noblest chapters are the chapters which deal with the monastic life. It is true that every now and then the monasteries grew corrupt, but by and large, the monastic life meant that perhaps a million human beings during the centuries decided to abandon normal life on this earth, and as a symbol of their devotion to God, they took a vow of complete poverty. They were not going to own anything. They held to the Gospel mandate, "Give away what thou hast. Give it to the poor and follow me." Therefore they chose a completely spiritual life. There are today tens of thousands of people who still live under that choice. Their poverty is a symbol of their spirituality. This is true, not only in Christianity; the great Buddhist religion has a vast monastic population. All saints are beggars. They own nothing and live by alms.

By startling contrast, we do not have in Judaism a single beggar saint. We aid the poor. We try to overcome their poverty, but we never dream that poverty in itself is a mark of saintliness. On the contrary, poverty can often corrupt character and break morality. Perhaps one of the reasons that we never have adored poverty as being in itself spiritual is that we knew too much about poverty! There is no spiritual history among any other people which begins with as much abysmal poverty as that with which ours begins. Our history begins with four hundred years of slavery in Egypt, during which we were not even free to move. We lived under the lash, with dried crusts of bread. How, then, can we ever glorify poverty? After emerging from Egypt, we were forty years in the desert, where if you wandered off in the wrong direction, you would die of thirst. By the racial memory, even the food came down by a miracle from heaven.

Therefore, the Biblical promise to the people was: "Some day things will go well. You will not have to worry about food. You will not have to worry about water. God is bringing you into a land flowing with milk and honey." Thus Moses, in his last speech, in the Book of Deuteronomy, speaks to these starvelings of forty years in the desert. He tells them of the future, how well things will be: "God will bring you into a land of springs and rivers, a land of pomegranates and figs, a land of wheat and barley, a land from whose hills you will dig iron and copper. God will bless you. It will be well with you."

Then Moses thinks, "They are going to become better off; in that there is a danger." So he turns from the lush description of comfort and says, "But beware, when your flocks and your herds will increase, your heart may be lifted up in hauteur, and you will look around and say, 'My hand and the power of mine arm have gotten me all this.'" Thus he touches with clear insight upon the first spiritual danger which comes to men and women when things start to go well with them, when the anxieties of poverty are finally left well behind. Their danger is a self-delusion, a delusion of grandeur, "My hand and my strength . . ."

Of course a man's own energy and a man's own ability count, but what porportion of his good fortune is due to causes beyond his energy? I did not know Mr. Benjamin Fairless. I met him at one or two meetings. But something fine was quoted from him in his obituary. He, of course, would not have denied that he had brains and energy, but he said, "I am a mighty lucky man. If my father had not emigrated to America, I would be digging in the coal mines of Wales." With the same energy, with the same brains, thousands of Americans would be living under other circumstances, as second-rate cattle dealers in Bavaria or minor merchants in Warsaw, and would be using the same brains and expending the same energy. The hand and the arm and the brain count, but more than we achieve ourselves is given us. It is essential, as Moses told those people while they still were in the desert, to avoid the delusions of grandeur, to learn and relearn modesty. When you learn modesty, you will learn gratitude, and you will keep on an even spiritual keel. You will not strut in self-delusive pride.

In that same speech, Moses uses three verbs which express the danger of delusions of grandeur and express the attitude of gratitude and decent modesty. He describes the flocks, the herds, the fields, the pomegranates, the figs, and he says: "You will eat, you will be satisfied, and you will thank."

Nowadays, in England, the nobility, the lords and the ladies and the earls, do not count for very much. They do not have too much popular respect, nor for that matter, too much money any more. But there was a time, not further back than fifty years, when it could be truthfully said that an Englishman "dearly loves a lord." The doings of the lords and the ladies were avidly read; read most, I believe, by hard-working parlormaids and scullerymaids, because to them this was heaven. Just think: to wear those wonderful dresses, to ride in carriages, to go to garden parties, to eat in restaurants in Mayfair — that is heaven on earth! To the poor, the life of the upper level was thought to be the greatest happiness imaginable. So, they devoured the society pages which bought them the opiate-vision of earthly paradise.

Of course, those who were thus described as wearing fine clothes and alighting from carriages and rushing to garden parties were not one-tenth as happy as the poor scullerymaid imagined they must be. They are rushing around looking for happiness. Scripture indicates that when things go well with us, we are in danger of being miserable in a special way. It is interesting that tradition insists that the unhappy Book of Ecclesiastes was written by King Solomon, although the book itself does not say so. Why was King Solomon insisted upon as the author? Because he was the man in the whole Biblical history with whom things went best. In that land flowing with milk and honey, which the previous generations were unable fully to enjoy because of constant invasion, in Solomon's reign the land was at peace. He extended his borders. He was the richest and the most successful of all the Biblical Kings. So tradition picked the man with whom things went best and had him say, "I tried every happiness. I went from enjoyment to enjoyment. I tried mirth and found it mad." He did everything that his vast resources could suggest to him and ended up by saying, "It is all vanity, vanity of vanities. It is a weariness to the flesh."

One of the sure reactions when things go well with us is not only our personal delusions of grandeur, but our strange disappointment as to the availability of happiness. The reason we always imagine that we **should** find happiness, and yet generally we do not, is due to our incorrect but normal logic. When a man is poor and struggling, when he is uncertain about the food bill or a proper roof to house his family, he is right and logical when he says, "If only things went a little better with me; if I had only a little more income, the problem of food would grow less and the problem of a house would cease to bother me. Just a little more, a little more . . ."

He is quite right. But then he draws the incorrect generalization, "If I had **much** more, I would be still more comfortable and I would be still happier. Once I can afford it, I will buy every joy, and I will be truly happy." That is a pathetic and often a tragic delusion. You can buy pleasures, but they will soon cease to be pleasures. You can never buy happiness. No matter how expensive the articles are that you buy, by the time you have thrown away the wrappings, you have thrown away the expected happiness.

That is why King Solomon, if he indeed was the author, devotes almost the entire book to describing everything he did and all the money he spent and all the display he made, and how all of it left him disappointed; that there was no happiness in life and it was "vanity of vanities, a weariness to the flesh."

He raises a problem, but he does not solve it. He does not, as you would expect in a complete book, tell us what he **should** have done, what is the true way to happiness. But he does give a hint at the end. The hint seems to imply, "The trouble with me was that I thought I could buy it, and it is wrong. Perhaps happiness does not lie in the expensive, but in the simple." So he says, "The **daylight** is good. It is a pleasant thing to see the sun."

One of our main difficulties when things go well is that we lose our taste for simple things, and it may be that it is in the simple things that happiness lies, but we do not even know that. We do know that life has a big disappointment for us if we think that as things go better with us, we will be that much happier. This is the delusion. Perhaps our only way is to hold on to our capacity for enjoying the simplicities of life, the family and the friends, and the quiet conversations. "It is a pleasant thing to see the sun." It may be that happiness will come from itself and by itself. This much is certain: Happiness cannot be successfully pursued.

A month or two ago, the President called into active service some portions of the National Guard. He had his purpose; I suppose it had to do with making a show of strength in the Berlin duel with Khrushchev. Whatever it was, he called into active service part of the National Guard. It was very disturbing that quite a number of the soldiers (it may have been exaggerated by the press) started bitterly complaining about their inadequate food and their unsuitable shelter. They may have been right; things may not have been properly prepared for them. But the Pentagon was greatly disturbed by it. Later they showed that only a few had complained and things were not really bad. The President, however, paid attention to it, and he has reacted by increasing the regular army, and will send these National Guard boys back.

The Pentagon was disturbed because of a previous experience of a few years ago. The Pentagon remembers that a number of allied United Nations' soldiers were captured by the Chinese and the North Koreans who proceeded to "brainwash" them. Quite a number of the American captives were successfully brainwashed and became pro-Communist, repeating the Red libels about America poisoning the air and whatnot. That did not disturb the Pentagon too much. But then the Pentagon discovered that of the Turkish soldiers of the United Nations — plain, unlettered peasants — not one of those captives were successfully brainwashed. Only Americans were.

What worries the Pentagon is that we do not have our old moral stamina. We have lost it somewhere along the road. We do not have the power of resistance. It may be that the increased comfort of American life, compared, say, to the life of a rough Turkish peasant, has created in us a definite weakness. In addition to the delusions of grandeur when things go well, and in addition to the fact that we imagine that we can buy happiness, there is also a certain degeneration, a certain weakening of the moral fiber. It may be so. It is possible to say that our children no longer need to have the rugged pioneer qualities. We may say this if we were sure the world would remain safe.

But suppose things do get rugged, are the children, whom we have sheltered, strong enough within themselves to take hardship as the Turkish peasants took it?

That is a question basic to the Biblical Book of Job. Job had things go well with him and he had a lovely family too. He started to worry, "Maybe my children are too well cared for, and they are losing moral stamina." The children used to give a party every day to each other and Job, according to Scripture, had a special sacrificial service every day for his children, because he was afraid that the easy life was weakening their spiritual strength. The children never came to the test because, unfortunately, they were all killed in a catastrophe, and Job alone was now subject to the test of stamina. He had lost everything, his children, his health, and even his friends. They came to see him, and instead of consoling him, twitted him with having secret evil in his heart, or else God would not have punished him. Job defends himself and after many agonizing dialogues in the book, Job concludes that whatever strength he has left is his conscience. "I will hold firm to my righteousness."

Ultimately the source of strength is ethical strength. Otherwise we have nothing within us to sustain us in time of trouble. It is abundantly clear that there is need for more moral strength in America. We had better concentrate our education upon it. The culture of the conscience is needed as an antidote to the inevitable softness which comes from comfort. It may well be that the rebuilding of ethical decency is the central problem in American life today.

In most civilizations there developed an aristocracy for whom things went very well. They got their possessions either by conquest or by earlier commercial activities.

These aristocracies always, without exception, grew corrupt and rotted away, for reasons that the Biblical analysis explains. But the rotting away of the aristocracy, and the last one being the English aristocracy (the rest are now gone) was not of crucial importance. They are, as Voltaire said, "just the froth on the top."

What we have in America in this regard is something which has never happened in the world before. The aristocratic privileges of not being worried where the next meal is coming from, of having a secure home, of being able to purchase the pleasures of life, to travel around and see the world — for the first time in the history of man, three-quarters of a great nation has it "well with them." Certainly three-quarters of America does not have to worry whether there will be food for a meal. Certainly three-quarters of America have a decent or a fairly decent place to live in. Never in the human story were the miseries of poverty dispelled so far, and never in the human story were such a proportion of people in a great nation as comfortable and as well off as the Americans are. Therefore the problem posed by the Biblical analysis of the danger of this particular human experience becomes, perhaps for the first time, a broad national problem.

We know what America must need and what it must heed and what it must fight against. The delusion of grandeur, that we are the greatest, the best, and the strongest, is beginning to be shaken. A little more gratitude for our privilege will strengthen the individual and strengthen the nation also. As for the second danger of which the Bible speaks, the belief that happiness can be bought, we are now sunk deep into the mire of that delusion, "If I only had this or that; one more object and I will be happy." No, happiness is not in these things. Convenience, yes, and comfort; but do not imagine it is happiness. There is happiness in simple things, perhaps; we do not know. But to chase pleasure will lead to heartbreak. It is now not only a small aristocracy which is in danger of this disillusion, it is three-quarters of a nation, and that situation can grow into a massive moral debacle.

Our life, by its very success, brings us to grave danger. We should be grateful for the Hebrew Scriptures which concerns itself fully with these earthly matters. We should be grateful that those who wrote the Bible concentrated their attention on the problems of the earth. To our own country and to all who need the lesson, comes the counsel which we have described, from a land ten thousand miles away and from a Scripture two thousand years old.

IX

WHEN LIFE IS DULL

In the oriental religions, Buddhism, Hinduism, a word frequently used is "Maya," which means "illusion." "Maya," illusion, is applied primarily to human life itself. It is the belief and the teaching of the great Asian religions that the whole of this life of ours is a sort of dream, a dream within a dream. Therefore we should not devote ourselves too much to seeking its joys, nor should we fear its threats. Since it is all an illusion, some day we will wake up and know it.

The Christian Church in its classic faith does not say quite that life is an illusion. To Christianity, life is real but relatively not important. This life on earth is just a vale of tears. This is the brief period when we must bear our cross. The redemption, the eternal salvation is what really counts. This life is real enough, but it has only the reality of a brief preliminary to eternity.

Now, if some of the greatest religions in the world, the philosophic Asian religions and the ethically noble Christian religion, all agree in the deprecation of human life, we must assume that there is a good reason for these great thinkers and spiritual leaders to brush this earthly life aside. There is logical reason for it. The logic obviously

Sermon delivered January 21, 1962

is that this life of ours is often more a burden than a joy. Sickness comes, troubles accumulate; it is hard just to keep going day after day. Bobby Burns once said, "Life is a galling load upon a weary road."

In addition to its burden, life is often unjust. How many people in this world suffer unfairly! By no stretch of the imagination can we say they deserve it. So if life is burdensome and life is unjust, it is no wonder that the great religions of the East and the Christian Church said, "Do not pay too much attention to it. It is not worth your devotion. Devote yourself to heaven."

One can sense this mood in the hymns. Some of the beautiful Christian hymns express this value-emphasis on eternity. The Negro slaves, brought here with unspoiled minds from the Stone Age life in Africa, caught the heart of their new religion. You remember the spiritual in which the man sings, "By-and-by, I will lay down this heavy load." This is our life: By-and-by, I will lay down its burden. As for the miseries of life, its undeserved suffering, we remember the grand hymn, "Come ye disconsolate, where'er ye languish; earth has no sorrow that heaven cannot heal." Do not bother too much about your sufferings in this vale of tears. Heaven will heal them all for you. This is the logic and the justification for the attitude of the great religions of the world when they say that this earthly life is of no great consequence.

The Biblical Judaism, for reasons that are beyond our fathoming, selected the opposite road and stoutly insisted that this life on earth is precious and beautiful. It insisted, one might say, in spite of the manifest facts. When the Bible speaks of a reward for merit and for decency, it says, "I will reward him with long life." To the Hebrew Bible, the more life, the better. If it takes this exceptional road of saying that life is a privilege, not a burden, then

Judaism has to face the problems which the other religions do not have to face. The problems of the bitterness of life have to be solved in the Old Testament.

The Book of Job, which discusses the injustices of life, could only have been written in the Old Testament. That book could not have been part of the New Testament, because in the New Testament one would say to Job, "Do not make all this fuss. Life will soon end and heaven will make it all up for you." But since Biblical Judaism took the stand that earthly life is precious, then it was compelled to defend the thesis. That is why such subjects are dealt with in the Old Testament and only in the Old Testament.

Among the evils of life, the Hebrew Bible deals with that strange and mysterious sickness of the soul which overcomes almost every civilization, sometimes at the height of its physical comfort; that mood which Shakespeare describes in **Hamlet,** when "life is flat, stale, unprofitable." When in a period such as this people madly seek distractions which will occupy them all day to keep them from thinking, then almost every life has long periods when life drags and it is dull, boring.

The Book of Ecclesiastes is especially devoted to a man's description of what his life is like. Everything, he says, is boring and life is meaningless. But the cure for the feeling that life is "a weariness to the soul and the flesh," is not found in that book. The answer is scattered in all the other books. Let us try to distill from the various Biblical books what counsel Scripture gives us at the times when we think — as we all think at times — that life is dull.

One of the illusions which we have when we are young is that life is going to be thrilling all the way through. When we are young, we imagine that if we can only attain what we want to attain, if we can only enter the profession or get into the business that we dream of, life will be exciting. This is a great word with young people, "exciting." Things always have to be "exciting."

This illusion leaves us quickly. The young lawyer discovers that his twentieth case is not quite as "thrilling" as his sixth; the twenty-seventh, twenty-eighth, seem to be largely the same thing, and he begins to feel a sense of disillusion, that life is becoming routinized, repetitious. The young doctor, after being in practice for a while, begins to believe that all the patients are saying the same thing and he can predict what their complaints will be, and his work becomes a repetitious routine. So it is with every human profession and livelihood.

One of the first disillusionments with life is this awareness of its repetitiousness, of its routine nature. Scripture understands that clearly enough, and that is what King Solomon complains about most. We remember his words in the first or second chapter of Ecclesiastes. He says everything is repetitious; what was, will be; what will be, already was; there is nothnig new under the sun; and that, he says, is what makes life weary for him, "a weariness for the spirit and the flesh."

Scripture implies its response to the complaint of the dullness of repetition. The Jews were in Egypt for four hundred years, enslaved in Egypt, doing the same uninspired jobs, the same stone-dragging, stone-chopping, for five generations, four hundred years. Yet we do not hear any complaint from them about the dullness of that relentless routine. Possibly it was because they could not speak out. These were mute, gagged centuries. But they **were** redeemed from Egypt. Now they were no longer under the slave routine and were marching through the free and spacious desert. We would expect that life would now be a little more exciting and interesting for them. Yet almost all the bitter complaints, the mean-hearted complaints of the people of Israel uttered anywhere in the Bible are uttered in the freedom of the desert. All their outcries, all their sneerings at Moses, their leader, are heard here: "Why did you take us out of Egypt? You want us to die here. We remember the wonderful food we ate in Egypt. Look what you are feeding us here," complaint after complaint. Why was that? Because the desert was, also, routine; not a routine of repeated tasks, but a routine of scenery.

They had to go over the same dunes, and one oasis was like every other. It was all an endless marching under the glaring, blazing sun for forty years. This routine frayed their spirits and life was unbearable. Their complaining under the changelessness of their desert days finally ended when the younger generation was convinced that they were no longer going over the same track, like a treadmill; when the younger generation finally knew it was marching forward to the Promised Land. Once they were aware that they were now no longer going in circles, but were going toward a destination, their complaints immediately stopped. Life ceased to be dull.

Clearly there is an implied answer here. There is a remedy to the dullness of routine in the awareness of progress. Only that lawyer can continue to practice in happiness who is convinced he learns something from every case; that no case is an exact repetition of the case before. And only that doctor is any good in his later years who understands that every patient is different from every other, and the same germ produces different results in different people, and he has something to learn from this particular sickness in this particular patient.

97

The sense of learning, of advancing, is the grand answer to the supposed routine nature of life, because then the repetitiousness of life, to the extent that it exists, is a blessing. We could not live long under the excitements that we imagined in our early years life needed. A certain amount of dullness, a certain amount of automatic routine is necessary. But lest the routine benumb us, we must always have a sense of growth and progress. This was said clearly in the Bible right at the beginning of the desert wanderings. The people complained at once, and God gave Moses these magnificent words: "Do not cry to Me. Just tell the Children of Israel to march forward." "Just to march forward," to have a sense of progress is the best answer to the dullness of life's inevitable repetition.

One usually does not think of a banker as a person who will become a literary man, and certainly not a best seller. Yet there is a banker, Edward Streeter, who has had three best sellers. His first best seller came when he was a young man, in World War I. Edward Sreeter was the author of that famous comic correspondence which some of us will remember, **Dere Mabel.** Then a few fears ago, he wrote **The Father of the Bride,** which became a best seller; and just this year, he has written a third best seller called **The Chairman of the Bored.**

The man who is the hero of the novel, the head and brains of the corporation, decides the time has come when he has to retire. He does so, and he becomes the "chairman of the bored." His life is now empty. The idleness is eating him away. The story ends with his finding another business with two other men who, likewise, had retired and were existing under the boredom of idleness.

We are all beginning to realize the effects of idleness upon the human personality. Obviously it is a mistake for people to look forward so fervently to years of idleness. For what reason do we object to the fact that we have four or five million unemployed in America? We do not need their labor. Our farms already overproduce. It costs vast fortunes every year just to store the surplus, because we do not have the heart to dump it into the ocean. If we had half the farmers, we would produce all that we need and more than we can give to the hungry of the world. Workingmen in New York have just won a five hour day. All that is good.

Yet there is something wrong about it. What is wrong is the growing idleness of the employed, and that applies to corporation executives as well as to the workingmen. The loafers of life, both compulsory loafers and willful loafers of life, do themselves hurt. They sin against their own happiness. It is not natural and it is not productive of joy for a human being to be idle. As much as routine may do, so idleness, also, leads to the dullness of life.

Why should we mind if the labor unions get a bigger share of the profits? There is nothing morally involved in who gets which percentage. But the moral question is: What are you going to do with the rest of the day? What will your life be like if your work takes only a few hours? Idleness is self-defeating, whether it be that of the head of a corporation who pretends to be important, or the workman who does as little as he can. It is always self destructive.

The Bible describes a happy woman. It is in that famous last chapter of the Book of Proverbs. Usually we speak of it as a description of the noble woman. It is really a description of the happy woman. She is described as working, working in a household, of course, but somehow finding time to engage in profitable business, and sometimes, in addition, finding time, as Scripture says, to

99

"stretch out her hand to the poor and to the needy." The climax of the chapter comes with this unforgettable sentence: "She does not eat the bread of idleness," which is the most indigestible food, the most corrosive food. Scripture's happy, enviable woman works and her life is full.

The Bible is very chary about calling people happy. The Bible is much too full of insight to throw around carelessly the word "happy." As far as I can remember, there are only three types that the Bible calls happy. One is, "Happy are those who walk on the righteous road." Another is, "Happy are those (who feel close to God) who dwell in Thy House," and the third is, "When thou eatest the labor of thy hands, happy art thou and it is well with thee." The dullness of indolence is as bad as the dullness of routine and needs, in every human life, a conscious, disciplined cure.

In the early part of the 1800s, a Swiss businessman, Henri Amiel, wrote his autobiography. When it was translated into English, it was warmly received. One of the things he says is relevant to our theme. Amiel said that the masterwork achievement of the art of life is to attain a fine old age. He does not say that it is a gift, but an achievement.

In this sense, few of us **achieve** a fine old age, for the simple reason that we never work at it. When we are in the fifties and in the sixties and might perhaps have prepared our character for the future, we fail to do so, for we do not admit that we are anywhere near old age. So when it comes, it always comes as a half-shock. It always takes us unprepared. What, then, is the good of Amiel telling us that to **achieve** a fine old age is a masterwork? We never get started on that job. We become suddenly aged, and what we are, we are.

100

Scripture describes how old age captures us by surprise and leaves us helpless in the new circumstance. An old man is often surrounded by the routine of life because he never taught himself to walk away from it. Moses in his old age described it by saying, "I cannot go forth and come in. I am confined to my place." One's rooms, one's apartment, even the scenery becomes monotonous. As for the joy of work, most of the strength or the opportunity is now gone. To this monotony and idleness, add the further curse of loneliness. One of the most pathetic words in Scripture is when David says, "I am forgotten in peoples' hearts as if I were already dead." So loneliness adds to the dullness of age. I suppose the bitterest expression of it is not in the Bible, but in the poem of Thomas Hood, who says of an old man, "When he is forsaken, broken and shaken, what can an old man do but die?"

It is such a resigned and defeated conclusion which would be horrible to Scripture. We notice that the Bible is full of praise for the aged. I doubt whether any other ancient literature speaks more glowingly of the aged and makes more radiant promises that the aged will "flourish like a palm tree," "verdant in old age." How does the Bible, which knows life, make a prediction which seem so self-delusive?

The Bible praises old age intelligently. Old age is always praised specifically for its wisdom. Age is the time to contemplate. It is the time to think over the experience, to weigh what you have read, and judge what you still can read. Above all, it is the time to have the wisdom of faith. King David says, "O God, forsake me not when I am old. Cast me not, O God, off from Thee when I am old."

The real tragedy would be to be old, to be lonely, to be helpless, and in addition to all that, to have an empty heart and a dull mind. What Scripture offers as the consolation of the dullness of age is the inner consolation, the growth of quiet wisdom and the assurances of faith. That is why the Bible says, "Even youths may grow weary, but those who wait for the Lord shall increase their strength." The revival in age is mental and spiritual and that is its "verdant blessing."

There was a good deal of debate in the second century of the present era as to certain books, whether they should be admitted into the Bible or not. One of the books that was debated was Ecclesiastes, which speaks of the dullness of life. The book was almost rejected; and certainly what shocked the Jewish teachers of the second generation was a phrase which the author uses in the second chapter, after he describes how dull and repetitious life is. He says, "I hate life." It is indeed a human feeling, but to have King Solomon say it and for the rabbis to preserve it in Scripture, where it might be a guide for others, was impossible.

You must not hate life. You must face life, know its troubles, meet its troubles, and then you may perhaps be fortunate enough to find it sweet enough and rewarding enough. It is necessary to face the fact that we delude ourselves in our youth; that life cannot always be thrilling. There is always routine in it, but we must learn that progress and growth are the answers to the dullness of routine. There is plenty of idleness, willful and enforced. Only creative work of some kind, voluntary or necessary or even playful, is the medicine for the paralysis of idleness. And as for age, there is always a chance to attain the "verdancy of the mind," the radiance of the wisdom which is its unique blessing. Moses said to his people: "I put before you a choice. Choose ye life." In his words is one of the grandest mandates of Scripture: Let your life be affirmative. Life is worth an active choice. We can make it worth choosing. "Choose ye creative, simple and thoughtful life."

102

X

WHEN LIFE
HAS STRENGTH

The famous and tragic philosopher, Friedrich Nietz-sche, despised the Christian religion. He also despised the Jewish religion which gave Christianity birth. Just what Nietzsche despised about Christianity and Judaism is rather strange. What even skeptics admire about the religion which springs from Scripture was precisely that which he despised: He despised the **ethics** of the Bible. This is a surprise, because what is there to despise? That people should show mercy to each other? That nations should practice justice with its citizens? That nations among each other should strive for peace? This is the summary of the Biblical ethic. What can be wrong with it? Why did Nietzsche have contempt for it?

Nietzsche described the Biblical ethic by the insulting term, "slave ethic;" in German, "sklaven moral." What he meant to say had some reality in it; that the sort of ethic which springs from the Bible (mercy, justice, peace) is for the benefit of the weak; that a strong man does not need it; that justice and mercy protect the helpless. The whole ethics of Scripture, he said, was concocted by the weak and the anemic of the world, for their self-protection.

Nietzsche was bitter, but he was brilliant, and there is some small justification for his describing the Biblical

Sermon delivered February 17, 1963

ethics as "slave morality." Yes, it did spring out of weakness. If our ancestors had never known weakness and never endured great trouble, they might never have evolved the ideals of mercy and justice. Mercy and justice would hardly have arisen in the powerful, military state of Assyria or of Babylonia. It is precisely because of the weakness of our people that they were sensitized to ethical needs.

Let us visualize what their life was on their return from the Exile. Here was a tiny little Jewish community in a devastated land; about them on all sides, the great military powers of the ancient world. The little community asked itself, "How can we exist in a world of force? We do not have any material power. We are poor, and even the walls of Jerusalem behind which we might hide, have not yet been rebuilt."

Thereupon, one of their prophets (it was Zachariah) said at that time, "Do you want to know by what strength you will live, you little Jewish community? Not by military power," said he, "and not by physical strength, but by God's spirit will ye survive." In other words, the essential strength of a people is spiritual!

So it is quite true that a time of historical weakness provided the proper soil which was watered by the tears of the anguished and thus produced the crop of the Biblical ethic. To that extent, Nietzsche was right. Biblical ethics **was** created by the weak. But that makes it all the more real. It is not that the Bible scorns material and physical attainment; but it saw the powerful Assyria which had terrorized the world disappear completely, and the Babylonians who had conquered them disappeared, and the Persians who conquered them disappeared. They decided that in the life of nations there must be a source of strength deeper than armament.

Yet the Bible is not unrealistic. It knows that a man can draw strength from material things, of course. Let him accumulate much property and it makes him feel strong. Let him have success in any field and he feels confident. Let him be blessed with grand health and his walk along the street is like a dance. The Bible does not despise these material realities. Yet it knows that man is born to trouble. What will you do when your possessions begin to melt away as they ultimately always do, and you will have to face straitened circumstances? What will you do when your success tastes like ashes in your mouth? With what, then, will you puff up your chest? What will you do when health begins to fade? Then where will you find your strength? These are the crucial questions asked in Scripture. What is the source of the **inner** strength? The outer sources of strength are obvious and they are good and they serve. It is good to accumulate. It is good to be successful. It is a blessing to be healthy. But some day you will have to face crucial tests. Are you preparing? What is the source of the spiritual strength; not the might and not the physical strength, but the spirit? That is an original and a basic question in Scripture. What is the source of the vitality of the spirit in man that can give him the courage to face the buffetings of life with strength and dignity?

Sigmund Freud sent his successive doctrines into the world like a man shooting a cannon. His theories came like projectiles against the consciousness of the world. Every one of his doctrines created a shocking impact: the doctrine of the sexuality of little children; the doctrine of the bitter contest between daughers and mothers and sons and fathers. Perhaps the last doctrine which came from his own time of trouble was the most shocking of all and the one that will live the longest. That was when Sigmund Freud announced that in all of us there is a

105

Death Wish. It was an astounding thing to say. We had been told by everyone, all writers and all doctors, that we have a blessed possession in the Will to Live; and here Freud says that we actually have a will to die. But he is proving to be increasingly correct. You see it especially when you do not carry the idea to its extreme: Do not think of the death wish as suicide, but ask the question, is there not in us, as Freud says, a tendency to move away from life; to move towards death, let us say, half a death wish, when tasks get heavy, when problems get complicated and we want to run away from them? It can even be suggested that alcoholism is a little death. It is obviously an escape from life. This tendency when problems get bad to wish we were out of life, the death wish, is spiritually weakening. It often weakens the body too. It certainly saps the courage.

Yet what Freud thought he discovered, he actually only rediscovered. Does not the Bible say that a man has a choice: "Behold, I put before you life and death. Choose ye life." The man must decide for the life wish, to live with strength. The practical question is how it can be done. We cannot wait for crises. How does a man develop in himself beforehand, the avoidance of the death wish, the cure of the habit of running away? How can he strengthen in himself the willingness to move towards life?

Scripture clearly indicates how: Moses, at the end of his career, calls his disciple Joshua to him and says, "Be strong and of good courage." It is a strange ideal to make into an imperative. Who does not **want** to be strong? Yet it remains a fact that strength is often a decision of the will. How can that will be mobilized so that we wish rather to meet life than run away from it?

Moses continues: "Be strong," he says, "because it is you who must lead this people over the Jordan into the land that God has promised them." You have a task which summons you to strength and to life. Thus Moses implies a general rule of life, that every task we have to face is crucial, for it says to us: What will you choose? To avoid, to excuse, to escape? Or to confront and do and solve? Our strength is lost or built up with every task.

Is not Joshua's decision repeated in every person's experience? Does not every young, harrassed mother, when the children are sick or the rest are noisy, and everything goes wrong, wish she were out of it, wish she were dead, or at least sick; or would like to have at least two months of rest in the hospital? She is tempted by the desire to escape from life, and yet she finds strength. She faces this complexity of jobs, the fifty trivialities that join together and become as massive as a mountain; and to the extend that this young woman faces it, to that extent does the self-indulgent young person become an adult.

Thus our first source of strength is a decision to do. That is not surprising as a Scriptural idea. In what other religion is God described as an Eternal and constant Creator, Who works, Who builds? God always says to us, "Who shall go for us? Whom shall we send?" And blessed are those who fight down the death wish and summon their will to action and say, "Here am I. Send me." The first journey towards strength is the step that we take towards the next task that awaits us. That is basic in Scripture.

A historic language like English is a museum of ancient phrases. There are phrases in English which we understand in their modern meaning, but which we are sure once had a different meaning, and how they originated is often impossible to know.

We say a thing is "good and strong." Today we mean it that the thing is **very** strong. But "good" and "strong" do not really hang together. "Good is ethical. "Strong" is physical. Whatever the origin was of the phrase, "good and strong," combining the ethical with the material, it is there in the museum of the English language and perhaps may be due to the influence of Scripture. One of the chief sources of human strength, according to Scripture, is not only the will to act and thus to fight off the habit of running away from life, but also it is the conscience. The "good" is always related to the "strong."

We can see this as we read the very first chapter of the Prophet Isaiah. His description of his people is all in the metaphor of physical sickness, "sores on the body," "aching of the bones," "fading of the sight." He describes the people of Israel as "the broken people," "the broken in body." Then for the cure, he says: "Learn to do justice. Learn to plead the cause of the widow and the orphan." In other words, the source of their strength must be their ethics.

Now, that may sound naive to most modern people. We tend to consider the ethical life more or less as residual. We are not living in a very firm ethical era in many ways. Yet in a sense the most modern thinkers hold to it in other terms. Students of the mind believe that the source of human ineptness is as indicated by Sigmund Freud. In his book, **Psycho-pathology of Everyday Life,** one of the first published in English by Dr. Brill, a physician in New York, Freud discusses little things in daily life, such as stumbling in speech. Instead of saying a certain word which you intended to say, you blunder into another embarrassing word somewhat like it. Why does it happen? He starts to explain these stumblings in daily life and, from that, he goes deeper into the whole personality.

Though Freud claims to have nothing to do with morality, yet the essence is the same thing that Scripture says in moral terms. The reason that we stumble and are weak, according to the most modern understanding of the human personality, is that there is something in us which we suppress; something in us that we are ashamed of. The psychiatrists say that we ought not to be ashamed of it, but we are ashamed of it. Thoughts, past experiences, past imaginings which ran through our mind—all these things we suppress. And although suppressed in us, they rise again to confuse us in daily life. So it is what we suppress which makes us stumble in speech and falter in action.

Scripture says what we suppress is the unethical, the evil action, and the evil thought, and that bad conscience makes us indeed falter in speech and stumble in action. Of course there are people who can be as evil as one can imagine and yet who are strong. There are people who have such impudence that they can malign you when talking with someone else and, the next hour, meet you and look at you with frank, open face. But for most of us, our weakness in dealing with people is that we are divided. Possibly we had said something about them, or we had wished them harm, and when we meet them, we are weak before them.

Of this, at least, we are sure: If our conscience is clear (to the extent that we poor human beings can have an absolutely clear conscience) to the extent that we have nothing to apologize for, to that extent we are strong in the presence of others. Yes, "good" is "strong!" The English language remembers it and Scripture proclaims it.

Last Wednesday evening, at the second of our new forums, we heard a poet read his poetry. He read well and his poetry was communicative. As I heard, there ran through my mind the old problem involved in the creation of art.

Let us consider the problem in relation to poetry: In order to want to write a poem, the heart must be stirred with great emotion. But when it comes to the actual writing of the poem, the poet must know the rules of grammar. He has to be careful, to strike out one word, put in a better word. This mood of careful writing is far from emotional. It is an exercise of intellect. So here we have a basic difficulty with all art creations. It needs powerful emotion to start with, and then needs cold technique. But the two moods cannot go together. How, then, is art ever produced?

An answer is given by one of the great English imaginative poets, Wordsworth. He says that art is accomplished by "emotions remembered in tranquillity." The difference between the artist and us is this: He can carry over his emotions into a tranquil time when he can use his intellect and his skill. We all have emotions, but most of us forget them and, therefore, we are not artistic. Only the man who can recall his emotions in times of tranquillity can turn his feelings into art of enduring value.

So it was with the art of life, as practiced by the creative artists of Scriptures. We can see the process in the Book of Psalms. King David and the other authors who followed him are tranquil now as they write. They are creating art. Though calm now, they remember their emotions, their triumphs, and their sorrows.. King David's fears, all the terrors that pursued him, all the hostility which assailed him, are all in his mind now. But he is tranquil and he is carefully writing a psalm and rebuilding the structure of life.

Almost always, in thus rebuilding life against those horrors that they remember, rebuilding it in times of tranquillity, the psalmists often use the metaphor of a fortress: "The Lord is my fortress, my strong rock in Whom I am secure."

We may think of our life in the same metaphor. What assails our fortress? When we come to worship, enter the House of God, we have times of tranquillity. For the hour, we are at peace. We read the grand diction, carrying memory. It awakens in us deep emotions while we are in this hour of calm. Scripture would bid us, in these moments of tranquillity, to remember our past emotions. Let us remember how our fortress, the fortress of our life, was almost destroyed by sudden raids of attacking forces. Do we not remember the first time we saw a film before our eyes and in that instant we were sure we were going blind? Do we not remember that first ache in our chest, when we were sure we were getting a stroke of some kind? This fear left us ten minutes later. But that first assault should show us all how weak we are, how suddenly our fortress can be attacked by the raiding horseman of panic. How can we prepare the defensive strength of the fortress of life?

Often we train our defensive forces too late. When something serious happens to us, then for the first time, we try to find faith. But it is very difficult. It is as if we had ignored all previous raids, but now that the fortress is seriously attacked, we are summoning untrained levies to defend it. We are spiritually untrained. The source of

111

strength, trust and faith in God, must be carefully built. In these moments of tranquillity, when we recall, if only for a moment, the terrors which assailed us, we must begin to build up our trust in the Eternal God and leave our destiny in His care. As we train ourselves toward faith and trust, we can begin to say with the Psalmist: "The Lord is my fortress. Why need I be afraid?"

Nietzsche, when he despised what he called "slave morality," was expressing only the negative side of his doctrine. He had a positive side too, his idea of the "Superman." He believed in a Superman, born to rule and master, who tramples over the rights of others and represents strength. This is one of the most tragic delusions which have entered the human heart, that a person can endure indefinitely like a Superman. The material strength always fades. Our people discovered it early. It is much wiser to prepare our life for defense, and build up strength for the time we need it. Scripture's method, not stated systematically but breathing from almost every part of that great book, is that our strength comes from three sources: from the will, from the conscience, and from the spirit.

From the will must come a battle against the death wish, a facing of every task. From the conscience, a cleansing of that moral devisiveness that makes us weak. And from the spirit, in these moments of prayerful tranquillity, a slow development of the habit of trust. Thus may we be able to say as the years go by: "Even youths shall faint and be weary, but those who wait for the Lord will renew their strength."

XI
WHEN LIFE
HAS WISDOM

The most famous of all the mosques in the Mohammedan world is the mosque of Saint Sophia, in Constantinople; Istanbul, as it is now called. On the model of its architecture are built almost all of the important mosques in the entire Moslem world.

It would seem rather curious that this great classic mosque should have the name of a Christian saint, Saint Sophia. The reason is that this was a Christian church before the Turks conquered Constantinople in 1453. But even for a Christian church the name is strange. "Sophia" is an abstract noun. It means "wisdom," as in philosophia," which means "love of wisdom." So the saint after whom this magnificent church is named is called "Saint Wisdom." But it is strange that an abstract should thus be personalized and now be thought of as a sacred individual. Strange, indeed, but not without precedent. In the Bible, too, wisdom is personalized, even though it is an abstract concept. In the Book of Proverbs, wisdom speaks, walks the streets, calls forth to people to listen. Wisdom personified is the chief speaker in this beloved Biblical book.

Thus both the Greek Christian tradition which built the church of Saint Sophia and the Jewish tradition which

Sermon delivered February 24, 1963

113

wrote the Book of Proverbs, personify this abstract concept and speak of wisdom as a person. The reason for this goes right to the root of what we call "wisdom." It is based on the clear difference between knowledge and wisdom, a difference that perhaps can be made clear by an analogy.

Let us consider: In the winter, fuel, coal or oil or gas, is brought into a building. That fuel is put into a complicated system of machinery, furnace pipes, and radiators, until finally the fuel becomes warmth which is something rather abstract. The warmth is the purpose and, we might say, the ultimate goal of the fuel. What fuel is to warmth, knowledge is to wisdom. Knowledge is what you take in and put through the complicated machinery of the human personality; and if it attains its ultimate, genial result, then just as the fuel turns into warmth, the knowledge turns into wisdom.

The only machinery which can transform the fuel of knowledge is the human personality. Therefore, we cannot find wisdom in a book, which is inanimate. There we can only find knowledge. Therefore whoever tries to transmit the goal of knowledge, the warm radiance of knowledge, tries to do so through personality. Hence, Plato has the man Socrates speak in dialogue all through his books So, too, the embodiment of the Roman wisdom in Marcus Aurelius, who speaks to us through his personal diaries, his "Meditations."

Thus the best way of understanding the Biblical concept of wisdom is through the Scriptural personalities; not to look through the Bible for scattered texts which mention wisdom, but to look for the individuals through whose psyche knowledge was converted into the geniality of wisdom. Who, then, are the people whom the Bible calls "wise"? As we observe and spend a moment in their presence, the concept of wisdom can be transferred to our own understanding.

Tennyson, in his visionary poem, "Locksley Hall," said that "knowledge comes but wisdom lingers." What he means is clear enough. You can get knowledge early. But it takes a long time until you transmute it into wisdom. Since, therefore, it does take a long time, the general feeling is that wisdom is associated with the aged who have lived a long time "Old" and "wise' go together.

But if this is so, Scripture presents a puzzle: The oldest men in Scripture are in the Book of Genesis. For some psychological reason, they are described as living to immense ages, not decades as we live, but century after century. So we would think that these old people who lived to eight or nine hundred years, would be described by Scripture as "the wise," "the aged wise." Yet there is no one among all the ancient worthies in the Book of Genesis so described. In fact, even in the Book of Exodus, not Aaron nor Moses, who lived to a hundred and twenty years (which is the basis of our Jewish good wish) not even they, praised as they are for other qualities, are ever called "wise."

The first person to be called "wise" in Scripture is a builder and an architect, Bezalel. Bezalel is introduced into the Bible (it is right in the middle of the second book) with God's words: "Behold, I have called forth Bezalel; and I have filled him with the spirit of wisdom; and he will build the Tabernacle here in the wilderness."

From this identification of the builder as the first person of wisdom in Scripture, "I have filled the heart of Bezalel with wisdom and he will build," obvious conclusions come quickly to mind. First there are certain

115

types whom the Jewish tradition does not particularly consider wise, though others might so consider them. Some sage in his mountaintop fastness in a Buddhist monastery in Tibet, meditating eternity, isolate from the world, is surely a sage. But he is not what we consider a sage. To us, sagacity, sageness, must show itself in life, in the midst of life, in the action of life. We conclude that to escape life in order to be wise is not, to us, the right path to wisdom. Wisdom must show itself in action.

We conclude, further, that it must show itself in constructive action. And since the first construction that is so described as an act of wisdom is a sanctuary, a tabernacle, we conclude that the finest wisdom is that which manifests itself in constructive institutions which voice and evoke human ideals: political institutions, educational, philanthropic, religious. There are people who are very clever, and wherever they turn, their cynical cleverness destroys things. They are smart, but they are not wise. The first person described as wise is the man who, in the desert, amid a recalcitrant people, out of sparse material, built a sanctuary—a strange, but significant, characterization.

The Bible, as we note, is very chary about handing out compliments, especially compliments as to wisdom. It considers this a rare quality. Having waited a book and a half, through Genesis and half of Exodus, before it found the young architect Bezalel to call "possessed with the spirit of wisdom," Scripture now waits six books before it finds a second person to praise. This is in the Book of Kings and it is Solomon, the son and successor of David.

But having waited six books, Scripture now becomes lavish and speaks of Solomon as wiser than all the wise men of the East, and wiser than all the sages of Egypt. If he was so superlatively wise, what was the nature of his wisdom? Again we are confronted with a distinctive personality, whose nature is described at the beginning of his career. When his father died and he as a young man became king, he went to the shrine city of Gideon and offered sacrifices. After the sacrifices he fell asleep and God appeared to him in a dream and said: "Ask what I shall give thee"—what a grand request from the Infinite Benevolent! What if the Omnipotent were to ask us, "Ask what I shall give thee!"

Solomon answered in the dream (he remembered the whole dialogue, what was said to him and what he responded): "O Lord, Thy people is multifarious and difficult. Give me a heart of wisdom, that I can understand and justly judge Thy people." Then God said to him: "Because thou hast not asked for power and not asked for vengeance over thine enemies, because thou hast not asked for wealth, I will give thee all these blessings. But above all, I shall give thee a heart of wisdom." Immediately thereafter comes the story of the two women, each shrieking with rival claims, and how Solomon saw the reality beneath their words and with wisdom arrived at justice.

Solomon represents the type of wisdom which reads the hearts of people. This is not an easy achievement because everybody in life walks around with a mask. Everyone is disguised. Not in vain does Scripture say in the Book of Samuel: "Man judges by the outer sight. Only God judges the heart." How can we read what people really are? Their words deafen us. This person speaks bitterly, not because of what has just happened, but because there is a certain bitterness in the heart, long resident there. This woman talks with extra sweetness to hide the fact that she dislikes the woman she is talking to. This man talks with great confidence. Behind the bold words, cowers his nervousness. Can we really read people's hearts? And if we cannot, how can we do justice? How can we bring the harmony which King Solomon brought, so that his kingdom grew and was blessed? But when it is possible, it is the mark of true and great wisdom.

Watch committee meetings, watch the general meetings of any organization, and you will understand how difficult it is to read the heart. Most men take part in the debate that goes on constantly at all meetings. They answer the words which just were spoken, as if the words were really significant, or more significant than a mere index. "You said so and so; I said so and so." What was said is not deeply significant and the answer is not significant either. The wrangling on the surface, the battle of masks goes on in every human meeting. Blessed is the organization which has a man who, behind the anger of the words and the battle of sounds, reads the heart; and understanding what people really want and do not or cannot express, he achieves harmony and friendship in the group. Such a person who sees the heart of people and achieves harmony has a touch of the wisdom of Solomon.

There are three books toward the close of the Bible which are called, as a group, as a triad, "The Wisdom Books." They are Proverbs, Ecclesiastes, and Job. The Wisdom Books are not Jewish. That seems a strange thing to say, but is not meant to be startling. Although they were written by Jews and written in Hebrew and are part of the Hebrew Bible, these three books are not Jewish, for they have nothing in them of the Jewish past or specifically of Jewish memories. In these three books, in Proverbs, in Ecclesiastes, in Job, there is no mention, as in every other book, of the deliverance from Egypt. There is no mention of Abraham, Isaac, and Jacob, the ancestors to whom we constantly advert. Even God is not described as the God of our Fathers, always simply as God. In other words, these three books are written by Jews in order to express that which is above the specifically Jewish, to voice the universal quest for wisdom.

The third and the greatest of these books is Job, the biography of a Gentile sage, a man from the land of Moab, carefully described as not a Jew. He is the embodiment of "The Wisdom Books." Just what wisdom he embodies is something that is magnificant in humanity, whenever it is found. It makes a person, in the modern phrase, an "unforgettable person," when the specific wisdom of Job is found in him, wherever he may live and to whatever religion he gives his loyalty.

Which human wisdom is it that Job represents? Job began in prosperity, surrounded by a family, himself in good health. Then calamities strike him, one after another. All of his blessings disappear and he is left lonely and sick and with an embittered wife who wants him to curse God and die. The whole magnificent dialogue throughout the book is a demonstration of Job's determination that no matter what has happened to him, his basic faith in God and the universe will not be destroyed. So the climax sentence in the book is: "Yea, though He slay me, yet will I trust in Him." This is the spiritual attainment of the Moabite, Job.

But is **this** wisdom? Is this not rather a description of staunchness, of spiritual power of resistance? Why, then, is this heroic, unyielding Gentile the hero of "The **Wisdom** Books"? What is the wisdom in it?

Job's wisdom is a deep and subtle wisdom. It is the wisdom of a sense of proportion and a scale of values in life. We slowly arrive by an unconscious process at certain faiths by which we live. We believe that the world makes sense, that it is basically benevolent, that we are not alone and disregarded in the cold infinities of space. We rest secure in this belief. Then something tragic happens and we throw it all away in a minute. Because of events that occur, many of them transient, because of little sufferings and sometimes only minor discomfort, a person abandons the basic faith upon which, more than he realizes, his life is built. In this he is unwise. For what he has done is to add to his calamities the miseries of cowardice and chaos. Where is the wisdom in that? That is why Scripture says: "The fool saith in his heart there is no God." The Bible is not making a philosophic argument, but is giving a psychological characterization. The man who will throw away everything upon which he relies in the world just because things go badly with him this week, or even if things go seriously bad with him, has gained nothing and lost much by making the world meaningless and destroying his own hope. We all walk in darkness, but those who have faith believe that the dawn will come, and others who reject faith, stumble in a perpetual night. So it is deep wisdom to keep our sense of proportion and not let what happens recently destroy what is the foundation of life.

This understanding is universal. There is a great pagan statement to the same effect. It is Aeschylus who says in the tragedy, "Agamemnon," "That man is wise who in calamity does not rage against the gods." He does not base his life-philosophy upon what just happened to him. That is the profound life-wisdom of the great Gentile sage whom the Bible has made the hero of "The Wisdom Books."

We spoke of personified wisdom, "Saint Sophia," and in the Book of Proverbs, "Wisdom" calling in the streets. It is noteworthy that when she calls in the streets, summoning people to be wise, she calls to youth. Why to youth? It is not that youth has a monopoly on folly; there are enough silly, middle-aged people and foolish old people to indicate that we all need wisdom.

But it is a long process to transmute the raw material of knowledge and, therefore, it is necessary to begin early to acquire it. Perhaps each stage of acquired wisdom belongs to one of the stages of life. In youth, when we are still in the rebellion against the discipline of our elders and tend to be destructive, it is a mark of wisdom for a young man particularly to begin to think in a new direction and ask himself: What can I achieve in the world? What can I build? If he begins thinking in these terms, he is getting a glint of the wisdom of Bezalel the architect. A man in middle life is surrounded by people who are laying traps for his unwariness. He judges people as he finds them and therefore tends to be cynical. It is good if he can look into the hearts behind all the pathetically human "acting-up" and all the fearfulness, and see the poor, cowering, timorous creature who seeks only safely in a menacing world; and then, understanding people in all their antics, becomes able to achieve some harmony among them. That is a touch of the wisdom of Solomon. In our old age, when the forces of the universe set an ambush for us and we must walk with forced courage, it will be a blessing if we will not let chance troubles destroy the basic meaning of our universe. Thus we may gain a touch of the spiritual heroism of Job. In the Book of Job, that great wisdom chapter, the twenty-eighth, there is a description of people digging for wisdom, as in a mine. The phrase is used: "The worth of wisdom is above rubies." A ruby does not have to be as big as a brickbat to be valuable. A little ruby is precious. Whatever little bit of wisdom we have, be it the wisdom of Bezalel or of Solomon or of Job, whatever it is, it is our grandest possession and is the precious jewel of our life.

121

XII

WHEN LIFE HAS GRACE

In the Greek mythology, the goddesses play an important part. The great goddesses, each with her separate name and her separate influence, are of course well known. Then there are goddesses in groups, bevies of goddesses, as it were, the nine Muses and the three Graces.

The nine Muses have a very clear function. Each one is a patroness of a specific art: Terpsichore, the goddess of the dance; Erato, the Muse of lyric poetry; Thalia, the Muse of drama, etc. But the three Graces are not clearly defined as to purpose of function. They are a triad who somehow shed a certain radiance on life, give a certain likableness (a certain glamour, we say today) to human existence. Yet though the function of the three Graces (and the concept of grace) is thus a vague one, and apparently not too important since it was left to a group of minor goddesses, nevertheless it is remarkable how this vague mood has penetrated into the consciousness of man and left its words and its impress upon so many different branches of human organized thinking and human instructions.

A king in Christian Europe is nearly always referred to as ruling "by the grace of God." Nobility of a high

Sermon delivered March 3, 1963

order is addressed as "Your Grace." What has "grace" to do with it? In the Christian religion, in the Catholic religion, the greatest prayer, most frequently uttered, addressed to the Virgin Mary begins, "Hail Mary, gratia plena," "filled with grace." In the great battle between the Protestant and the Catholic Church, part of the struggle lasting for centuries, was over the definition of the words "Divine Grace." Even in law, which must be cool and logical, when an English Tribunal (and an American too) decides that a certain promissory note is due on a certain day, there are added three days of "grace."

So here is a term, vague, hard to define, yet it has penetrated into many areas of human thought. Evidently it has some potency as an idea, and we would expect that it would be found plentifully in Scripture. It is found there in a specific way, in a way we could, perhaps, anticipate. Knowing as we all do that Scripture is primarily and almost exclusively devoted to the concept of God-inspired ethics, then even this little addition to human life called "grace" has pentrated into the concept of Jewish ethics also, for any general idea, if it is found in the Bible at all, will have some connection with the ethical life.

We can realize that if we stop and contemplate the famous and oft-quoted verse in the Psalms, and look at it with new eyes: "Worship the Lord in the beauty of holiness," we see at once that the word "beauty" and the word "holiness" are not a normal wedlock of words. "Beauty" is a term in aesthetics. "Holiness" is a term in religion. What has aesthetics to do with the ethical religion of Judaism? Yet here they are wedded. They are wedded also in the story of many a great Biblical hero, described as having grace. Numerous times in Genesis, we are told that Joseph found grace in the eyes of those who met him.

123

Thus is grace tied to ethics in Scripture. What can we anticipate as to their true relationship? We may say, thinking ahead, that since the Bible is not concerned exclusively with personal and individual salvation, but is deeply concerned with the ethical health of a community, then a person's individual ethics must have such qualities as to exert a moral influence beyond his person. A man can be ethical and yet utterly unlikable. He can be what Robert Burns called "the unco' (uncouth) good." If a person's righteousness appeals to other people as unlikably self-righteous, then whatever ethical power he has, fails to exert an influence, and thus he fails in an ethical duty.

Since society is central in the Scriptural concern, ethics in Scripture needs a certain grace in order to spread its light into the lives of others. Just how ethics can make use of grace is a matter that is worth our searching out this morning in the pages of Holy Writ.

In the English national hymn there are the words, fervently sung, "our gracious king" (or queen) "God save our gracious king." What is "gracious" about a king? A king is powerful. A king is privileged. But what is specifically "grace" in a king?

Scripture answers that specifically in one of the Psalms. In Psalm Forty-five, the writer (a Levite) sings in praise of the king and describes the grace proper to the king in these words: "God has blessed you, Your Majesty, and has poured grace on your lips." So to Scripture, a noble characteristic of a man of influence, of status, is grace in speech!

This is a theme of which we moderns know a great deal. We see conscious grace in speech, carefully

124

worked out in the skyscraper offices in New York, and delivered with a charming smile to us from every television station. Yet why is this consciously concocted grace of speech, half the time at least, repellent to us? Because an inevitable fact about it obtrudes itself upon our consciousness. We see this man speaking these words which were given to him to say, for which he is being paid. He says them with gracious smile and a voice full of charm, yet half the time we hate it because we do not believe him. We do not believe he cares about what he says. The grace is bought and paid for.

Grace in speech needs to have, at least, sincerity behind it. A man must believe what he is saying. But even sincerity is not exactly what makes speech truly gracious. A man may be sincere; he may talk to us of what he knows; but he conveys clearly that he knows he knows it, and knows that we do not. We have met many such learned people, who talk to us either in private or in public, as the French would say, "from a height downward." A man talking "down" in his speech, although he is very sincere and although he knows well what he is discussing, expresses in every tone of his voice a definite contempt for his auditor. This is always graceless and always repellent. Whatever he wants to say, even though it is valuable, is hindered in its influence by our resistance. We listen to him. We shy away from his deprecation of our uninformed mind, and we say, "Yes, he knows what he is talking about, but . . ." The "but" means, "I cannot stand him and I reject what he says."

But when a person, in public or in private speech, understands that the people he is is addressing are cultured, even if they are not expert in the particular subject that the speaker is discussing; that they are expert in other subjects, greater experts than he; or even if they are not expert in any intellectual subject, at least are experienced in life and may know better than he how to live; in short, if a speaker has respect for those to whom he is speaking, then in his tone and in his words there is a blessed graciousness. That is true grace of speech, and that is why it is an ethical quality, and that is what the beautiful verse in Ecclesiastes says: "Divre Pi Chochom Chayn," "A sage! The words of his mouth are shining with grace."

We Jews have received training, an early and stern training, in the tasks of charity. In the earliest levels of Scripture, we are told exactly what to do for the needy: to leave the corner of the field unharvested, not to gleam too efficiently, but leave it for the poor. When our ancestors went to Jerusalem, so the Bible says, to celebrate the Passover, they had to be sure that the stranger and the homeless celebrated with them. All these requirements of charity were drilled into us. They constituted the first nationwide adult education in social responsibity that mankind has ever had and has not often duplicated. But with this training, Scripture takes a step in the direction of grace and says: "Zadik Chonayn V'Nosen," "The righteous person gives wth grace." That is a term which has spread from the Bible into many cultures.

We speak of a gift given with "ill grace" or with "good grace." Sometimes we may be glad that our great charities are organized into such huge machines that the recipients overseas are spared the knowledge of how much ill grace is often involved. It is good that they do not know what battles we have to engage in to get contributions from certain people; what pressure has to be exerted on a certain man by his competitors; how we have to bribe him with his picture in the Jewish press; and how, finally, after all the pushings and all the threats, he

126

reluctantly gives and with "ill grace." It is good that the recipients, wherever they are, do not know anything about that. But, also, they miss those who give happily and with "good grace" too.

Perhaps the real knowledge of the graciousness of a gift is seen in our individual relationships. When we give something, thinking that we want to please our friend, and we accompany the gift with a certain mood that indicates it gives us pleasure to give it, that is a gift with good grace. Any act of generosity is a kindness, but generosity with grace is a benediction.

So to grace of speech there must be added grace in giving. So says the Psalmist: "He who giveth graciously, tenders honor to God Himself."

Some English words cannot be traced back to their origin in Anglo-Saxon or in Norman-French because they are invented words. English has many words just concocted for the purpose of concealment. Often it was desired to avoid mentioning God, not to "take the name of God in vain." So all such curious-sounding words as "golly," "gosh," untraceable as to their origin, were invented in order not to say the word "God." When we use the Enlish phrase, "Goodness gracious," it is simply a disguised substitute for "God's grace." "God's grace" is a phrase which is not to be uttered lightly, certainly among Christians. It is one of the central concepts of Christian theology. We adverted to it in passing some time ago as the basis of the great dispute between the Protestant and the Catholic Church. It is relevant to know just what it implied.

The Christian Church basically holds that man has inherited sin, the sin of Adam. This is the classic Christian theology. But how can we be saved from this inherited taint? There are two ways, each suggested respectively by one of the great branches of the Church. The Catholic Church says we are saved by human "works," by how we live, by participating in the sacraments which have a sacred power. It is by these "works" that we receive God's help and are saved from the inherited sin of Adam. The Protestant sects tend to say the opposite: Nothing that we do, none of the sacraments which are mere ceremonies, will ever save man from the inherited sin of Adam. Only the free gift of God's grace!

This debate between works and grace is one of the great themes, the operative themes in Christian thought for centuries. No wonder that the English language has found a way to avoid expressing God's grace lightly; and so we say "goodness gracious" instead of it.

"God's grace," not quite in this theological sense, is found in Scripture. It comes from the Bible. We speak of God as "Chanun Verachum," "Gracious and Merciful." Of course we do not seek God's grace because we need to be freed from an **inherited** guilt. Judaism is more concerned with accumulated guilt, the bitterness, the resentment, the wrongdoings which we accumulate in our lifetime and which we feel need the free will gift of God's forgiveness. Upon God's forgiving grace, we build the most holy observance of our year, the Day of Atonement, on which day we say, with whatever solemnity our personality can summon, "Not in dependence upon our own righteousness do we make our supplications to Thee, but upon Thy gracious mercy alone."

So God's grace, His free will forgiveness, is one of the divine qualities available for human emulation. To be able to forgive, to add to grace of speech and to grace of giving the grace of forgiveness, is difficult. It explains to us the nature of the charm of the Bible's hero, Joseph,

128

the boy wonder of the Bible, of whom Scripture says frequently, "He found grace in the eyes of his master." He found "grace in the eyes of the prison warder," he found "grace in the eyes of Pharaoh." What was the source of this radiant graciousness in him?

At the end of the Joseph saga we see, retroactively, a quality that must have begun early in his life. When his father died in Egypt, Joseph, the viceroy, had been for many years the benefactor of his brothers and his brothers' families. But when Jacob died, they were terrified. Now they feared that Joseph would exact his vengeance for what they had done to him years ago, when they were young men. They thought the presence of their father was all that had restrained Joseph and were afraid of what would happen to them now. They came before Joseph to plead with him: "Brother, forgive us." He looked at them with astonishment. He had long wiped out that bitterness from his heart. He said: "Am I God to predict the future? God wanted all this to happen. Thus the lives of hundreds of thousands of people were saved from famine. Why should I not forgive you? Of course I forgave you long ago."

We can see, then, retroactively what was the source of Joseph's grace. That boy, brought to Egypt as a slave, had grounds for abundant resentments in his heart. How callously was he treated by his own brothers, tied up in a pit, sold to Arabs as a slave, brought down to Egypt and again misunderstood and, later, falsely accused! One tenth of such miseries do not happen to us, and yet how much bitterness do we accumulate in life! Justified bitterness indeed, resentment against people which they richly deserve! Grace must therefore be a free will gift. It has nothing to do with people's merits. It is simply that we decide that we are not going to carry that burden of misery

129

in our hearts any longer. We get rid of it and life sweetens. This is the healing grace of forgiveness.

There is still no definition of grace. It is so many-sided! Perhaps, we may hazard an analogy: As knowledge accumulates into wisdom, so goodness may culminate in grace. Yet perhaps this is an overstatement. We should rather consider grace in the sense of its use in music: A grace note in music is an extra embellishment. It is not essential to the melody, but adds to the attractiveness of the song. It is an embellishment, a decorative addition.

Then we may say that Scripture asks us to add an embellishment to our ethics because we do not want the ethical life to be ungainly and clumsy. Of course, if it came to choice, we would much prefer the righteous and the rough to the sly and the smooth. But it need not come to such a choice. The substance and the beauty can merge. What we are concerned with is not a **central** matter, not wisdom, that grand culmination, and not inner strength, the spiritual power to endure, not the grandeur of the saint or of the hero, but the mood of the lady and the gentleman—just that. May God Who is abundant in grace remove clumsiness and ungainliness from our life and spread his graciousness over our daily path.

XIII
WHERE IS MY GOD?

There is a popular Jewish proverb: "It is hard to be a Jew." This proverb is of Continental origin and reflects the social conditions surrounding Jewish life in the old world for many centuries. How could it be easy then and there to be a Jew? Always a minority, almost always a despised minority, attacked by a brutalized peasantry and scorned by a sophisticated upper class, bearing burdens at every turn of the road: "It is hard to be a Jew."

This proverb arising out of the environment expresses and epitomizes a social situation. But the proverb is correct, also, in a deeper sense than the social one. It is equally true that in spiritual, one might say a philosophic sense, "It is hard to be a Jew." The Jewish concept of God, the heart of any religion, is in itself a difficult concept. Let us compare Judaism with Christianity with regard to its concept of God. We are not comparing the two religions as to which is true and which is not true; that is always a futile discussion and no matter who carries it on, it is never unprejudiced. We are not discussing rightness or wrongness of the respective religions. We are discussing what you might call the psychology of a philosophy. What is that attitude of people to the two God-ideas?

Sermon delivered February 2, 1964

That the Christian idea of God is easier to accept than the Jewish is manifestly not true. After all, the Christian concept that God is a Trinity is a mystery, as the early Christian theologians themselves admitted. This three is not three, but one; and, furthermore, the second person of the Trinity is God, and yet human, God incarnated in a man. That concept is surely difficult to accept, whereas the Jewish concept of God, a pure monotheism, the Living Intelligence which creates and rules the world, agrees with the attitude of most of the philosophers.

So one can say that on the face of it, the Christian God-conception is harder to accept than the simple, pure monotheism of the Jewish God-conception. That is manifestly true. But the Christian God-conception—and this is the point—though harder to accept than the pure monotheistic Jewish one, is easier to retain. It is easier to remain Christian, as far as the God-conception is concerned, than it is to remain a Jew.

Just consider: It is Christmas and the children are shown a lovable, radiant infant in the manger, and they are told that the infant is God. Is it not easy for a baby to love God, for an infant to love another infant? It appeals to the child's heart at once! But we tell our children that God is "Invisible," "Eternal"—what can this mean to a child?

So, too, in early adult life when the human career becomes complex with moral problems, the Christian can think of Jesus as a companion who walks by his side on the streets of an eternal Galilee! Of course, we also say, "Noah walked with God," "Abraham walked with God." But we take this to mean a remote metaphor. To a Christian, to whom God is a man, it is not merely a metaphor. He can see himself in his perplexity having a companion who says, "Are you going my way?"

In the later years of life, when life's burdens are heavy, a Christian can say, "I think of him who died on the cross and with him, I am bearing my cross." Furthermore, Protestants should not be too scornful about Catholics who now give divinity to a woman and make of Mary virtually a God, to be adored. Think what it means psychologically to an old, broken Italian woman with no joy in life and no health and nothing but misery, when she prays to Mater Dolorosa, the "tear-stained mother"! Is not such a God-idea easy to hold to?

When you compare all this with the Jewish concept of the Infinite Presence, invisible, omnipotent, how can this philosophic language retain an emotional reality? Of course Scripture saw the difficulty of holding onto the pure, ethical, monotheistic God-conception. It saw this early. After all, when we consider the Scripture as an intellectual enterprise, we remember that it came to a world of people where polytheism was omnipresent and everywhere God was visible in images. There was no question as to where Beal was or where Zeus was; one saw his embodied presence. Yet to simple people from prophet to woodchopper, the declaration was made: From now on you must believe in an Omnipresent Invisble. They knew at once it would be difficult to retain such a pure concept.

The greatest minds and hearts of Scripture bitterly complained that they themselves have difficulty in feeling close to God. That is the meaning of the anguished cry that occurs at least twenty times in Scripture: "Where is my God? He is far away, just when I need him most. O God, why standest Thou afar off in my time of trouble?"

We modern people, living in a time of difficulty and world confusion, ought to have a special, sympathetic understanding of the great, creative spirits in Scripture who found it was hard to be a Jew spiritually. It ought

133

to be of some importance to us to trace down the experiences which led to their anguished cry. When did they say it? When is it most difficult and how and when was the difficulty overcome? That is the purpose of our discussion. One might call it the psychology of Jewish God-conception.

There has been much speculation during the last century as to how religion arose among men. There are many theories. All the differing theories have one element in common, namely, that certainly it was the power of nature which impressed itself upon primitive man and created a sense of power greater than he. All the antique religions are nature-religions and all the antique gods represent a nature force: the storm, the sea, the mountains, the rivers. All these old religions are created, or at least influenced, by the impress of nature upon the bewildered mind of primitive man.

We always say that Judaism came into this polytheistic world with its various nature gods and said, "There is only one Creator, one Master of nature." That is true, but the truth goes much further: It was not only that Judaism clarified the natural confusion and proclaimed one system, one law, applying to the grain of earth and the furthest nebula, which is the basis of all science. It is not only that, but Judaism also said, "There is another source besides nature for our conviction of the presence of God. That other source is human history." It is not only what happens in the natural world, but what has happened with you and with your family. God is to be found not only in space but in time, and so they introduced into the human mind the concept of the God of history.

That explains why the story of the people of Israel and the Bible begins with a great impact of divinity upon human history, the deliverance from Egypt. There you have the basis for a strong God-conception, a powerful God of justice Who sees evil and, by direct punishment, destroys evil and redeems the innocents. Thus a great, historic force brought God near to our people, and so they were constantly God-conscious when they considered the Exodus from Egypt, the historic event, as important as the Creation of the world at the beginning of Genesis. Genesis begins with the God of nature. Exodus begins with the God of history.

This concept of the God of history, God the Deliverer, certainly should bring man near to God and God near to man. Yet note what the Psalmist says (it is the first use of the anguished cry, "Where is my God?"). He says: "Mine enemies encamp around me to eat up my flesh and they say, 'Where is thy God?'" If history had stayed at the mood of the Exodus, if history had stayed triumphant, the God of history could be easily held in the human heart.

But unfortunately "the enemies camp around" and history which begins triumphant becomes quickly tragic, and this little people who first proclaimed the pure God-conception for the world has had the most tragic of histories. "Where is my God" was a repeated cry when "the Assyrians came down like a wolf on the fold," and destroyed the Northern Kingdom; and after them, the Romans, and after them, one destroying force after another, up to the Nazis in our time. When history is thus tragic how can one continue to believe in the God of history? One can only repeat what the Psalmists cry: "Where is my God?"

In times of historic tragedy the great God-conception tends to fade and people are less religious, not because of conviction but in emotion. Why is it, then, that this people which, having seen the tragedy of history more continuously than any other people—if only because it has survived to see it more often—and which should be expected to have the vaguest God-conception, have nevertheless held so long and so firmly to its faith? It must have been a sheer effort of will on the part of our people, a refusal to lose God entirely, a sort of spiritual stubbornness.

I read last week a Hebrew biography of Rabbi Meir Shapiro of Lublin, in Poland, the founder of a Yeshivah there who had the good luck to die before the Nazis came. He was a scholar. He was also a Chassid, a leader of that ecstatic sect. He wrote books, founded a Yeshivah, also was quite a musician and wrote hymns. His Chassidim, his sect, sang lovingly the hymns that their Rabbi wrote for them.

Now they were, of course, herded together and marched toward the furnaces of Auschwitz. There is very little record of how the various types of Jews acted on their way to inevitable death; but these Chassidim of Lublin sang their teacher's hymn and as they marched, they chanted the words: "Our hands are powerless, our strength is gone, but our Father lives." They kept on insisting, "Our Father lives," and they or their kin lived to see history become triumphant again after every tragedy. They lived to see the other half of the historical picture: that a people crushed, somehow lays down new foundations; old communities reestablished, or new communities founded in a new world.

It is no wonder that the anecdote is told over and over again that when Frederick the Great, the skeptical Prussian monarch, the friend of Voltaire, said to his chaplain, "Give me one logical argument for the existence of God," the chaplain said, "One? The one irrefutable proof is the existence of the people of Israel on earth. That they have continued is contrary to all reasonable laws of history."

It is evidently written into our consciousness that God will often fade from our minds but that He can always be recovered. When history is triumphant, God is near. When it is tragic, He fades from our minds. History can become triumphant again. So it has been with us, and so it can be for all.

The great German philosopher, Immanuel Kant, was not a religious philosopher. He was what is called a critical philosopher. But in certain of his sayings he has a religious mood. The most quoted saying of his is: "Two things fill my heart with awe and wonder, the starry heavens above and the moral law within."

He considered "the moral law" to be an almost inescapable sense of what is right. This sense was to him one of the basic data of human life. Of course Judaism is rooted in the soil of that idea. It is the first religion which made of God an ethical force, a God of justice. The God of justice is easy to believe in when you see "the moral law within" manifesting itself in outer life. When you meet decent people, clean-hearted men and women, when you live in a decent community, it is easy to believe in God because His justice and mercy manifest themselves in life.

But what shall we believe when the experience comes, as it came to the Prophet Malachi who said, "Nobody is doing right. All are doing evil. Nobody bothers even to ask, 'Where is the God of justice.'" When you see corruption, when you see one corrupt person—that is all you need—who triumphs in his corruption, your reaction in whatever language you use is, "Where is God?" The

137

prosperity of the wicked is one of the oldest questions in theology; and when, especially, corruption overtakes a whole society, as has happened time and time again, then God seems to flee to the distant nebulae.

At times such as ours, when we cannot find a clean novel, when there is hardly a single influence in a teen-ager's life urging him or her towards decency and re-straint, when everything moves to corruption; in an age such as this when "the moral law within" seems to be no law at all, God seems far away indeed.

It is so and will always be so. But the ground for holding on is the conviction that "the moral law within" is a very troublesome quality. Nobody is quite at ease in evil, as we can see by the way every criminal apologizes by saying, "Everybody is doing it." Every person who acts wickedly has some proverb whereby to justify him-self. The moral law—whatever that conscience is—is at least a disquieting factor, and no society remains per-manently content with its corruption.

Therefore it has happened frequently that there comes a time in a corrupt society when a fresh breeze seems to enter from an open window and sweep away the poi-soned air, and the society becomes decent again. In the bawdy Elizabethan society there rose up from the hearts of man moods which eventually became a new religious attitude, the Puritanism which clarified and cleaned all English society. This Puritanism became too petrified and it was brushed aside, and English society entered a sec-ond period of corruption in the Restoration of Charles II. The corruption was not only in England. The whole so-called "rococo" period was a period of this so-called "gal-lantry." Most of the dirty poetry that was sold under the counter up to the last few years when books of any kind can now be sold over the counter—most of the dirty poetry came from the time of the Restoration. The world was corrupt and it continued in corruption through the early Georges, and then came the Victorian period during which people became trustworthy again, people became decent again. Victorianism became stodgy and it has gone now.

But we see that every corrupt period so far is part of an alternation. The sense of shame begins to accumulate and people, first of all, become bored with bawdiness (how much variation can there be, after all, in dirty jokes?) They get tired of it and a fresh wind comes and clears the world. That is the way it has been in the past. That, please God, it can be again. If it comes again as it has come previously and the world gets clean again, then it will be as Scripture says: "Let the wicked forsake his path and call upon God. He is near."

Shakespeare tells many jokes. Some of them are coarse, but all his coarse humor he puts in the mouths of coarse people, the mob. Whenever he has a joke spoken by one of the class that he considers superior, that joke always has some deeper meaning. It is wry and meaningful humor.

In **Much Ado About Nothing,** one of the chief characters says, "There never was a philosopher who could endure the toothache." You can philosophize about history or you can philosophize about social manners and morals, but when you have a jab of physical agony, all your philosophy flies out of the window. "There never was a philosopher" who could keep up his philosophy when he has physical pain.

The Psalmist, likewise, speaks of his physical torments, and evidently it was both physical pain and be-

139

reavement because he says: "My tears have become my bread. Where is my God?" When we are in individual, personal trouble, in sickness, our religion is shaken because we always consider it an injustice. Why me? What have I done? Why do I deserve it? And in bereavement it is worse because it is half unselfish, at least. In bereavement we often think: Why should he have had to die so early? It is not fair. So when the "tears become our bread," we ask, "Where is our God?"

We know well that there is no good answer to that question. There is no adequate **religious** answer for the apparently undeserved suffering of decent people; and also there is no good irreligious answer. What is the usual irreligious answer? How good is it? The irreligious answer is that this is the way nature works. This is no answer to the human heart—it is a shrug! There is no strength and no consolation in that. As for the religious answer, it is difficult "logically." How can you reconcile apparently undeserved suffering with the God of Justice?

So this remains a prime problem and puzzle in life, religious or irreligious. Yet the difference between the irreligious failure to answer this question and the religious failure is that religion, at least, holds out the hope of consolation. One is perpetual night and the other is night that moves towards a dawn. The Psalmist who says, "My tears have become my bread. Where is my God?" (it is the Forty-second Psalm) continues and he says, "When can I again join the pilgrimage to the house of God?"

What the Psalmist is really saying is, "My sorrows and my pains have isolated me and I live in my own world, surrounded by my own miseries; and I feel as if I am abandoned by man and God." "When," says the Psalmist, "will I again be a part of human society? When

I join the pilgrim throng again and come to the house of God and see friends around me. I know they have suffered at least as much as I have suffered and have outlived it and are now strong again. I see them and I believe the time will come when my tears will dry and my strength will return."

Religion does not **solve** the problem of God and suffering. Nothing has solved that problem, so far, but religion says: You have suffered enough. "Comfort ye, comfort ye, My people."

We began by discussing Christianity and how much easier it is to hold onto a concept of God Who is incarnated as a man. Of course, Jesus of Nazareth was not a Christian. The religion of Christianity was founded upon the fact of his death and his believed-in resurrection. He was a Jew, and when he died in agony, he also uttered a Jewish agonized cry. He said as the Gospel records it, "My God, My God, why hast Thou forsaken me?"

Those words were not original with Jesus. What would a Jewish young man quote in agony? He would quote **Tehillim,** the Psalms, and this is the opening verse of the Twenty-second Psalm: "Eli, Eli, loma azavtoni." Once we recognize it as a Psalm quotation, we realize it is part of a whole group of quotations—unhappy quotations—voicing sorrow that God seems so far away just when we want Him near. "Where is my God? Why standest Thou afar off," David cried, "in my time of trouble?"

All these anguished cries give us a new avenue of understanding the Bible. What do we usually understand to be the true greatness of the Bible? We understand that it is very great literature, and it is. We understand that it has ethical idealism, and it has. But it has something else that is unique in classic literature in the world: It is tremendously and heartbreakingly sincere.

No other book, no other literary foundation of any other religion is so truthful about the fading of religion in the hearts of its greatest men. The Bible tells us a truth about our faith: Nobody is forever strongly religious. The fading of the reality of God occurred to David and occurred to the Prophets, and it is normal for us all because the God-conception is so pure and so exalted.

Scripture can be understood as a dialogue. When history becomes so tragic, when the world becomes so corrupt, and life is so unhappy: "God, why art Thou afar off?" And the Divine answer is: "You are walking in darkness. But keep on walking and those who walk in darkness will see again the radiant light."

XIV
WHOM SHALL I FEAR?

We are all occasionally angry, but thank God we are not often in a blazing rage. Whenever we see a person thoroughly enraged, we are deeply disturbed and embarrassed because the person in a blazing rage is a human being dehumanized. He does not look normal, his face pales, his eyes blaze, his fist clenches. He can be murderous. It is as if he is possessed by some demonic force. The hideous spectacle of a blazing, murderous rage is so disturbing that it is very difficult for us, then, to appreciate the fact that this destructive emotion is actually one of nature's blessings to the animal world. Without rage, animals would not survive to the percentage that they do. Nature is, as has been said, bloodstained, "red in beak and claw," and animals often have to fight for their lives. They never fight—could not fight—cold-bloodedly. Nature blesses them with the gift of rage and this violent emotion stirs up the adrenal glands and the proper chemical is poured into the blood and the tone of the muscles is intensified so that the animal can fight violently for its life. Then, after the battle is over, the rage disappears. But we human beings, inheriting this life-protecting instinct, have exaggerated it disproportionately to our life-needs; and rage which is a blessing in animal life, can easily become a curse in human life.

Sermon delivered February 9, 1964

There is an analogous, inherited emotion which especially concerns us today: Fear, like anger, is a blessing, a protection in animal life. One of the memorable sights in South Africa is the animal life in the great Kruger game preserve. One of the most frequent sights there is a herd of impala, these slim, beautiful gazelles, each not more than five feet tall. These gazelles, slender-legged, large-eyed, large-eared, graze calmly until some little noise is heard in the distance. Then their ears raise and they freeze into immobility. Fear has taken possession of them. If the noise is repeated and it is interpreted as danger, they flow away like a stream and disappear before one's eyes. If the noise is not repeated, the fear vanishes at once, the alertness is relaxed and the impala go on feeding.

This life-protecting instinct of fear, like the instinct of rage, also is exaggerated in human life and becomes dangerous. We might say that if rage is a fire, fear is an acid which corrodes us.

Clearly it is central to the task of all character guidance, that which we receive and that which we give to ourselves, to learn how to manage our human exaggeration of the nature-given instinct. So Scripture, whose central task is (as it would put it) the building of human beings in the image Divine, Scripture which means to reshape the character of man, faces the problem of our chronic, human perversion of the natural instinct of fear. The Bible is full of comment on the question, but in a series of books as Scripture is, the various comments do not always easily harmonize with each other. Many of them seem mutually contradictory. But we may assume that there is a substratum, a basic attitude as to how life should be lived in confrontation with the problem of fear. The search for this basic attitude is the purpose of our investigation of Scripture today, under the heading, "Whom (and what and when) shall I Fear?"

The Book of Psalms is generally called the Psalms of David, but David is not the author except for about twenty or thirty for sure of the hundred and fifty psalms. His are the earlier psalms. When you read these early Davidic psalms, you are struck with their leading mood: King David is always talking about the dangers he is in; dangers from enemies, people who "camp about him," people who lie in ambush for him. This concern of his gives a true picture of David's actual life experience. He was always in danger. As a shepherd lad leading his father's flock, there was the danger of lions which were frequent in Judah in those days. As a young man on the verge of his twenties or perhaps a little younger, he wandered into King Saul's court and fought Goliath. Then madness seized King Saul and he suddenly hated the boy whom he had loved, so David fled for his life. For a number of years he lived the life of a wandering fugitive, with King Saul always sending expeditions to capture him. He was constantly in danger. When he finally became King, he had to endure rebellion, revolts by his most beloved sons. His life was that of a man walking through an ambush. This is reflected in the Psalms: He is always speaking of "enemies."

A number of times David says: "God is my stronghold! Of whom shall I be afraid?" It does not mean that he was **not** afraid. With enemies lying in ambush for him, he had to be alert. But somehow he felt that his faith guarded him against the exaggeration of fear. What he believed amounts to this: Every human being, to a different degree, depending upon temperament and the reaction that we awaken in other people, has enemies or half-enemies, people who do not like us. They would not be sad if harm came to us; and so would actually do us harm. Since they may really endanger us, we need to have enough fear for alertness, in order to protect ourselves.

145

But here is where the weakness of human nature enters. It was Bergson who said that in humans, the mind takes the place of the instincts. I do not remember now whether Bergson meant that to be a compliment or a complaint. But it is certainly a fact that the human mind often perverts the natural instincts. It is natural and right that we should fear. But our fears become unnatural. In animal life, when danger of an enemy is past, the animal forgets immediately. But we do not easily forget. We will remember a mean word for years and some hostile act, often a minor one, will remain in our minds all our lives. And so we pile up the memory of hostility, writing our own miserable psalm of life until finally the fear which should have been temporary in face of danger becomes a permanent mood, and our life no longer seems secure. This useless remembering can even grow into a madness.

Of all the letters we sometimes receive from unfortunates, patients in mental hospitals—they are all sad, but the saddest are those that come from the paranoiacs, those who see enemies all around them; and not only all around them, but even enemies within themselves. They write about the demons that have entered into them and are eating them up and destroying them. Such madness is an exaggeration of a mood found in our "normal" life. It is only a question of degree. We all have a tendency to paranoia, to remembering "the enemies," of remaining afraid too long after the danger is past.

It is the function of the spiritual forces in our lives to provide an antidote to this poisoning of ourselves. That is what King David means when he says: "The Lord is the stronghold of my life. Of whom shall I be afraid?" When there is danger, I need to be afraid and alert. But when the danger is past, I return to a confidence in my inner strength.

The Divine source of confidence, something to trust in life, sometimes works through a human agent. In England the fears piled up due to the hostility and the half-veiled threats of Hitler. The fear accumulated to the verge of national panic. Then after Chamberlain came Churchill, who gave his people a sense of "inner stronghold." The fear in Chamberlain ended in Munich, The renewed sense of strength in Churchill produced "their finest hour."

Clearly it is the urgent necessity in every life to stop remembering the hostilities which have passed; to use the instinct of fear as nature intended it to be used, as an alertness against what lawyers call "a clear and present danger," not as a preservative of past hostility. It is in this task that we need every reassurance of our faith. When God sent Moses' successor, Joshua, into the Promised Land, there were dangers and enemies to face. He knew that Joshua would be brave enough to face them and afraid enough to be alert. But after each separate danger was past, God's counsel to Joshua remains for every life: "But be strong and of good courage."

We sometimes call a person a Stoic. Thus we use the name of an ancient philosophy and make it into a common noun. The old Stoics were brave people. Their courage was derived from a doctrine which is more easily admired than emulated. The Stoics taught that we should all live "in harmony with nature;" that whatever happens to us is a natural happening, and since it is natural and we, too, are a part of nature, we must accept it. Whatever happens is not what Shakespeare called "the slings and arrows of outrageous fortune." Nothing that happens is "outrageous." It is all natural and so we must bear it without complaint.

The Stoic philosophy of living in harmony with na-

147

ture is a doctrine for a chosen few, for great philosophers. For most of us, living in harmony with nature is not always so appealing. We do not consider nature a source of unmixed blessing. On the contrary, the same natural world that gives us the warm zephyrs of May, brings us the tornadoes of September and October. The same quiet, green landscape can explode into a destructive earthquake. The germ is part of nature; the virus is as natural in the universe as we, and if the virus seeks his prey and we are its prey, it is an act of nature too, is it not? Nature is a constant source of danger.

It is not only the fear of human enemies, but also the fear of the dangers that life itself brings to us. Our fear of nature is normal except when the human mind begins to exaggerate it. It is not so much the unnecessary remembering, as with hostility. Here the misery comes from our imagination, our anticipation of natural dangers. We have too much imagination. We see in every little discomfort a premonition of something awful, and our vivid picture of a dire future destroys our joy and our confidence in life. That is why the Psalmist says, "Be not afraid of evil tidings." The operative word here is "tidings," "news." We always anticipate bad news and that anticipation of ours is a self-destruction. So the Psalmist says, warning us not to be afraid of "evil tidings" (this is the Ninety-first Psalm): "He will give His angels charge over thee to guide thee in all thy ways."

Now that is poetic, figurative language. What the Psalmist means is that there is a certain angelic power, a certain protective power in us that should guard us against being terrorized by evil tidings. There is an inner strength. There are powers of bodily defense which we never think of. We have only to think of how many thousands of potential infections our bodies' defenses have in our lifetime thrown back defeated! And what of the magical healing power of nature which with a mysterious engineering power spans over and heals every cut, every burn! We have "angels," a protective power in us that should keep us from the terror of evil tidings.

Scripture does not say that evil does not come—why should it not come—we are part of nature and share the fate of all natural things. Certainly evil comes and it is our duty to face and protect ourselves as much as we can. But to keep on looking for "evil tidings," that can become a sin against our psychic health. The strongest words of the Psalmist are in the Twenty-third. David knows and we all know the future that we all will face. He does not say it will not come and he does not pronounce such nonsense as, "There is no death." But he speaks like a man: "Yea, though I walk through the valley of the shadow, I will fear no evil." There is time enough for the tidings. It is for us to face today what we have to face.

All this counsel is clear enough if it were not for the fact that there is in Scripture a mass of verses that seem to say the very opposite. What we have cited thus far warns us against remembering too much of past hostility and over-anticipating the natural dangers. Yet in the Proverbs there is a famous verse which says: "Blessed is the man who feareth always." How can Scripture say, in self-contradiction, that it is a blessing to fear? In fact, there are at least a hundred verses in Scripture which call upon people to fear; but usually, almost entirely, it is to fear God.

The Biblical word for "religion" is "Yiras Adonoi," "the fear of God." Now that we state it, we are aware of being embarrassed at the Scriptural characterization of religion as "the fear of God." This embarrassment is not a natural one; it is an induced one, created by certain

Christian propagandists who tell us, "The Old Testament religion is a religion of fear. It always speaks of fearing God. But the new Testament religion is a religion of love." Of course, all such contrasts are unfair. They are always prejudiced, generally obtained by leaving out the verses that would favor the opposite side and leaving out on their own side the verses that would hurt their case.

In the first place, the New Testament also speaks of religion as "the fear of God." In the Book of Acts when there is the praise of a certain centurion, he is described as "a just man in the fear of God." In the Epistle to Corinthians, Paul says to the churches, congratulating them, "You have grown and prospered in the fear of God." So there you have it: Religion as "the fear of God" is not the mark of contrast between the two religions. Early Christianity and the parent religion both consider it proper to characterize religion as "the fear of God."

We have to acknowledge all these texts and, if possible, get beneath the surface of them. Some scholars say that "the fear of God" does not mean the terror of God; that "Yiras Adonoi" means the "reverence for God." Of course that is true to some extent. The "fear" that we have for a mortal man cannot be of the same quality as the "fear" for an Infinite Reality. The latter is a sort of purified, ennobled fear; it is an awe, a reverence. These scholars are right, it does mean reverence. Still the word "fear" is used and fear is an element in it. What does it mean when Scripture says: "The fear of God is the beginning of wisdom"? How do we understand it? How is it related to the instinct of fear?

Scripture explains itself clearly: There is a Psalm (Thirty-four) in which the Psalmist speaks to us as if he were our father and we are his children. He says, "Lechu Vonim . . .," "Come, children, listen to me. I will explain

150

the fear of God. It means," he says, "Keep thy hand from evil and thy tongue from speaking slander."

So "the fear of God" seems to mean the fear of those things which would be displeasing to God. In other words, the fear of sin; in fact, a fear of a special type of sin. In the Book of Leviticus, in the "Holiness" portion which we read on the Day of Atonement, certain special sins are mentioned and always in connection with the fear of God: "Curse not the deaf," "Put not a stumbling block before the blind." A little later, "Oppress not the weak, but thou shalt fear the Lord, thy God."

Now it becomes clearer: The fear of the Divine displeasure is mentioned in connection with those things that we can do with impunity, free from the danger of human punishment. You can curse the deaf; he will never hear you and never know of your malevolence. You can put a stumbling block, a stone, in the road of the blind, and he will stumble and hurt himself and never know who did it. You can do harm to the weak and they will never retaliate. For those evil deeds that are "safe," about which you do not need to fear human retaliation or punishment —what you can safely "get away" with—"Fear the Lord!"

In other words, it means practically to fear your own weaknesses. We know we are never as good as we may seem to be. We know what we might do to others if it were not for the fear of detection and punishment. In those cases where we are confident that we have nothing to fear, we should fear offending the God of Justice. That is the ethical-emotional meaning of the Jewish God-conception. That is why religion is called "the fear of God" and why such "fear" is called "the beginning of wisdom." Partly it does mean awe and reverence and partly it means a never-ending fear of the possibility of doing evil. That is why **The Ethics of the Fathers** said: "Never trust your-

151

self till the day of your death." God is ever-present and I will always be afraid of displeasing the God of Justice and Mercy.

Among the popular "inspirational" books there was one published a few years ago with the grand title, **The Conquest of Fear.** It is a good title, but a false one, because it promises more than it can ever fulfill. We cannot conquer fear. Fear, like rage, is one of the inherited instincts and it will always be with us. In fact, fear **should not** be conquered. We could not protect ourselves without the alertness and the excitement to self-defense which it gives us. But, being human, we have marred a natural instinct. We have kept the fear of enemies too long in our minds. We have anticipated dangers with too vivid an imagination.

We might characterize what Scripture has accomplished as a grand enterprise in mental hygiene. It says: Fear cannot be conquered, but it can be rechanneled. Since you **must** fear something, then fear the displeasure of the God of Justice. Perhaps the doctrine can be summed up as follows: Fear God, but never fear man. Fear your own weaknesses, but do not fear what has not yet happened. If you can thus rechannel the inherited instinct, you have climbed to a good height from which you can see the right pathway for decent living.

XV

WHO IS MY BROTHER?

Thomas Babington Macaulay was a famous man in the early days of the Victorian era, and his fame continued to some extent down to our day. He was a historian of note. His **History of England** is still readable. He was a statesman. He helped in the government of India during the days of the Empire. He was an essayist. But he won a place in the hearts of England by a narrative poem. He was the author of the much-beloved boy's ballad, **Horatius at the Bridge.** At least two generations of English school-boys and many American boys, I am sure, knew long stretches of the epic by heart.

The poem **Horatius at the Bridge** is set in the early days of the Roman Republic, but the narrator of the story lived two hundred years later, in the troubled days of the Roman Empire, in the days of bitterness and dispute when all the different social classes in Rome hated each other and all of them together were oppressed by the growing corruption of the Roman Emperors. The supposed narrator looks back two hundred years to the idyllic, peaceful days of the Roman Republic and tells the story of what he calls a number of times, "the brave days of old," the days of Horatius. He describes his social philo-

Sermon delivered February 16, 1964

sophy (as far as a child's poem can have philosophy in it) in these words, contrasting his own unhappy times with the happier days of the Republic. He says:

"Then none was for the party
    And all were for the state;
The rich man helped the poor
    And the poor man loved the great.
Ah! Romans were like brothers
    In the brave days of old."

Since this poem is no longer taught in American schools, it is probable that men have grown up now and reached their professional standing who never saw the poem at all. It is not too great a loss; the poem is not particularly deep, but generations have loved it. So it would be possible to make a psychological experiment with a psychologist, which is always fun. Pick a young psychiatrist who is now practicing his profession and is just chockfull of doctrine. He has never seen the poem **Horatius at the Bridge.** So we give it to him, saying, "Read this poem and give us your reaction to it." He would read it and come back and would probably say, "A fine poetry, full of action and with a grand, lilting rhythm, but you know the whole philosophy of it is simply wrong. This author, whoever he was, just did not understand family psychology. His narrator believes that when people lived together in friendship, lovingly and affectionately, that was due to brotherhood; that when they quarreled later and were bitter, that was due to a lack of brotherhood. We can assure him that the facts of life prove the very reverse. This Mr. Macaulay did not know the truth about human families, or perhaps his own family was exceptional. Now we know that brothers do not have peaceable relations; on the contrary, when different temperaments are forced to live together in one family, the friction is greater, and certainly competitive rivalry exists among brothers. We

154

psychiatrists speak of 'sibling rivalry,' the special quarrelsomeness which exists among brothers. So when he is describing the wonderful, peaceful days of the Republic, how can he say that Romans were like brothers? It is just the reverse. He should have said they were like pals; and when he describes the quarrelsome days of the Empire, then he should have said they were like brothers, because that is the way we psychiatrists say brothers really are; they are constant rivals."

That sounds a little cynical to us. Yet before we let ourselves denounce it, we must remember that much of the same negative judgment about brothers is found in Scripture itself. The Bible's description of the first pair of brothers on earth ends in murder, in fratricide; and as for the next important pair of brothers, Esau and Jacob, one has to flee for his life before the other. So it is evident that the modern idea of "sibling rivalry" is nothing new to Scripture; it was well aware of the bitterness that grows among brothers and why.

This Scriptural realism creates a problem in our understanding of the Bible. There is apparently a fundamental contradiction in Biblical philosophy. For when Scripture envisages its ideal of social life, it describes it exactly as Macaulay's narrator did. It speaks of a future built by human brotherhood. Thus brotherhood is equated with peaceableness. Clearly this spells a contradiction between the psychology of Scripture and its ethical idealism. If brotherhood actually is as the Bible describes it in the stories of Cain and Abel and Esau and Jacob, how can it call world peace "brotherhood"?

But so deep a contradiction is highly improbable in Scripture which is essentially consistent. It is possible to find in Scripture one verse apparently contradicting another. But to have so profound a contradiction between

155

what Scripture knows well about family bitterness and yet to describe the peaceable future as "family brotherhood," clearly cannot be possible. So it is only a seeming contradiction; and as we analyze this seeming contradiction, we may well reach a greater depth in our understanding of Scripture. There is a likelihood that the Scriptural concept of brotherhood, as it bridges that apparent contradiction, is creative and original. To find Scripture's deeper concept of the meaning of human brotherhood is the intent of our question: "Who is my Brother?"

The Book of Exodus tells of "the birth of a nation," the story of a people, its deliverance, its adventures. The first book of the Bible, Genesis, has little to do with peoples and nations; it is the story of individuals and their families. The whole Book of Genesis is a sequence of family chronicles; and in every important family chronicle there is bitterness between brothers: Cain and Abel, Esau and Jacob, whom we have mentioned; and finally at the end of the book, Joseph and his brothers. Scripture concludes that Jacob had to run away, to make another career in the land of the Aramaeans. Joseph had to run away, to make another career in the land of Egypt. From the almost inevitable rivalry and quarrelsomeness in family life there springs an impulse to leave home. It rather typical for a brother to go away to a different land to build up his independent career.

The psychiatrist would agree that Scripture is right. The thing to do, he would say, is break the family bond, go somewhere else, build a career independent of your family. That is part of the process of growing up. This the psychiatrist would say, and this Scripture says too. A person goes away from home and finds new friends, so we are told in the Book of Proverbs: "Sometimes there are friends who are closer than a brother." All that is normal; you must build a new life, your own life, with your own friends.

But then Scripture goes further and says in the same book: "A brother exists for times of trouble." When trouble comes into a family, when a parent dies, the brothers and sisters start gathering from far places. Perhaps they look at each other somewhat distantly, but in time of trouble they learn to appreciate that they are brothers and sisters. Then gradually, as they move into middle life and beyond that into age, they find that they are closer to each other and have become precious to each other. There comes a time when we know that brother and sister are the only bond we have left with father and mother who are gone. Those with whom we may have quarreled, of whom we were perhaps a little jealous, have become part of our life, cherished in a profound unity.

So Jacob comes back from a far country. He and Esau, who might have killed one another twenty years earlier, now fall into each other's arms and weep and kiss each other. So, too, Joseph, sold into slavery by his own brothers, finally reveals himself to them: "I am thy brother Joseph," and what he says tells the story of his emotions. He says: "I am Joseph. Is father still alive?"

One of the most beautiful truths of life is revealed when a family of brothers and sisters reestablish their old-time bond. It is a truth stated and restated in Scripture and reveals that the Biblical concept of brotherhood is not a naive one, not a static one. It is a dynamic concept. Brotherhood in a family is not something given (except in a biological sense). It is something achieved. We must rebuild our brotherhood. Once that is achieved in a family, once brothers and sisters, often aging, know that they are one in heart, they are to be described in the words of the Psalms: "How beautiful when brothers dwell together in

157

unity." The phenomenon is heartwarming because it is an emotional and ethical achievement. Brotherhood is something we must **rediscover** and win again.

Jewish people are keen and alert, and they are also introspective; they like to talk about themselves. It is strange that after a hundred and fifty years of Jewish intellectual talk about Jews, Judaism, Jewishness, our writers and speakers have not yet settled the question of their own identity as Jews. What does it mean to be a Jew? Are we race, nation, or religion? One can still get this old argument stirred up anew. Is it not curious that after a century or two of such debates, we still do not agree or know what we are?

Perhaps the reason for this indecision is that Jews are not **exactly** definable by any of those terms. We are certainly not a race, if we mean "race" in a scientific sense. There are only five races. Even in the semi-scientifc sense when we speak of the English race, the French race, even in that sense we are not completely of common descent. Of course it is largely true that we are of common descent because of the fact that the oppressions in the past have drawn half-Jews rather away from us than brought them to us. So by the process of subtraction, we are more or less of a common descent which may unscientifically be described as "race." But the very variation of our features indicates a variety in our biological inheritance.

Are we a nation? Certainly not. A number of Jews have built a nation, a justly beloved nation, but all the Jews of the world are not a nation. We are part of the nations in which we live.

As for religion—we **wish** that religion were the correct description! The Jewish religion represents our great-

158

est attainment, that of which we ought to be most proud, which we ought to try to make most real in our life. But when we think of perhaps a third of the Jews of the world who have lost their religious attachment, can we say that they are no longer Jews? Are they not our fellow Jews? Evidently even our most preferred definition does not quite fit the facts. We are a more or less anomalous social group which is very hard to define or to fit precisely into the customary categories. That is why Jewish intellectuals have had such difficulty coming to an accepted self-definition.

Since that is the case, we are not surprised that Scripture has still another inadequate or incomplete definition that might well be added to "race, nation, and religion." Scripture speaks frequently of "Bes Yisroel," "the Family of Israel," "the household." In other words, we are a family. We know at once that is a good definition; we can tell by the way we annoy each other! Just like brothers and sisters, we Jews have an unerring skill in mutual irritation! Nothing makes us angrier than the misbehavior of a Jew. There can be twenty numbers racketeers in Pittsburgh, and the one name we will see in the list is the Jewish name. And, contrariwise, in lists of people who have achieved greatly, we note the Jewish name at once. Our reaction of irritation or pride to our fellow Jews is exactly a family emotion.

Therefore, as with the blood family, people go away from the "Family of Israel" to seek their career elsewhere. This happens chiefly at the college age, when young people begin to wonder why they should be "burdened" with this particular identification for which they are not responsible. So there is a certain percentage of these who become alienated from the "Family of Israel." But, again, this alienation is frequently but gradually overcome. We always find young people, young men and women coming back to their Jewish affiliation. Some, of course, are permanently alienated and are lost, as a brother who never finds his family again; but the majority of our young people start by discovering qualities in their Jewish kinship which they begin to find acceptable and then often admirable. Some attach themselves to the various campaigns aiding Jewry over the world. They work on committees. Some are attracted to the local charitable organizations and do or guide social work among our people. Some become officers of the various Temple clubs and organizations. So gradually the "household of Israel" reintegrates itself.

If we look upon Jewry as a family which always seeks to rediscover its unity, we will see that it is astonishingly successful. It is not an overstatement to say that the "Family of Israel" has never weakened basically through the ages. It is doubtful whether there is an historic group which remains as deeply integrated a family as ours. After two thousand years of being aware of each other and quarreling and disagreeing and debating, we are still remarkably united. The little nation of Israel taxes itself heavily in order to make room for Jews unlike themselves, of different skin color, with different history—and they open their doors and keep them open! American Jews tax themselves every year for huge sums in their campaigns to help Jews whom they have never seen and will never see! I doubt whether such a sense of mutual family responsibility can be paralleled anywhere in the world.

But this family feeling is always something that has to be rewon. There are always members of the family who run away, but always a decent proportion slowly comes back, and Jewish brotherhood is always magnificently reestablished. So Scripture in the words of King David says: "Who, O God, is like the people Israel: a unified people on earth." Our Jewish family unity is always an achievement which must be reattained in every generation.

A century ago, when radical or agnostic criticism of Scripture began, most of the attacks were centered on the Book of Genesis and its account of the Creation. This account was scorned as totally unscientific.

The center of the attack was the Creation of Man, and the charge is correct. It is unscientific. Our scientific idea about the origin of humanity on earth is that man is one of the last in a long chain of animal evolution. But Scripture describes him as being there right at the beginning; that is, unless we believe that each Scriptural "day" meant an era or a millenium and the statement that man was created on the sixth day meant that man was created late. But all that is speculation. On the face of it, the account of the Creation of Man in the first part of Genesis is certainly unscientific.

The criticism is justified, but it is unimaginative. It does not appreciate Scripture's intention. The Scriptural author makes use of the scientific picture of his day, but his intention is not scientific, it is ethical. The whole narrative has a moral purpose and the imaginative reader must ask, not what the scientific picture is (that is, of course, out of date, as our scientific picture of world-origin may be out of date ten years from now) but what was its ethical intention? Once we look upon it with imagination, we can see that one of the basic ideals of the Bible is revealed in its account of the Creation of Man.

God created the animals by whole species; he created the birds, created the lions, created the tigers. He did not create humanity. He created a man and then a woman and then a family. The Rabbis, sensing an implied ethical ideal, asked the following question: "Why is it that all living things were created by species and man was created only as an individual?" They concluded: "That was in order that every human being shall know that we are part of the same family and no one shall say, 'My blood is better than yours.'" So the initial ethical declaration of Scripture is that there is not only the biological family and not only the Jewish family, but also all of humanity is a family. That is why Malachi, the last Prophet, says: "Have we not all one Father? Has not one God created us all?"

We notice that Malachi uses the word "created." He refers backs to Genesis. If there were no such ideal in Genesis there would be no such statement in Malachi. Malachi's statement is often quoted, but people generally fail to quote his complete statement. After saying, "Have we not all one Father," he says, "Then why do we deal treacherously one with another?" If we are brothers, why are we so murderous?

That is a real and a tragic question. If we would have to answer the prophet's cry of anguish, we would say people are murderous because they resist the idea that they are really brothers. Men and women fight to maintain their belief that they are different and superior to all others. This idea of superiority recompenses them for every personal failure. If actually in your heart you know you are a nobody, then your consolation is, "At least I am better than this black-skinned man." We seem to need this delusion to console us for our many failures, and therefore we all fight to maintain and to emphasize the differences between us. A difference of language is sufficient for our pitiable purpose; a difference of language between two adjacent nations is enough for a thousand years of war. A difference in skin color is sufficient for deep-rooted hatreds and scorns and slavery.

The answer to Malachi's pathetic question, "Why do we deal treacherously," is that it is because we insist that **our** difference is a superior difference, and if not individually, at least racially or nationally we are superior. Therefore all our instincts of self-praise fight the belief that we are all brothers. Clearly brotherhood between races and nations is, like brotherhood in the family, not something to be fobbed off with idealistic words. It is something to be attained, attained at a price, at a price that begins with being truthful about ourselves: How much better are we? Why do we have to boast of our skin or our descent to bolster up our weaknesses? Step by step, street by street, neighborhood by neighborhood, person by person, we have to win the sense that we are all children of Adam. This, like the unity of a family and the unity of Israel, is a toilsome process, a Scriptural goal; and the very struggle to attain it is an evidence of moral maturity.

When Joseph—pampered young Joseph, wearing his coat of many colors—was sent by his father Jacob to his brothers who were far away feeding the flock, he wandered on the way and a stranger met him. The stranger asked, "Where are you going?" And Joseph made the simple answer which became a famous sentence. He said, "I seek my brethren." Those words, often quoted, are the real Scriptural Jewish answer to "Who is my Brother?" "I seek . . ."!

Brotherhood is a search, a quest. Scripture's concept of it is that it is not a fact, it is a process, it is a mandate, it is something slowly to be attained, in family life, in Jewish life, in world life. So to answer our question, if

163

we ask of Scripture, "Who is my brother," the answer is, "He whose hopes I honor, he whose sorrow I try to share, and he whose kinship I hope to merit." To the extent that we attain brotherhood, to that extent will the world be more lovable and more secure.

XVI
WHERE ART THOU?

Christian theology is an imposing structure. It took many centuries to build. Its foundations were laid by Saint Paul, Saul of Tarsus. Its walls were built by the Church fathers, and it was finally roofed in by Saint Thomas Aquinas in the Middle Ages.

This imposing edifice has as its cornerstone an incident in the third chapter of Genesis. The incident is of course well known, but the use of it by Christianity may not be so clear to non-Christians. At the beginning of the Bible, we are told that first Eve and then Adam ate the fruit of the forbidden tree. Christian theology develops this incident as follows: The act of Adam was a sin which was never eradicated. It is inherited by all human beings, Adam's children. Since that original sin is an hereditary sin and an innate corruption in all of us, it is far beyond our power to atone for it. Since we did not commit it, we cannot be cleansed of it, and it is a permanent stain upon human nature. Therefore, in order to cleanse men of this hereditary sin, we need a supernatural purification, namely, that God must be born on earth as a mortal so as to be a sacrifice for the otherwise irremovable sin with which Adam has corrupted all his descendants.

Sermon delivered February 7, 1965

165

That is the essence of the Christian theological system and it reveals in this regard how the daughter religion grew up differently from the mother religion. The Scriptural story of Adam and Eve's disobedience in eating the fruit of the tree is, of course, discussed in the Jewish commentaries. But it is an extraordinary fact that the incident of which the Christian Church made so much, amounts to virtually nothing in the Jewish tradition. There is almost nothing in the tradition dealing with the sin of Adam.

What the tradition does fasten on would sound strange to a Christian theologian, but it is not strange to us. It was not the sin itself that is talked about; it was what came after the sin: Adam in the garden hears God's voice, and God says, "Where art thou?" This question bothered the rabbis. They said, "Why should God ask, 'Where art thou?' Does God need Adam to tell Him where he is hiding?" They were always on the search for seemingly unnecessary questions which had deeper significance than at first appears. "Why, then, does God ask, 'Where art thou'?" To which they say that God merely wanted to evoke an answer from Adam and thus to start the conversation between God and Man.

In this explanation we see something significant which we may never have noticed before in Scripture. God began with the question, "Where art thou," in order to start a conversation. Now that we think about it, we shall see that the entire Scripture from Genesis to Chronicles is nothing but a long conversation. It is a dialogue. Sometimes it expands into a trialogue, but it is always conversation. Touch any part of Scripture and you will see that it is a conversation: Even the technical, legal parts in Leviticus, Numbers, and Deuteronomy are given as a conversation between God and Moses and are repeated in

166

conversational form between Moses and Israel. The whole moral teaching of the Prophets is not through books but through conversation, through public speech addressed to the people and the people answering. God, speaking to the people through the Prophets, says (in Isaiah): "Come, let us reason together saith the Lord," "Let us have a conversation, let us argue together." The whole of Scripture, its basic literary form, is primarily a dialogue. That may help explain why the Bible is the great religious classic. Religion itself may be described as a dialogue between the Eternal and the transient, between God and Man, between heaven and earth.

Conversation, then, became a classic vehicle in religion. That is what the more solemn term "communion" means: talking with God, hearing a question and giving an answer. This conversation found in Scripture continues in human experience as long as the Scriptural religion itself continues to exist in the hearts of men. We are to understand how our faith expresses itself: We are asked questions and we are expected to give answers. To the extent that this dialogue continues even below the threshold of conscious enunciation of words, to that extent does God live in our hearts.

The question, "Where are thou," began this great dialogue and therefore it is the key which will admit us into the palace of Scriptural thought.

Sigmund Freud was a careful and an able student of Greek drama, and he based his whole system of complexes upon that literature. If he had been asked, "What does our present day human nature and our weaknesses have to do with a drama written by Aeschylus or Sophocles in 300 before the present era," he would say,

167

and quite wisely, that those old dramas are the summed up wisdom of the race, and the race's self-awareness of its problems and its difficulties are recorded in them. Therefore they may be taken, even today, as a pictorialization of the continual personal problems of Man. That is why Freud took from the Greek dramas the Electra complex, the Oedipus complex, and so forth.

Freud's transfer of these ideas from ancient times to modern experience is quite acceptable as a doctrine. But one cannot help regretting that Sigmund Freud is himself obsessed, haunted by a certain anti-Bible complex. He was not anti-Jewish. He was a loyal Jew. He went frequently to the B'nai B'rith Lodge in Vienna and lectured there. But he was anti-Bible.

If Freud had studied Scripture with half the zeal with which he studied the Greek classics, he could have found in them adequate prototypes for the various states of human nature, and he might have devised different complexes entirely, especially if he had looked without contempt at this Adam story where the famous question is asked. Adam has just hidden himself. God says, "Where are thou?" Adam answers God, "I was naked and I was afraid and I hid myself."

That answer ought to fascinate psychoanalysts. How that dream, that nightmare of nakedness, of helplessness, recurs from time to time, leaping up from the murky depths of the human subconsciousness! This sense of being totally defenseless and unable to hide is a revelation of the basic fears that haunt us from our infancy. That is when this dream of running naked through the darkness in panic (as Adam runs away to hide) is stored up in our minds.

These childhood fears tend to be pushed out of our consciousness as we grow up. The work of life, the joy of developing our abilities, of finding our place in the world, all these creative and self-encouraging activities drive the fears away. But the old fears of being "naked and afraid" in the world rise up again in the latter part of life, and Shakespeare in his intuitive genius saw it. He must have had this Adam-statement in mind when he has old Cardinal Wolsey say to his servant: "O Cromwell! Had I but serv'd my God with half the zeal I serv'd my king, he would not in mine age have left me naked to mine enemies."

Thus do the old dark fears begin to invade us again. Old people begin to be afraid they will be lonely, their loved ones will go, who will take care of them? They often fear, unnecessarily, they will be penniless; nothing seems safe to them and they become pathetically conservative. Then they are increasingly afraid of sickness. The various fears accumulate until finally the aging person is terrorized!

That is when God's question comes: "Adam, where art thou?" Why are you walking on this ghost-haunted road? Have you no faith? It becomes clear that the religion which we were taught as children, we have to relearn when we pass middle life, because we begin to lose our way and find ourselves panic-stricken on a dark, specter-haunted road. We must learn again to have some confidence in people's decency, that there will always be somebody to care for us. We will not necessarily be left helpless. There are still skilled doctors in the world and we will be cured from many an ailment that terrorizes us. "Adam, where art thou?" Find again your faith in life. No older person is religious again, no older person has recovered his faith unless he is able to look at the process of aging fairly and bravely. The mark of the religion of an aging person, as to whether he has recovered it or not,

169

is to be able to say with all his heart: "Yea, though I walk in the valley of the shadow, I will fear no evil for Thou art with me."

This conversation which began with Adam, continued with Abraham who said, "Here I am." It went on with Abraham's children. Then the conversation widened into converse between God and the whole people of Israel. With the people of Israel it first began with the same theme as it had with Adam who said, "I am afraid and I tried to hide myself," the theme of courage.

But soon the theme of the Biblical conversation with the people of Israel changes. It moves from personal courage to moral character. The whole conversation with the Prophets, which occupies a third of the Bible, and much of the conversation of Moses in his last year with his people, was on the problem of character, since this people was being built into something new in the world. It was not only its monotheism which was attained in the midst of a polytheistic world; it was also the moral reconstruction of this handful of people in a world of every sort of corruption, of sexual perversion, of every form of brutality and callousness. This people was being continually hectored into decency by the denunciation of their teachers, who gave them no rest, who never allowed them the slightest scintilla of self-encouraging complacency, and never rested until they became a people of mercy, of decency, of cleanness of home life.

Without that moral virtue, they could not have endured. When we count the various explanations for our miraculous continuity, we must count also the character, the decency, the dear family life which the Prophets had built up in our hearts. How else could a people live? Our

170

exiled families were not dispersed, but stayed loyally together through all their emigrations and immigrations. It is our decent family feelings which kept us alive.

Through the ages, whenever we wandered off from the old ethical standard, some leader would rise and say, "Israel, where art thou?" What has become of all the teachings of the past in your heart? Immediately there would be written a new ethical literature, following the mood of the Prophets. If an historian would study these ethical books bibliographically, from the point of view of their dates, just when the ethical literature appeared, in which centuries, he would always see it was in a century in which the people's morality began to get a little besmirched, and the leaders of the faith felt the need to ask the question, "Where are you?"

Suppose, then, the question is asked of us today. Without making too much of it, would there not be some impulse in us to repeat Adam's old answer, "We are ashamed. We ought to hide ourselves"? How sure are we now that the Jewish family is what it had been for centuries; that the children reverence the parents, that the parents are worthy of reverence; that Jewish students at colleges devote their hearts and minds in the old way to the love of learning, and appreciate the privilege of being taught; that Jewish people, young and old, have something of the old cleanness of life which was our glory; that Jewish authors, with their talents, think that they should have a special responsibility to that historic decency of the people from whom they are descendants? Suppose these questions are asked of us today.

We do not have statistics on the matter. Statistics of decency are very hard to accumulate. None of the scientific inquisitiveness of questionnaires can help us much.

But we have a feeling that if we are asked today in reference to our social-moral character, "Where art thou," we might very well want to hide from the question.

Surely the time will have to come, as it came often in the past, for the Jewish people, wherever they live, not to be content to be "like everyone else." Of course we are no worse than any other group. Our boys and girls in school are no worse. Our families in their family life are no worse. Children handle their parents and parents handle their children in just the same way in Jewish and Christian homes. But is that a consolation, that we are "just the same as everybody else"? If that is all we are, then the Prophets have lived in vain and Moses has wasted his career.

We were meant to be something special, something of an example, and there is no shame in being proud of that. We were trained from the very beginning to prove that a whole community can be decent and kind. Of course the kindness still lives with us; for that we need not hide in shame as Adam did. We are still the most generous, open-hearted, open-handed people in the world. But I believe that our cleanness has become a little dirtied. Maybe the time will come soon, as it has come a number of times in our history and in the history of the world, when a period of sexual and other corruption and literary filth will be followed by a reaction towards decency. The Elizabethan rowdiness was followed by the Puritan reaction. The Restoration in the time of Charles II was afterwards followed by the Victorian strait-laced epoch. These moods go in alternation.

It may therefore be about time for the world, and particularly for us, to hear again the question: "Where art thou?" How much of the past decency has been lost? It is about time that the world may soon begin to clean itself again. If that time comes, as it came in the past a number of times, then it is not too much to hope that our Jewish authors, who have used their talent in imitation of all the filth that is found in the printed book today, will now use their talents for the revival and the cleansing of our generation.

The Prophet Isaiah was the one who extended the dialogue between Eternity and Man one further step. It was extended from the individual Adam to the people Israel, and Isaiah thought of a dialogue expanding to the entire world. God now opens a conversation with the whole of mankind. But Isaiah says of this conversation that it is "a voice crying in the wilderness." The phrase gives us a picture of some noble person who could no longer stand the life of human society. He wants to preach against it, but no one will listen. So he goes out into the desert and raises his voice. He speaks aloud but no one hears—"a voice crying in the wilderness."

The furthest extent of the Biblical colloquy, the speech between God and the nations, the concept of human brotherhood and therefore human peace, which Scripture brought into the consciousness of man, was for many, many centuries "a voice crying in the wilderness." No one listened. The nations continued their brutal blood-letting without cessation. Century after century went by and it was not yet a conversation, only a soliloquy on the part of Scripture, until 1896, when a Jewish engineer and statistician named Ivan Bloch decided that wars in modern times have become too expensive and ought to be abolished, and he persuaded the Czar to found a Hague Court of Arbitration. It was from that Jewish impulse that the soliloquy became for the first time a dialogue, really, among nations; unless we count the occasional "Peace of God" which the Church was able to bring in on certain Christian holidays, to prevent the feudal lords from fighting each other and desecrating the festivals; but otherwise, the peace-conversation was only one-sided. The Bible spoke and no one answered.

But in our time it is becoming a dialogue. First, the Hague Court of Arbitration; then that pious Presbyterian son and grandson of Presbyterian ministers, Thomas Woodrow Wilson, dreamed the Biblical dream and was virtually martyred for it, and then it has turned into the United Nations. Today it is a conversation; and if it is a conversation, then it ought to proceed in the classic way, and we ought to ask today of the nations, "Where art thou?" What is the present stage of comradeship and peace?

The answer is almost precisely Adam's answer: "I am naked and afraid." Never was mankind as naked, as helpless before hostility as it is today. It does not help us that we have two thousand missiles with atomic warheads, except that they scare a possible aggressor; that is their value. But if he does not scare, if he decides to bring down the world, if he decides that he can destroy us with his first attack, if he makes any mad decision—we are naked! Ten million Americans can be killed in the first action resulting from his murderous decision! Never was the world as unprotected as it is today.

The trouble is that we cannot hide ourselves. As the old Negro spiritual said, "There is no hiding place down here." What, then, is our hope? How can mankind's conversation with God and destiny continue?

Adam indicates it: He said, "I am naked and unprotected and I am afraid." Thank God that we are afraid. Thank God that the realization of danger has penetrated into the consciousness of potential aggressors all over the world; and that this fear, increasing, also increases our safety. The conversation between God and the nations is at this stage: What our idealism cannot accomplish yet, our terror may for the present achieve. And we might change the old Scriptural verse, "The fear of the Lord is the beginning of wisdom," and say that the security of the world lies in reading the sentence, "Our fear of our fate is the beginning of our safety."

The word "dialogue" has become a highly fashionable word in theological circles today. We no longer hear that ministers of different religions are "having a conference;" they always say today that they are having either a "colloquy" or a "dialogue." Dialogue is a fine way of dealing with the problem that must be met, the problem of the gulf that has existed between great traditions and how to bridge it. Only people at the highest intellectual level, discussing the fundamentals of their respective beliefs, can bridge these chasms. For such a purpose, mass meetings are not needed; we have to have colloquies and dialogues, informal, leisurely, and selecting the right people for them.

If that is a good technique, then one can understand the lasting influence of Scripture. It has been from the beginning a dialogue, a conversation; not a mandate, but a "come, let us reason together." The original question of the conversation, "Where art thou," reverts into the human consciousness at crucial times. When we are losing our courage and become fear-haunted, the question is asked, "Where art thou?" When a people trained to nobility becomes cheapened, the old question resounds. When mankind is naked to its enemies, it hears again, "Where art thou?"

This is the question which God asks, and waits for us to hear, to understand, and to give our response.

XVII
WHERE ARE
THEIR GODS?

Many attain success, but all must pay a price for it. Sometimes the price is excessive. A man may work with all his heart and mind to amass wealth; but having attained his goal, he may find that he has worn out his body and cannot enjoy what he possesses. Or a man may rise as high as he dreamed he would rise in his profession, and then find that he has entangled himself with so many responsibilities that he can never lay his burden down. Thus there is sometimes a heavy price for success. Sometimes the price is not so heavy and in these circumstances, life is a good bargain. But one way or another, a price must be paid.

Just as in the life of the individual, so success must be paid for in human history. When a social or political group attains some great material, cultural, or spiritual success, it has to pay for it, and sometimes very dearly.

In the history of the development of human religion, count Judaism as one of the outstanding successes. Think what it means as an achievement in the development of spiritual and social understanding. Here was a group in the midst of an idolatrous world. Somewhere and some-

Sermon delivered February 14, 1965

how the ambition arose to make this group the only non-idolatrous people in the world. It would not be too difficult to imagine that a few brilliant minds could evolve and hold onto the immense idea of an Omnipresent, Invisible, Eternal Mind. A great individual could achieve it. But this tremendous ennobling of the mind involved farmers, ploughmen, fishermen, men and women. It involved converting a whole people into philosophers, so that they could understand that what is invisible may be the greatest reality in the world. This grand goal was attained. Idolatry disappeared from our people, and we became the only people to worship a pure, spiritual Universal, the one and only God. In the history of human thought, such a mass refinement was a tremendous success, and a great price had to be paid for it.

The price can be estimated when we recall that the Bible frequently speaks of God as "hiding," "hiding His face from us." What does that mean? The Prophet Isaiah says it clearly. He says: "Thou art a God Who hideth Himself away." That simply means that it is difficult to hold on steadily to a great idea. The purer the idea is, the easier one loses grasp on it; it quickly becomes vague and unreal, and thus the Eternal One, the Pure, the Spiritual One, the Soul of the world disappears from our ken.

This never was a problem in idolatry. The gods never disappeared. A sophisticated idolator would know that his gods were meant to be a symbol of the forces of nature. So whenever he heard the thunder, he thought of Zeus. Whenever he fell in love, he thought of Aphrodite. And the less sophisticated idolator merely needed to step into the temple and see the statue of Zeus, and there is the god!

178

But if you once understand that God is the spiritual soul of the world, you cannot find Him so easily, but you can lose Him very easily. That is the price you pay for a noble God-conception. That is why Scripture frequently asks, pathetically, "Where is God?" Or sometimes people in Scripture will scornfully point a finger and say, "Where is your God now?" To hold onto the pure Universal Spirit is one of the great burdens and the great prices paid for attaining this high level in pure religion. In order to understand that this is more than a problem in the past history of human thought, but that it is a problem in day by day human experience, since God sometimes seems to become vague to us just when we need Him most, let us ask the Biblical question and see where and when in life the question, "Where is my God," becomes urgent and real.

Sometimes a poet can make us feel the reality of past history more than a historian. The historian gives the facts and may even interpret them. But sometimes a poet can make us sense what it was like to live in that period. The historians have written about the great invasions in nearer Asia; the Babylonians or Assyrians marching down from the North or the Egyptians marching up from the South, and always Palestine, this little buffer-state between, helpless. But Lord Byron describes emotionally the experience of living through an invasion by the irresistible Assyrian army:

"The Assyrian came down like the wolf on the fold,
 And his cohorts were gleaming in purple and gold;
 And the sheen of their spears was like stars on the sea,
 When the blue wave rolls nightly on deep Galilee."

The sweep of the lines give a picture that was both a historical reality and almost a personal participation. The small nation was like a flock of sheep, helpless, when the tremendous invading army "came down like the wolf on the fold."

That is a symbol of much of the history of this people of ours, helpless against powerful, irresistible forces. Cruel enemies came against us, "the wolf on the fold." Where, then, is the Shepherd to protect the "sheep"? This question, "Where is God," amid the cruelties of history, comes up again and again in Scripture.

God often seems vague to us when history is cruel and brutal, and history has frequently been brutal. Power has always dominated. Decency has always been victimized. If one would look at history cynically, one could say the only crime in history is not to be strong enough to kill before one is killed.

The brutality of history does not disturb the religion of the polytheist. A polytheist by definition believes that there are many gods; and if there are many gods, one god must necessarily be weaker than another. Thus when there is a battle on earth, the favorites of the stronger god defeat the favorites of the weaker god. The proof that this was their belief and their conviction can easily be seen: In antiquity, when the conquered people were taken away captive to be slaves in the land of the conqueror, the conquered gods also were dragged into captivity and put into the temple where they became minor parts of the pantheon of the victorious gods. So to a polytheist it is no problem that weaker nations are crushed by the powerful; that is the way it is both in heaven and on earth.

But to a monotheist who believes that God is the God of all the world and and a God of justice and the Father of all His children, how can he explain and endure

180

history when the mighty power comes down like a wolf on the helpless fold? This spiritual misery was made specific in the Bible. The Assyrian army marched down and encamped before Jerusalem, and the haughty Assyrian marshall Rabshakeh talks to the besieged Jews on the wall and he says, "Do not let King Hezekiah reassure you that God will help you. Where is the god of Arpad? Where is the god of Chamath? Did they help their people when my royal master's army attacked them?" So where will the God of Israel be?

That is a brutal question. It shakes the heart. Rabshakeh, the marshall of the Assyrians asked it first. Then in his heart Vespasian, the Roman emperor asked it seven centuries later, when Jerusalem with its beloved Temple rose in flames. All the brutal "wolves" of history, until the last "wolf" in Europe—the most ravening "wolf" of all—ask in clear implication: "Where is your God?"

But, alas, we do not have a strong answer that we can give to them or to ourselves. That there is evil, that there is brutality, we know. Therein does not lie our answer. Our answer to the Assyrian marshall who asked by implication, "Where is thy God," and to all his successors, is somewhat different: Not what is done by brutal strength—this we must accept—but what happens afterwards. To the Assyrians we say, "We will outlive your siege and your invasion." To the Romans we say, "We will be scattered from the homeland and still live." To every oppressor we say, "You drive us out. We return. You burn our ghettos. We will rebuild. You throw down our tombstones. We will set them up again and honor our dead once more. God is not visible in your brutal power, but God is visible in the power He has given us to recover." Because we have never given up, we are a living evidence to all the world that brute force cannot ultimately destroy, that the spirit will live.

There, then, is our God, in our ability to survive. It is a lesson and an assurance to all the children of men cowering in terror before the threats of destruction, that those who wish to live and those who have God in their hearts will indeed survive. We say to the "wolves" of history: We live because we believe in the words of the Prophet, "Fear not, my servant Jacob. You will pass through the fire; it will not consume you. You will walk through the floods and they will not overwhelm you." In this survival—there God is in human history!

The great statement of Immanuel Kant, repeated thousands of times, is still inspiring. He said that two things fill his heart with awe and wonder: the starry heavens above and the moral law within. To that great philosopher, the very fact that there is an instinct to decency, a moral law within the human consciousness, is just as awe-inspiring as the starry heavens.

One wonders what the great philosopher of Koenigsberg would think if he had lived to our day and had seen what a branch of psychiatry had done with what he revered as "the moral law within." Psychoanalysis, at least in its original Freudian form, destroyed the conscience as the source of reverence and awe. It said that in the first place, the moral law is not within; it is an imposition from without. They call it the "super-ego." All our decencies are forced on us. What is within? Bitter, mean, animal-like impulses, the wild "id" as Freud calls it, the untamed animal within us. So Freud might change Kant's statement and speak, not of "the moral law within," but perhaps of "the immoral law within."

In fact, when we think of the evil in people's hearts, we agree with Freud, rather than with Immanuel Kant;

and thus the sense of "awe and wonder," the presence of the Divine seems to disappear from our lives. This is particularly so when evil people are successful. That was stated by the Prophet Malachi who says: "They say that evil men find favor in God's eyes. Where then is the God of justice?" We ask this question often because it is our frequent experience that evil not only exists, but greatly succeeds. How many false men are in positions of public trust, successfully deceiving an electorate with the devices of publicity; and only those who know them, know that they are hollow men! How many men have reached heights in the industrial world through meanness and brutality motivating their ability! How many evil men do we know who are honored because people are afraid to speak the truth about them! What breaks down religious confidence in us is the success of the unrighteous!

This question did not trouble our distant ancestors. They always said, "The wicked are happy in **this** world; in the **other** world, they will get what they should get." But for us, we know that our problems should be settled in this world, and that we have to endure the fact that frequently evil is triumphant.

I just read a book entitled **Gambler's Money** by a man named Wallace Turner. He is a respectable and a trustworthy writer who has written for the **New York Times,** and he writes here about the financial situation in Nevada, where gambling is legal. He speaks of one chain of gambling casinos that takes in forty million dollars a year. What a flood of gold! That forty million has to be concealed from the income tax, for these people do nothing honestly. They have come up from the underworld. They have risen to these heights from the underworld. They have to hide most of that money. They manage to do it and then, eventually, when by devices they "hide" it and "redis-

183

cover" it, they put it into legitimate businesses. Many an honest businessman suddenly finds himself with a partner whose natural method of living is thievery and murder.

All this golden flood is corrupting American business life. We read about it and we say, "Where are the laws? Where is the government? Where is the conscience of the American people?" It shakes our faith in the strength of law and order and the decency of people.

In this regard a word of wisdom was uttered by the Psalmist. He said, "Fret not thyself because of evildoers." It will often happen that evil men are rewarded. Be sure your own conscience is clear. "Fret not thyself . . ." Well, we try, and we have enough religion in the sight of this injustice—enough residual religion to be confident that evil will not endure and continually triumph. Public conscience will awaken, laws will be passed. This sort of underworld success eventually corrupts itself. That is true enough. But in the meantime, we have to endure it as part of our life. We try to be patient and try not to "fret" ourselves, but the God of justice must forgive us if occasionally we murmur, "Where is our God?"

The classic problem in theology is called in English "the problem of evil." Generally it has a title that is of Greek origin, "theodicy." The latter part of the word means "justice." It means the problem of God's justice. That question always has two sides, the one we have just discussed, the prosperity of the evil, and the other half, the misfortune of the righteous.

In all the discussions from ancient times to today, the discussions take first one side of the problem and then the other. But the most intense discussion is on the second half of the problem. It is the misery, the undeserved misery of the righteous that sometimes makes the Eternal God fade from our life. The Psalmist phrases this with his typical vividness. What we would phrase in our more verbose language, "When undeserved sorrows come to me, it is hard for me to hold onto my faith," he puts in this way: "My tears have become my bread day and night, and they say to me, 'Where is thy God?'" When "our tears become our food" and all that can nourish us is our grief, it is then that the Great and Eternal One seems to fade from our life, and it is the most difficult time of all to rediscover Him. That is why the old scholar wisely said, "Do not try to comfort a person when his dead still lies before him." God has vanished into a mist for this person. You have to wait till the eyes see clearly again.

This problem has been thought about so much that many answers have been given. First of all, religion requires of the person whose "tears have become his bread" to understand that until our knowledge gets larger, until we solve problems which our mind is capable of solving, until we find the healing for certain diseases, premature sickness and death is the lot of us all. It makes no difference what we believe in, what our character is, sickness comes, bereavement comes, and ultimately death comes to us all. In that regard there is one lesson for the Godly and the Godless: Learn to accept what you cannot change. Learn to face what is inevitable. Courage is the beginning of cure, if cure there is. This stoicism applies to us all.

But the religious have something in addition to help them. They are holding on with all their strength to the conviction that life has a meaning and that, therefore, even human suffering has a purpose. The religious person can soon begin to believe again; his very sorrow may bring a purification to his heart. Precisely because he has suffered, he can understand other people's suffering. One rarely finds a person who has become more understanding and more gentle because he is happy and successful. If a man is happy and successful, he may be more generous. He can afford it better. But the capacity of sympathy, the fellow feeling for people in tragedy, only comes from one's own tragedy.

Only after we have suffered, and only because we have suffered, do we understand that there are other people who need our strength. That is what the Prophet meant when he said, "You are purified as silver is purified in the furnace of suffering." A religious man bearing his undeserved sorrow says, first, "I must bear it as all must bear it," then, "I trust I will find God again and so learn to believe that I will gain from my sorrows." The religious person has not triumphed over his sorrows until he can say with all his heart: "It is good that I have been afflicted, for thus have I learned Thy precepts."

Thus following the lead of the Bible's question, "Where is Thy God," we come to a general characterization of Judaism or, more specifically, of its Biblical foundation. We can see immediately that the Bible is not for children. The Bible can be good for children, but we always have to "sweeten" it for them. We have to simplify the stories and sometimes turn its tragedies into fairytales, confident that even through the simplification of the story the deeper meaning will somehow shine forth. But as it stands, the Bible is not for children. It is for adults. It is for mature adults. It is for people who can look at life steadily, realize what it is like and yet not be afraid.

Because the Bible was the uniquely spiritual success in the historic past, bringing to average people the understanding of the Infinite, it has put upon us all the task

186

of keeping hold of that delicate reality. So Judaism, all through the Bible and all through our life, is a constant struggle.

Nobody who understands life's reality should be serenely confident of his faith. We are always asking, "Where is God?" The very question and the various bewilderments that evoke it, whether it be the brutality of history or the triumph of the undeserving or the misery of the righteous—whatever it be, the very asking of the question is part of our religious quest. Led by this question, let us characterize our faith as follows: It never says, "Believe and you will be saved." We are not quite sure what it means to be "saved." No human being in this vale of tears is ever "saved." It is not, "Believe and you will be saved," but, "Seek ye Me, and live." "Seek ye Me constantly, and live ye courageously," is the mood of our historic and difficult faith.

XVIII
WHERE IS MY HOPE?

We are approaching the Passover, and the story of Passover enshrined in the Book of Exodus bristles with miracles: Rivers turn to blood, seas divide. The modern tendency is to dismiss all these miracles brusquely and to say they did not happen. While this opinion might be factually correct, it is nevertheless rather superficial. It would be much more understanding if, instead of dismissing those events out of hand as fanciful, one asked what was the emotional world of those great minds who wrote Scripture. What drove them to surround the story of the Exodus with such miraculous events? Clearly their world view was different from ours. To them the world was a wonderful place, a magical place, a miraculous place in which any wonderful thing might happen at any time; and therefore it was not unreasonable for them to feel that miracles must have occurred around the great Exodus of Egypt. So it was normal for them to embellish the historical account with all these magical events. People today are not that imaginative; they are matter-of-fact, and the general attitude of a modern reader would be to be content with the mere statement that those miracles did not actually occur.

Sermon delivered April 11, 1965

But no man is so prosaic or so shallow as not to sense one great miracle that did occur, and is still a miracle which cannot be explained offhand: the miracle of the Bible itself! The Bible itself is an astonishing world-wonder, and no logic based upon ascertainable facts can explain its unusual splendor. One only has to recall the fact that all the ancient world, without exception, knew only polytheism and the worship of the pagan gods. Yet only in this little land arose the understanding of the Universal Beneficent Spirit. Explain that fact by history! Explain it by archeology! It is a mystery: Why there, why to them, why at that time, when all the world was so diametrically different?

Or further: In all the world morality was narrow, restricted to one's own kin, one's own tribe. The word "morality" is from the Latin word "mos" which means "custom," and "ethics" is from the Greek word "ethos" which also means "custom." Yet this little people was the first to have a morality that applied to all the world. Why was it they who pioneered the great concept of universal morality? If anybody has an explanation for it, they have never given it in any book. The Bible is a miracle, or let us say, a marvel, an unexplained marvel.

There is one extraordinary mood in Scripture which is not generally discussed. Writers do speak of the extraordinary monotheism and the world-wide morality, but there is something else about the Bible that is just as wonderful. It is not quite so easy to describe, for it is a matter of mood rather than definite idea.

Let us put it in this way: Henry Thoreau, speaking of the United States, said that every man lives a life of despair, and that beneath all his games and amusements, there is this same concealed basis, despair. Thoreau's

189

judgment is not to be lightly dismissed; but he is to be listened to with some caution, because he himself was a sort of an "outsider." He looked upon the general life of people with some superiority and, perhaps, a little contempt.

Be that as it may, it is Thoreau's judgment that despair is prevalent and deep in people's hearts. History certainly gives some confirmation to that judgment. The ancient Greeks were supposed to be so sunlit and happy and life-loving. Yet in their genius, they produced the world's profoundest and most heartbreaking tragedies. No genius people could produce such great tragedies without tragedy being in their heart. As for the Romans, who were supposed to be so practical, the engineers of antiquity, whenever life got a little difficult for a Roman, he cut his wrists. Suicide was prevalent among the Romans.

Yet in the fifteen hundred years covered by the Bible, in all those generations, there were only two suicides. The remarkable uniqueness of Scripture is its buoyancy, its tremendous devotion to life, its indestructible conviction that life can amount to something. If there is any mood in all the ancient classics which is needed in modern life, it is that unusual buoyancy, this devotion to living, working, and achieving, found in Scripture.

So this last one of this year's Bible series takes its lead from the question asked by Job: "Where is my hope?" What is the source of this exceptional and miraculous optimism in Scripture?

There is something always interesting in the way in which quotations become quotations. A man will write a poem or a play, and one little sentence of that poem or

190

that play will somehow escape from its original literary environment, spread over the world and become a popular proverb. Evidently people who hear the play or read the poem for the first time are struck by this line, and they repeat it, tell it to each other, and so sometimes these words taken from the play will last for centuries and centuries. That is evidence that there must be great truth in it.

Alexander Pope wrote the **Essay on Man** more than two centuries ago (in 1733). Some early reader or some critic selected from it a line which has become a proverb: "Hope springs eternal in the human breast." This is certainly true. We tend to hope, sometimes automatically, and generally transiently. But it is only half a truth. Perhaps the more noticeable fact is the opposite, that **gloom** springs eternal in the human breast. It takes so little to depress us: Something goes wrong or there is some accident or somebody's verbal crossfire, and either for a long time or a brief time, gloom, anger, discontent come instantly into our mood. More gloom leaves its map upon the face of the average man than joy.

The literatures of the world have had a curious attitude to constantly recurring gloom, which is as natural and perhaps even more frequent than our hope. Writers often praise and even glorify that gloom. They consider it deeper than joy, and to some extent it is. A man tends to gloom and thus may also come to a critical judgment of society. Sometimes he sees life perhaps more clearly than those who are hopeful. At all events, in nearly all literatures there are praises of the mood of gloom. In the opening lines of Milton's great ode, he says: "Hail, goddess, sage and holy, hail, divinest Melancholy." Keats wrote an ode to melancholy. There is this streak of adoration for gloom found all through the literatures of the world.

Whether some would consider it to be a mark of superficiality or not, there is nothing of that mood in Scripture; not the slightest scintilla of praise for gloom as if it were a virtue. On the contrary, the Bible in many places describes this frequent mood of depressions as a misfortune.

To the Bible, losing hope is, first of all, a sort of a sickness that attacks the healthy soul. If one expects confidently something good to happen, but what is expected does not come and one begins to lose his hope, that mood of growing doubt is described in the words: "Hope deferred maketh the heart sick." When hope keeps away from us, its absence becomes a sort of a sickness, a deficiency, a disease of the soul. "Hope deferred maketh the heart sick."

Sometimes Scripture thinks of despair, not so much as a sickness but as a sort of a blindness, as in a sense it often is, for when we are in the mood of hope, we are looking towards the future. When we are in the mood of despair, there is a wall between us and the future. Thus it is in the Book of Isaiah: "We hoped for light and, alas, there was darkness; and we groped for the wall like a blind man." A vivid metaphor! When we are melancholy, we cannot see ahead; we just "grope" our way; gloom is a blindness.

Scripture goes so far as to describe a loss of hope as a death in life. In the Thirty-seventh Chapter of Ezekiel which is read on the Sabbath in Passover, there is the famous "Death Valley" scene: The Prophet is brought down in the valley of dead bones, and God says to the Prophet, "Can these bones live?" The Prophet answers, "Only Thou knowest, O God." Then the metaphor is ultimately explained: These bones are the spirit of the house of Israel. "They say our hope is gone. We are in exile. We have no future." Those who say their hope is gone are like the dead bones in Death Valley.

So in various metaphors, Scripture declares that there is nothing glorious or goddess-like in the mood of melancholy. The man who loses hope, loses his health of mind, his vision, and almost life itself. To Scripture a life without hope is virtually no life at all.

One of the curious things about Scripture are the moods which it selects to convert into commandments. Some things are commanded in Scripture that would seem to us at first glance cannot and should not be commanded. For example, Scripture says at almost every holiday, particularly at Succos: "Thou shalt rejoice." How does one rejoice if he does not feel very happy? Can joy be commanded? Or consider another Scriptural command: "Thou shalt not hate thy brother in thy heart." But suppose I do hate him; suppose I am in the habit of hating this sort of person and my hatred is by now inveterate, the automatic reaction of my emotions. Why **command** me not to hate? Is the emotion in my control? But that is exactly what Scripture means. All emotions are in our control, at least in their beginnings. Before we begin to pamper them and make them strong, any emotion has an early stage in which the mind knows exactly what is going on. That is the time, and when the emotion can still be controlled, and it is to that stage that the command is directed.

Therefore Scripture has its logic when it commands not only, "Thou shalt rejoice," and not only, "Thou shalt not hate," but also, "Hope thou." It does not blandly smile and say, "Cheer up," but sets forth specific circumstances under which it is possible for a person to build up hope.

193

It is always interesting to note how specific Scripture is. That is the difference between the Biblical literature and the Greek literature. The Greek literature was created by a people with genius for theoretical thought who always tried to generalize from specific instances to the great laws of nature. The Jewish attitude is always to try to bring the great doctrines of life down to specific instances.

Thus when Scripture commands us to overcome despair, it gives specific situations in which it is possible for us to do so. Consider this statement from Proverbs: "Discipline thy child because there is hope." The obvious meaning of the statement is that a parent should never think a child is too far gone to be corrected. A child is blessed with the faculty of rapid change. The child who is unbearable today may be adorable tomorrow or vice versa. A parent has no right ever to give up on a child. No child is incorrigible.

But the mandate has a deeper meaning than its family significance. It means that in a community, in a society, the greatest source of hope is that there is always a new generation; and with every generation of children, the world begins anew, a brand new day in history. So do not give up on children, do not give up on childhood, do not give up on the possibility of society making a new beginning. "Discipline thy child because there is hope."

In the Book of Lamentations, Scripture says that it is good for youth to suffer misery and bear burdens because "perhaps there is hope." Youth is given to wild emotional extremes, sometimes up, as the spiritual says, and sometimes down. Youth is capable of profound depression; is sure the world is lost, that there is no hope; that we elders have ruined it (as if we did not inherit it, as they will) and that there is nothing to do but go wild in one way or another.

194

Scripture says to the young man: "Perhaps there is hope." Do not give up yet. Prepare yourself for the future. You may be right in your hopelessness that there is no future. But suppose there **is** a future and you, then, are unprepared for it and are "a lost generation." So bear your gloom, fight your way out of it. "Perhaps there is hope." Go on with that gamble. Bet on the human future.

Scripture says (in Job): "There is hope for the poor." If one takes that statement alone, it has not much meaning. Take it against the background of Scripture: Scripture was the first to plan, to dream of a perfect society; to think of a world without poverty. It developed a system of sabbatical years in which debts run no further than seven years, in order that nobody should get deeper and deeper in debt. It proclaimed a system of jubilee years every fifty years in which all the sale of real estate ceases at that point and people return to their original holdings.

Whether the scheme worked, whether Henry George was justified in making that Biblical plan the basis of all his teachings, the fact remains that the Bible was the first to visualize a future for society, a future without misery without starvation. Scripture says: Never give up hope for society. There is hope for the poorest and the most miserable. That social optimism is the root of the Bible's Messianic ideal.

In this way Scripture tells us in its typically specific way how we may rebuild the hope when it seems gone. Childhood is always a new beginning, and one may say that youth always has the energy if it believes in the future; and as for society, there is hope for the slums, for the poor, and for the human achievement.

When we say that the Bible is not philosophical, we mean it is not **systematically** philosophical. But the Bible **has** a philosophy in the sense that every man has his own philosophy. The difference between a philosopher and an average man is that the philosopher's philosophy is systematic, is brought out into the open, reasoned out and made available. The average man's philosophy remains deep in him. Thus the Bible has its philosophy the deep source of its mysterious hopefulness. We can find a hint of it in the first great deathbed scene of Scripture.

Father Jacob is dying in an alien land. Around him are his sons. He is giving his final blessing to them, and he interjects an exclamatory phrase: "I hope, O God, for thy deliverance!" That phrase, by the way, taken from Jacob's dying statement, has been put into the night prayer. It is a puzzling statement. What deliverance can there be for that poor, broken, old man, dying in Egypt? What can he hope for? Yet his sons are around him; the grandchildren are there. There is a hope for the family even after Jacob is gone. The hope is in Him Who endures from generation to generation. God is the Guarantor of our hope. God validates our promises to the future. This thought runs through all of Scripture. "Our hope is in the Lord, our God." "Hope in God and strengthen your heart."

Perhaps the strongest expression of this implicit philosophy comes from the man who asks the question with which we began, "Where is my hope?" Job, that noble Gentile in Scripture, fights to hold onto his hope, but every successive misfortune tends to push him into the "slough of despond." Finally he says, in effect, "My hope in God is my last fortress, and I tell God that whatever He sends me, I still believe in Him and in the vindication of which He alone is the guarantee." So Job uttered the immortal words: "Though He slay me, yet will I trust in Him."

The Bible remains a mystery which in every generation we try to explain. How could such a book, so different from all others, ever come into being? In the earlier generations they explained it, one might say, from heaven downward, theologically. The explanation of the grandeur of Scripture would be, then, that since the Hebrew God-conception was noble, therefore their concept of life and human brotherliness grew great and full of personal and social hope.

This older explanation did not give us a satisfactory understanding of how the great God-conception came to our people. The word "revelation" is a little difficult for modern people to believe. They cannot easily believe in eternity making a breakthrough into mortal life. So it leaves the source of the God-conception unexplained to modern people.

Modern people therefore try to explain the Bible humanistically; that is, to explain its marvel from the earth up. They say a people having a certain temperament, courage and brotherliness, naturally developed a great God-conception to fit it. But that, unfortunately, does not explain where the people got that exceptional temperament.

Thus both explanations, the older and the newer, the theological and the humanistic, are insufficient. The Bible remains a mystery. But let us say that both somehow belong together, God and the native temperament of the people. Both the God-awareness and the people's mood combined to fight against the ever-present spirit of depression. The record of that struggle is Scripture.

197

Therefore Scripture says that despair is a sickness and a blindness and a death. Scripture says that we can, if we will, rebuilt our hope at the sight of a growing child or the struggle of an adolescent, and the progress of society. Especially when we derive our hope from the presence of God will it be strong and endure. Most clearly, the meaning of the buoyancy of Scripture is expressed in the verse: "Happy the man whose hope is in Thee. He goes on from strength to strength."

HIGH HOLYDAY SERMONS

XIX

THE FORGOTTEN GARDEN

There is a clock in Washington. There is one like it in Paris, and one in Greenwich, England. These clocks are guarded by government authorities and are kept running in precision to the fraction of a second. The purpose of these clocks is to correct all the millions of clocks in the respective countries and to protect the uniformity of our measurement of time. Every second is therefore precisely a second, every hour precisely an hour, and every year is the exact length of every other year. This exact equality of the length of the years, guarded by government technicians, is a mathematical fact, an astronomical fact. Yet everybody knows it is not a psychological fact. In nobody's life is one year precisely the length of another. We remember our childhood when the years seemed endlessly long. It seemed we were at the age of twelve forever. It took us so long before we entered our teens. Then we think of our later age. How the same three hundred and sixty-five days speeded up. It was only yesterday that we were forty, and soon fifty, and so on with increasing speed. In the afternoon of life, ten years move as fast as one year did in life's morning hours.

All this is psychologically true and known to all. Time either crawls or rushes, depending upon our age. Yet this

Sermon delivered September 28, 1962

201

fact, so real to the human heart, has undergone a surprising modification in modern times. One of the profound changes of modern age is a universal increase of the speed of time. Whether we are young or old, all of us moderns have a strange new feeling that for us and for the world, life has suddenly taken on a greater momentum. The years have speeded up.

That this feeling is real can be seen from a comparatively minor literary phenomenon. There has been recently a revival of interest in the American novelist of a generation ago, Thomas Wolfe. A biography of him was a best seller two years ago. A new novel about him is a best seller this year. What is it about Thomas Wolfe that he has suddenly come into a revived public interest? One of Wolfe's great novels was called, "Of Time and the River" and indeed the central theme in Thomas Wolfe is the sharp sense of the torrential rush of the river of time. One of his great metaphors, which took him page after page to develop, was the picture of a railroad train rushing and roaring through the dark night, away from the past into the mysterious future. Thus, Wolfe has a special appeal for us today because he expresses the new impetus, the new speed of the railroad train of history. We all feel, young and old alike, that events are moving faster than ever before, that the modern age is dashing through the dark night on a shaking, rattling, roaring vehicle, and we have no knowledge of our unseen destination.

To Thomas Wolfe, this noisy, rushing journey was a source of excitement and of joy. He was traveling away from a past which he wanted to leave behind him, into a future which he was certain held a great career. So while he could not, on the train's dark journey, know just where he was going, yet he gladly left his native town and faced the future with expectation.

I doubt whether Wolfe's exhilaration at the onward rush of time is shared by the average man today. We feel the speed but we dread the destination. We are not so eager or confident about the future to which we are rushing. This new apprehension puts man in a strange emotional predicament. He had been taught as a modern to scorn the past and to trust in the future. But now he is afraid of the future. Thus he has neither future nor past to trust in, and he is alone on a frail craft on the stormy torrent of time.

Therefore Scripture offers us a special doctrine of time. It is not modern, yet it speaks to moderns. The Book of Genesis starts history with what was good and beautiful, with the radiant Garden of Eden, and continues man's biography with his expulsion from its splendor. Evidently the Scriptural purpose is to remind us of a forgotten splendor that man may recover and treasure it again, and perhaps to some degree reestablish its good elements in the present world. The Bible would say: Believe in the future, but do not scorn the past. Out of what is good in yesterday, build your tomorrow.

So, on the New Year, on this most modern of new years, when time for everybody, young and old, has begun to speed on faster than ever before, and the future comes hurtling towards us, we turn back to the story of the ancient Garden and ask: What splendors did it have which now have faded from our life? Which of its ancient grandeurs might perchance be restored? Though we are in the headlong flight of time, we stop to ask which are the old treasures which we dare not leave behind, but must try to preserve to be a joy and a blessing in the onrushing future.

The Bible could have begun on some high mountain-top. It could have begun at an impressive seashore within sound of the thunderous surf, But God began it in a garden. There were trees in the ancient Garden, fruit trees and shade trees. There were bushes and shrubs and flowers. It is surprising how botanical the Bible is in these two first chapters of Sacred Scripture. Clearly it wants to impress us with the idea that man's original happiness was in the setting of a garden among the natural beauties of growing nature. From this Garden of nature, we were never completely expelled. The growing splendor of the world has always maintained our life and sustained our spirit. Expanding scientific knowledge has only deepened our awareness of the blessings of earth's garden to the life of man. The winds change the air, the trees bear fruit or give shade; yes, the very tiny insects in the earth convert the dead leaves and branches into fruitful soil. The complex balance of nature surrounds us, sustains us. We are part of the garden of life.

This relationship between man and nature began from the beginning, and one would assume that it would continue into the future. Yet one of the shocking novelties of our new age is that this ancient natural relationship may cease and that for the first time in history, we may seriously damage the growing world which surrounds and sustains us. This may seem a strange prediction, that man may destroy the garden of nature. But we have already had preliminary threats of what may happen. Just two generations ago, the magnificent forests on our North American continent, which took a thousand years to grow, were almost all destroyed by the greedy pursuit of quick wealth. But we aroused ourselves in time, developed a public movement for conservation, and began to save the forest again. Now in our time, the precious soil itself is being torn up for the underlying coal and the earth left a shambles, sterile and hideous. There, too, we are beginning to fight for the old garden, and see to it that the earth is restored to its creative blessing. But these two examples are really minor. They merely point to the new and disturbing fact that for the first time in the long history of earthly life, man with his machines, his mechanical saws, his giant earth movers, has, in certain situations, at last become more powerful than nature itself. Now if he wants to destroy his world, he is at last able to do so. This novel power of ours is expressing itself in new and horrifying ways. An American writer and scientist, Rachel Carson, has just written a deeply disturbing book. She calls it, "The Silent Spring." Her thesis is that in order to destroy insects, we are abandoning more patient biological methods of control and are spreading from airplanes wholesale poisons over the land, destroying all insects, harmful and beneficial, destroying the birds, destroying the blessed shrubs and leaving wide areas a brownish gray desert. Bird song is hardly heard any more in the countryside where chemical poisons are destroying the garden of life. But we do not need this naturalist to warn us. Have we not by now sent up the poisonous belts of radiation which have made the upper air noxious, and may forever, or for a long time, poison the very winds of life, and even lock the door before man's own great adventure? It is time we remembered God's question to Adam after he left the garden: Man, where art thou now!

There is much to fear about the future and there is something important to preserve about the days of the past. As in the past, so today and tomorrow we need the complicated yet normal balance of nature to sustain our bodies, and its beauty to nourish our spirit. What can we do? Of course, no one man can call a halt to the poisoning of the fields or the poisoning of the upper air. But the average man can know and understand what is happening to his world and build up his personal opinion, which becomes public opinion, and it is public opinion which moves statesmen. We know that it is possible to strip out coal and yet restore the soil. We know that it is possible to control certain insect life without wholesale poisoning of the fields and the suffocation of birds. We know that nations can find atomic means of self-protection without turning the winds of heaven into angels of death. There is enough science, or there can be enough science to preserve God's Garden of Eden for us. Let the cry rise from every heart: Save our fields and save our forests, protect our soil and clean the air. If we understand that we need the natural growing world to live in, if we see before our eyes the Eden which must now be preserved, then be sure that science will learn how, and statesmanship will find the way.

The writer of Genesis began, then, as a botanist, but he continued as a biologist. Having described the trees and bushes, he describes the living things, the birds of the air, the beasts of the field, the fish of the sea and, as a climax, the human race. This picture of animal life in the Garden is an unusual one. Living nature, there, was all peaceful. The animals march calmly before man and he gives each of them its name. The Garden is not only a world of beauty, it is a world of peace.

Now what good is this idyllic picture of the animal world at peace? Surely it is not true to biological life. Animals live on each other's flesh, and "nature is red in tooth and claw." But the picture of peace among all the living in that old dream-garden of Scripture has a profound human purpose. You will notice that when the Prophet Isaiah achieved the first grand vision of world peace, he picked up the language and repeated the picture of the Garden of Eden. He had the lion lie down with the lamb, just as in the dream-days of the past. The Edenic serenity

206

was meant to be an ideal never as yet attained but never to be abandoned, that the world can become an Eden of peace.

This dream, like all dreams, has flared up in the human heart and faded, and flared and faded again. Today in our life the color is gone from the picture of peace. It is characteristic of our world that people seem to feel that the onrushing train of time is moving towards a colossal crash. Our fears whisper to our minds that all our piling up of armaments, which are more powerful than any ever made before, is bound to result in their actual use, and their actual use will mean the death of mankind. So we all have the feeling and the fear that we are speeding forward towards a final explosion.

The many worthy men and women, particularly in England, who march in protests against the installation of atomic weapons, are, of course, nobly motivated. They want to do something. They want to say something. They want to protest the approach of the final explosion. Yet they are not more righteous than the rest of us. There is no responsible person and no national power in the world so actuated by blood-lust or by a hidden death-wish as really to want a modern world war. Yet this world-wide fear of war does not mean the achievement of peace. The great new powers, Russia and China, though they may not want war, certainly do want victory, and the victory over us. If, then, the Red world is armed and we are unarmed, they will without ceasing push us from position to position until there is nothing left for us but to surrender our freedom and live under their awful tyranny. This we will never endure. Hence, to be on equal terms in this cold war, we are compelled to arm. Protesting against the armament may be satisfying, but it is unreal. We know it is

dangerous to be increasingly armed but it is more dangerous to be inadequately armed.

The task of the free world is to continue the armed
cold war, to continue it stubbornly until eventually the
revolutionary fervor of the Red world will, like all such
fervors in past history, cool down to a mutual tolerance.
This is the task that requires endless negotiations, main-
taining conferences against all stubborn refusals, beginning new conferences when others finally faded away. This
is heartbreaking work for our leadership, and it involves
a spiritual contribution from the average people in the
lands of freedom. Our greatest spiritual danger today is
our excitement, panic, desperation. If we grow desperate,
then desperate leaders will arise to carry out our suicidal
will. Therefore every individual citizen must fight to
maintain his own patience, his own confident patience, to
contribute towards keeping the temperament of our country calm and strong. We must build up our personal
patience into national calm, and national calm means national endurance to last and outlast, until the Red revolutionary fervors die away and the world is secure once
more. This is no easy duty today, for the modern world's
mood is excitement, sensation. The news media look for
excitement and crisis. We are kept in a constant sense of
tension. Yet it remains each man's duty to fight the excitements and sensations and seek a confident quietness
within him. This is the best gift that we can give our leadership: a confident American people. We hold to the word
of the prophet, "In calmness and in quietness is our salvation."

The story of the Garden, which began with botany
and continued with biology, concludes with what we might
call psychology. It spoke first of the beauty of growing
nature and then of the peacefulness of the animal world,
and now moves into the heart of the first human couple
and speaks of their sinlessness, their innocence. Later,

indeed, they committed the sin of disobedience, but their life in the Garden of Eden, before that dramatic disturbance, was one of innocence, of a simple trustfulness of the soul. There was originally a beautiful simplicity about man, what the church would call "a sacred simplicity," "sancta simplicitas."

That man was once pure of heart and kindly in spirit is an idea which has long held a fascination over the minds of great writers. Rousseau, for example, in a famous essay, based his thought on the pristine purity of the human race, corrupted by civilization. This view was in a sense held by the average man up to recent times. We all felt that at least in childhood we were innocent. The great painters always pleased us when they painted angelic children. In some way or other, we all held to the picture of Adam in Eden, that we all began with innocence but that life corrupted us all.

But, alas, this sweet faith in basic human goodness has faded from modern life. Psychological studies of a certain school insist that even in childhood there are desires and urges that can only be called corrupt. And, also, modern history tends to confirm this scorn for human goodness. We have seen how a great cultured people mobilized the resources of science and used them for the mass murder of the innocent. What good, then, for us is the old Garden of Eden picture, cherished for so many centuries, the picture of the basic sweetness and innocence of human nature? Are we moderns not justified in our suspicions of people, of their motives and of their actions?

Nevertheless, we vaguely know that this new scorn for human nature somehow hurts us. We sense that it will be increasingly hard to attempt to build a satisfying life upon foundations of universal contempt and widespread distrust. Something of the trustfulness of the old Garden is necessary in our lives today.

209

Certainly we know that there is no true marriage without mutual trust. Perhaps precisely because we have met so many people whose motives are cheap and whose intentions are dubious, precisely for that reason we need at least one person in the world to whom we can give our heart with full confidence and in spite of all modern cynicisms whom we can trust absolutely and without reserve. When that faith truly occurs, and thank God it occurs often enough, there is a happy marriage and a blessed home. Two people have built for themselves a walled-in Garden of Eden.

And it is not foolish to carry some of that faith out into the world. Let us not permit this cynical, cheap, sensation-mongering world to destroy completely the simplicity of the Garden of Eden in our hearts. Not everyone is false. Not everyone has evil motives. The more people we find whom we can trust, the more the world becomes livable. People whom we trust tend to become trustworthy. Let us risk trustfulness to as many as we dare, and life around us will become more homelike and we ourselves, trusting in our fellowmen, will learn to find trust again in the human future. God guard us in the coming year against cheap and general cynicism.

Thomas Wolfe was a true symbol of the restless, noisy, forward rush of our restless, noisy age. He spent his life running away at full speed, yet one of his titles was, "Look Homeward, Angel." Occasionally, at least, he looked back to the angelic past of his early years. In this he was almost and unconsciously Biblical. Scripture describes mankind also as rushing away from the Garden of Eden, yet says, too, "Look Homeward." We live in a world where nature is being destroyed and the skies poisoned, where the danger of war means a threat of annihilation, and where contempt for the human spirit has led us to disillusion and cynicism. "Look Homeward, Angel," and you will see preserved in Scripture a vision of what the world might become, a blessed, growing natural beauty, a peaceful, united humanity, filled with homes of true-hearted faith. This, then, in these breathless times do we pause and wish for at the new kind of year. God grant a restoration of beauty to the growing world, patience in us to outlive our present danger, and the renewal of human trust that will make the world a home for all those who are dear to our hearts.

Amen.

XX
MY BROTHER'S KEEPER

There is always a mystery about artists and their art. There is much about them that has never been explained. Why, for example, does a young man in a certain business family insist upon becoming an artist, contrary to the mood of his home environment? Also, where do the artists' original ideas come from? What is the inner source of new thoughts, new colors, and new forms? An equally deep mystery in the field of art is the strange relationship of the public towards art. Why do certain art objects attract and others repel? Why did the great Egyptian architecture never revive in the later civilizations? And why was the Greek architecture admired, revived, and reshaped time and time again? There is a deep mystery in what mankind likes in art and what it persistently despises.

Perhaps the greatest surprise in popular art appreciation is the tremendous and enduring success of the tragic drama. It is surely unexpected. We would anticipate that people would prefer light and playful shows. They do indeed. Yet by far the grandest successes on the Greek stage and on the Elizabethan stage and on the French stage have been the somber, deeply disturbing, unhappy and often hopeless tragedies. It seems so unlike people to be attracted to tragedy, but they are.

Sermon delivered October 7, 1962

Why tragedy attracts is a question which was asked by the greatest of Greek minds, Aristotle. His explanation was that we identify ourselves with the tragic hero-victim. We recognize certain qualities in us which somehow resemble his, and when we see his fate, we are shaken. We are warned. We are helped. The tragedy is a cleansing of the spirit.

So said Aristotle. And so says Judaism. The old philosopher's description of the meaning of tragedy can well serve as a description of the Day of Atonement. On it we think of tragic failures and unhappy destiny. We speak of sins that we ourselves have never committed, but we know of tendencies in ourselves which should be watched and kept in check. Thus, as in the words of Aristotle, the somber drama of the Day of Atonement is a cleansing, a purification, an atonement of the spirit.

Since, then, the mood of the Day of Atonement is that of the tragic drama, it is appropriate to notice on this day that the Biblical book of Genesis begins with somber tragedy. The beautiful picture of the peaceful, brotherly Garden of Eden serves only as a contrast to the sudden unhappiness which descends upon mankind. The Book begins with double tragedy: first, a rebellion against God by Adam and Eve, then a violence against human life by their older son Cain. The first deed, being against God, is a sin. The second deed, being against man, is a crime.

The basic doctrine of the Christian Church is derived from the first tragedy, Adam's sin against God. But the basic mood of the Jewish faith is derived from the second tragedy, Cain's crime against his brother. That is why Christianity, dealing primarily with the sin of man against God (what it calls the Original Sin) has become a theology; but Judaism, dealing with the crime of man against man, has become a broad ethical tradition. This ethical tradition

213

insists that on the Day of Atonement, God will forgive our sins against Him, but our crimes against our fellowmen can never be forgiven until we pay for them and win back our brotherhood with our fellowmen. Therefore the tragic drama of Cain and Abel is central to the atonement thought. The theme of that ancient tragedy is clearly stated in a dramatic dialogue. God asks Cain after the crime, "Where is thy brother?" Cain answers, mockingly, "Am I my brother's keeper?"

This brief dialogue presents the basic question in all ethical living. Where is our brother, our fellow man? Is he far from us, or near? Is he part of our life concern, or relegated to the outer darkness? Are we moved by other people's sorrows, or are their troubles a nuisance, an intrusion upon our self-absorption?

This is an eternal question, but it is also especially modern. We moderns are not tough. We are sensitive and nervous. That is why psychiatry has become so widespread a part of modern medical practice. It is this modern sensitivity which raises the old ethical question in a new form. What is the **social** effect of our touchiness? Does it make us more aware of other people's needs, or does it drive us into selfish absorption with our own troubles? We must investigate ourselves as moderns and do it in a specific way. To what extent do we moderns sidestep the needs of our fellow men? In which way have we grown insensitive or callous to others, and in which directions must we rewaken our awareness of our interrelationship, our sense of being our brother's keeper? Once we understand that we must seek a new ethical sensitiveness, the drama of Scripture will tend to cleanse our souls and we will move towards fulfillment of our spiritual duty on the Day of Atonement.

214

In Soviet Russia the dominant official doctrine is called "materialism." But the word of greatest popular influence is not "materialism" at all. The people are taught to use the word "culture." They speak constantly of wrong actions as being "uncultured." A modern Russian is constantly eager to be what they call "cultured." The word is, of course, hard to define, but it has an important significance in Russia and in every land. Culture can be described as the relationship between the artistic and the practical, avoiding the ugly and the gross and seeking the finer and the nobler action. Culture is the enemy of coarseness, the aid to dignified demeanor. It means, perhaps, making an art of daily life.

Culture is not merely a matter of externals. It shows itself in external forms, but is a pervasive social influence. So it was always in the past. Cultured people exerted an influence, shaming the coarse and ugly manners, cleansing the rough and violent speech. Decent people, cultured people have always felt that they had a social duty to influence behavior, because cultured behavior leads to social awareness. Hence our famous proverb, "Handsome is as handsome does."

This brings up at once an urgent problem of the modern age. Are those who influence us leading us toward culture or to coarseness? Are our noted persons sensitive as to their influence upon the form of human behavior? To ask the question brings at once a negative and a disturbing answer. We cite a simple example. Millions of dollars were spent advertising a certain cigarette. The advertisement involved an ugly mistake in grammar. This corruption of speech, repeated endlessly in the hearing of millions, was continued and stressed. The protests against it by the educated were laughed at, and the error was valued all the more as good advertisement. Did not these people care that they were corrupting one of the most beautiful languages in the world and were increasing the prevailing carelessness of speech and coarseness of language? Of course they did not. Why, too, is it suddenly the modern fashion in advertising to bring in crude characters with strident and nasal talk, defiantly ungrammatical? Are they not aware that they are exerting an influence towards contempt for decent speech and general refinement? They seem to have no sensitiveness at all.

This matter of decorum in speech is not to be dismissed as inconsequential. We spend billions for education. We hope pathetically to develop a love for good literature and its moral influence. No one seems to care that the media of public influence are conducting a successful offensive against every high school and every public library. Add together all the cheap sensationalism of our day, all the coarse thumping music, all the ugly, shameless clothing on the streets, and you know that the mass media of our day are completely indifferent to the fact that the influence they exert is destroying decency and corrupting culture.

We bring to mind the classic proverb: "Evil communications corrupt good manners." We cannot easily change the cheapness of the modern world, but we can and should guard our own communications. Let each ask himself, what does my style of life do to those who may admire me and who imitate me? Am I helping to maintain the hard-won decency and slowly accumulated culture of the human race? There is a special modern duty incumbent upon us all nowadays. It is the plain duty for people to be ladies and gentlemen; to aid by our demeanor, within our small circle, the preservation of good taste, of cleanness of speech, of dignity in demeanor, and of all which culture means. Never be insensitive to your example. The standards of your fellowman are partly in your keeping, as yours are in his. Our mutual awareness leads us to our mutual discipline. In the culture of decency, we are ever each other's keeper.

Older men tend to become pessimistic about human nature. They get into the habit of believing that people are no longer as good as they used to be. This judgment is due to their natural and unconfessed idealizing of their own early years when things, they are sure, were better in every way. To be pessimistic about the changes in human nature, to believe that people are getting worse instead of better, is one of the hazards of getting old, and we all must guard against it.

Let us ask it as an objective question to be answered in his mind by everyone, young or old. Are people better than they were or are they not as good? This is, of course, difficult to answer because it deals with character, and character, like culture, is a complex word containing many meanings. Without going into the matter too deeply, it is fairly safe to say that in all likelihood human character is better in some ways and worse in others. In some ways the character of the average modern man is definitely better than that of his great-grandfather. We are certainly more tolerant, more openminded about varying degrees of behavior in other people, less likely to blame and accuse people for what we consider wrong. There is, of course, danger in our own tolerance, but there is clearly a virtue in it. There is perhaps another modern virtue, although that, too, contains a danger. We are less solemn. We believe more in laughter and in fun. We do not consider it wrong to take more and more time away from our work for pleasure and amusement. So we are more tolerant to others, and are more easygoing about ourselves.

Yet as we have improved in these regards, we have deteriorated in others. There are many ways in which we

217

are not as good as our ancestors, or even our grandfathers, or even perhaps our fathers. A generation ago, very few people would buy things which they could not afford. Now our whole economy is based upon universal debt. The vast national debt of great nations, spending literally billions for the most expensive armament ever manufactured, all this vast national debt is only a molehill compared to the mountain of private debt accumulated by almost all the newer families in the modern world. A vast proportion of our families are already bankrupt and will remain so. We are not concerned whether this new mode of living in debt is good or bad for business. It may be good today, and may be tragic tomorrow, when there will be a reckoning. Our concern is the moral problem. What is the ethics of taking things and enjoying things that you have never earned and that you will perhaps never pay for? People say, "Live it up." Is this not a revival of the Biblical sin, "Eat, drink, for tomorrow we die?" Does it not mean a vanishing of the older virtue of responsibility?

It seems clear that character has changed. People are, indeed, more tolerant and more fun-loving; that is perhaps good. But they have lost the basic cement which holds the moral personality together, the firm sense of personal responsibility. If this loss concerned only the way a person lives, his indifference to tomorrow, his hunger to enjoy things today, it would be bad enough. But such personal irresponsibility becomes quickly a social irresponsibility. As we grow irresponsible to our own future, we lose the sense of responsibility to others. We repeat almost every day the sarcastic answer of Cain to God, but we translate the Bible into modern speech when we say it. Instead of saying what Cain said, "Am I my brother's keeper?" we look upon others and we say, "I couldn't care less." "I couldn't care less." There is the modern moral debacle. When the publicity men for the wild living movie stars keep on publicizing the actions of their

218

charges, are they concerned with the fact that the example of the drunkenness and sexual corruption of these highly paid darlings will have a corrosive effect on the character of the American youth which idolizes them? They brush that influence aside. They couldn't care less.

Once upon a time there was such a thing as public opinion, because of which the whole atmosphere of social life helped people overcome temptation and live decently. There is very little public opinion today on the side of ethics. All the more does the individual become vital, we to others and they to us.

I wish here to say a word of loving recollection for our dear teacher and older colleague, Samuel Goldenson. The essential meaning of his life was decency and purity. He exerted a constant influence and always for the good. God grant us many such in our ethical strivings. We all need help these days. We are each other's keeper.

There is a classical reading recited every Day of Atonement. It is from the Prophet Isaiah, who talks on the meaning of the Day of Fasting. In his powerfully oratorical manner, the Prophet heaps scorn upon the ritual side of the observance, the fasting and other physical self-affliction; and then turns to the real meaning and evidence of true atonement which should take place every day of life. He describes it in the Biblical fashion in plain and specific words. True atonement, he says, is "to break bread for the hungry and to bring the homeless into your habitation;" in other words, to feel and to fullfill the obligation towards food and shelter for those hungry and homeless; that is to say, that we should, in a practical and material sense, be our brother's keeper, keeping him from hunger and homelessness.

219

While we are evaluating the moral changes of our modern day, let us be careful to count generous charity as one of the new and great virtues of our time. Never were the various little philanthropic groups so magnificently organized and united in great community funds, saving expense, raising sufficient money in every city of our land. Bread and shelter, of which Isaiah spoke, have become the active concern of devoted groups of citizens in an energetic annual campaign in every city in America. This is a firm step towards righteousness. More than that, in every country of the western world, there is no longer any need for the family of unemployed men to starve because of the stoppage of wages. Food is now amply provided. There is no need any more in a western country for aged people to fear that the time is coming when they will be penniless and shelterless and forlorn. We now have the welfare state; and whatever we would say about it in political campaigns, no party would ever abolish it any more. We are now fulfilling the mandate of the Prophet through our central government. And still more than that: In the last generation or two, food and medicines had been sent in times of great disaster, dispensed openhandedly, for example, by Herbert Hoover in Russia, dispensed this very day generously in the earthquake areas of Persia. But nowadays such munificent international help does not wait for disaster. A country like ours, and we are proud to say chiefly a country like ours, has given away billions in dollars and billions worth of food and machinery to almost three-quarters of the nations of the world. Never has human generosity been on such a grand scale as in our day. Never has the word of Isaiah on the Day of Atonement been so magnificently fulfilled.

In the last three or four years our community funds have a new worry in the field of organization. They had organized all the separate charities in the community for the obviously beneficial purposes of better collections and distributions. Yet no sooner are the charities organized, than new ones arise, outside of the fund. When these new ones are brought in finally, still others arise. This phenomenon is annoying, yet it points to one weakness in the vast charities of these welfare days. They do not meet the need for expressing our personal generosity. In fact, without meaning to do so, they tend to supplant the opportunity for personal benevolence. More and more people get into the habit of just writing their check or paying their taxes and thereafter excuse themselves of any personal charitable effort. They pay for the mass benevolence and feel they have done their duty.

Indeed they have. They have done their duty to others, but they have neglected their duty to themselves. The dramatic dialogue with Cain spoke of **thy brother** and **my brother** and Isaiah spoke, "If **you** see a man." The need of our soul is to do direct deeds of lovingkindness. We must seek for them, rejoice in the opportunity to do them, be grateful for a chance to help us express ourselves generously. We cannot live decently without personal deeds of lovingkindness. Whenever I show mercy to a specifc person, whenever I do a man a favor without expecting to be paid back in kind, whenever I do pure kindness to some human being, I have participated in that ethical dialogue between man and his fellowman which purifies the soul. And that day, whenever it comes, is a day of true atonement.

Modern architecture is radically different from Gothic and Graeco-Roman classic. Modern painting is another color-world from the painting of Rembrandt and Tintoretto. Art is ever changeful in its forms and people's tastes slowly follow in the footsteps of the creative artists and

221

gradually learn to appreciate what we never understood before. But there will always be one permanent art appeal, the powerful and imperious appeal of the tragic drama. As in the days of the Greeks and the days of Shakespeare, people will always come to hear and see the drama of human misdeeds and punishment. What they see and hear will afford what Aristotle called "a purgation, or cleansing, of the soul," and what Judaism calls "the spiritual atonement."

Each age will need its own type of purifying atonement because each age forgets in its own way that it is its brother's keeper. Our own age is one of increasing coarseness, of mounting irresponsibility, and of transferring the joy of lovingkindness to the huge social machine. Understanding that, we hope that God will help us find the sensitiveness which we, as moderns, especially need; that we may exert what influence we have towards the culture of daily decency, towards a rebirth of simple responsibility, and towards the blessed opportunity of personal kindness. We in our relation to others, they in relation to us, must approach each other's hearts again. When I see you carry your burden with courage, I will carry mine with confidence and strength.

Amen.

XXI

JACOB'S LIFE
Every Man's Life

Each of us can be better than we are. Each of us can be less irritable when contradicted, less impatient when delayed, less bitter when thwarted. Although we know that we can be better than we are, we always need to be reminded of it. The purpose of the High Holidays is precisely that, to remind us of our finer possibilities.

There are many ways in which this potential goodness of ours can be brought home to us. The American poet suggests one way in his famous lines:

"Lives of great men all remind us
We can make our lives sublime."

This method of reminder by high example is used in Sacred Scripture or, rather, it is used by the post-Biblical teachers and preachers who by their commentaries elaborate and illuminate the careers of the great men of the Bible, in order to throw their radiance upon the lives of average men and women. There is, for example, the Scriptural life of Abraham, the lonely pioneer who left home and kindred, who made himself a homeless stranger, all for the sake of a noble religious ideal. There is Moses, the strong and patient leader, who through two generations of endurance carried on his own shoulders

Sermon delivered September 18, 1963

223

the incredible burden of a rebellious, quarrelsome people. There is also Job, the tragic hero of suffering and pain, who demanded justice from God for his unmerited agonies and yet, in the deepest darkness of life, never lost his faith in the justice and mercy of the Eternal. These men and such like them are true heroes and, as the poet properly says, such heroic persons stir us average people to a renewed belief in our own grander possibilities.

Yet these exalted human types are really too noble for us. We know ourselves too well and are aware of our limitations. We read about Abraham, but we will never leave the familiar world for the sake of an ideal, as he did. We are not likely to carry the burden of leadership of a rebellious people, as Moses did. Nor can we hold on to our faith when life crushes us, as nobly as did the Biblical Job. These great men may bring us light, but it is a momentary light, a lightning flash in the darkness of the night. For us to be more lastingly influenced, we need examples closer to our daily life. We need to know of everyday people who, although average, have achieved what we want to achieve, unpretentious people who have been as courageous as we would like to be courageous. There, too, Scripture comes to our aid. For the men and women of the Bible are not only those exalted characters of exceptional heroism and strength. There are everyday people in Scripture, with our weaknesses and our failures, yet who have achieved what we would like to attain.

Such an everyday human being is Jacob, one of the Patriarchs, a man of weakness yet of strength, a man of selfishness yet of nobility, a man of fear yet of courage. Jacob is not the towering hero. He is just a

224

human being, in brief, a man like ourselves. It is precisely because of his everyday humanness that he is named as our true ancestor. We are called "children of Jacob," or by his later name, "children of Israel."

Jacob is Everyman and we, his children, share his average, human weaknesses. But he attained much that we would like to attain. So we think of him on this day, when the trumpet call of tradition reminds us that we can make our life "more sublime." His struggles and achievements may well be a blessing to us on this beginning of a New Year.

There is a curious controversy over the career of Jacob. It is an old dispute between Christian and Jewish theologians. Many Christian Bible commentators actually dislike Jacob, while the Rabbis in the past defended him. We might say that Jacob is like many of his descendants, a victim of scorn and anti-Semitism. What have these non-Jewish scholars against our father Jacob? They say, rather typically, that he was cunning and would do anything dishonest for his own advantage. The older brother Esau, a simple hunter, an outdoors-man, was cheated out of his birthright by the cunning father of all the Israelites. The implications against us are clear and need not be elaborated.

But the Rabbis of old rushed to our ancestor's defense. They say that after all, both brothers were twins. If Esau were older, he was older only by a minute. Furthermore, the birthright, whatever privileges it brought, was despised and rejected by Esau. He sold it for a mess of pottage. No one compelled him to sell his birthright. He preferred to satisfy his transient appetite to all the spiritual burdens of family seniority. Why blame Jacob

225

for buying it and not blame Esau for selling it? Besides, taking the blessing from his father Isaac was not Jacob's idea. He was unwilling to do so, but his loving mother, Rebecca, urged him and forced him into the plan.

But all this defense on the part of the Rabbis is only negative. It is in the nature of a rebuttal to the hostile contempt. More significantly, they have a positive description of Jacob which concerns us more, because their description of him indicates their personality ideal which, of course, must touch our own life. Their description, based upon the Bible's, portrays a contrast between the two young men. Esau was an outdoor man, a rover, an activist. Jacob was a homebody and a scholar, a meditative young man.

Now it is clear that the two descriptions of the twin youths describe two qualities which really are not separate but are, both of them, inherent in every youth. We all have some of the "Esau mood" in our youth, the wild, restless action, and we have also the "Jacob mood" of quiet, innner brooding. The percentage of the two moods varies with the individual, but more significantly, it also varies at different eras in human history. This present era is a time when some of our direst dangers come from the fact that the youth of the world is in the wild dynamism of its "Esau mood." In all the half-developed countries of the world, a chief source of civic disorder and bloody riot are the youths of the colleges. In South America, in Asia, the youth is violent and is a constant source of revolution and destruction. Even in our secure country, young people abandon the calm atmosphere of school too soon, are mad for action, high speed, danger and destruction. There is a special menace in our age, due to the "Esau mood" in the youth of the world.

We begin to appreciate nowadays the ancient ideal embodied in the life of the other twin, the youth who was to become our father Jacob. Youth needs the quiet of its long, slow thoughts. Youth needs to meditate to discover its own personality and to believe in the value of learning and studying that it may rediscover the truth that all the past ages live in the latest generation. The inner, meditative thoughtfulness and even the silence of youth is one of its greatest blessings, and the most urgent quality which the world must contrive to make acceptable again.

Who knows and who cares about whose fault it is that modern youth all over the world has turned to the wild Esau and has abandoned the quiet and studious Jacob? Partly it is due to the uncertainty of the world's future, and I do not know who is to be justly blamed for that. Partly it is due to the wild rush of modern transportation, available to too many too soon. Whatever is to be blamed, our need is nevertheless clear. We have done much for child education. Now we must improve youth education. We must use the discoveries of psychology to calm the restlessness of the youthful heart. We must reestablish a love for learning, a faith in the value of thinking and a belief that the future is worth preparing for. Methods will follow the understanding of the problem and our acceptance of the task. We all must see that it is dangerous for the wild mood of Esau to dominate the youth of the world as it does today. The world will be much safer whenever we reestablish the other mood, just as natural to youth, the meditativeness of young Jacob for, as Scripture says, "Even youths shall faint and grow weary, but those who wait for the Lord and meditate shall renew their strength."

A new novel has appeared a few weeks ago. It is by a clever young Frenchman named Couteaux and is entitled **Gentleman in Waiting**. It is a light book, clever, amusing and, as many modern novels are, a trifle bawdy. But it carries a serious philosophy which has a significant meaning for our time. The thesis of the book, which is evident beneath all its light playfulness is that the age of hard work, indeed the age of any work at all, is now out of date, and a new era of universal idleness is rapidly on the way. Due to the progress in automatic machinery, which is of course real enough, less and less work from fewer and fewer people is needed, and we must develop a new ideal, the ideal of universal idleness. The story tells how this young Frenchman, not out of laziness, but out of principle, lived on his wits and his charm and ended up as a universally adored saint, the new apostle of noble idleness. To the extent that such a novel should be taken seriously at all, one should say that if this is really a gowing modern ideal, to do less and less work in life, it is certainly contrary to the ideal which built our American society. America has followed what economists have called "the Puritan ideal," in which energy, vitality and work were considered not only valuable for its necessary results in taming the wilderness, but is also to be revered as a mandate from God, Who wants His children to toil in order to achieve. In fact, the old Puritan ideal is much older than the Puritans. It goes back to Scripture and is seen in its splendor in the life of Jacob.

This meditative youth, this introverted brooder is compelled to leave home, and in the country of his new residence, his whole life changes. He suddenly becomes a man of action, a man of restless work. He toils with muscle and with mind for over twenty years. He works in order to be able to support his wives and maintain his family. He uses brain and brawn to build up an estate so that he and they may have security. The energetic activism which was dangerous in youth as an "Esau quality" of wild energy, becomes a virtue in middle life when Jacob changes from the meditative youth to the creative man. Work in our Jewish tradition is more than a necessity. It is an ideal. The Puritans rediscovered it because they were an Old Testament people and studied our Bible. They realized that long before the story of our father Jacob, God Himself gives His children a divine example. He gave us the example of rest for one day, but the blessing of creative work for six days.

That new French novel is indeed playful, but it voices the beginning of a dangerous modern mood. People are working less, even those who have important work to do. They are trying to get as much pay for as little work as possible, and this applies to management as well as to labor. They dream of early retirement without realizing how empty an idle life can be. No person can have self-respect if he loafs away the days and the weeks and the months and the years, nor can he have mental health. If the direct work of earning a living is in some lives no longer needful, there is much work to be done in communities, charities, to help, communal work to share. Jacob, as creator and worker, should remind us to repent for all of God's precious time we have squandered in idleness except for what is needed for rest and recreation. From his normal life must come the eternal mandate that man is a child of a working, creative God. "Whatever thy hand findeth to do," said the Bible sage, "do thou with all thy might and thou shalt find blessing in it."

The great Roman orator and statesman, Cicero, was also a practical philosopher. One of the works that he has bequeathed us might be called a psychological classic. It is entitled **De Senectute,** "concerning old age." The title explains its purpose. It is meant to be a guide as to how to be happy though old.

The very impulse on the part of a busy statesman to write such a booklet points up one of the prime problems of our human life. We never really learn how to live. We really cannot learn enough to guide us all through our life. Every new stage in our existence is so different from the preceding that it requires a new technique, a new doctrine and some new ideals. There are people who were wonderful as youths and were a disappointment as adults. There are some who were able and creative and admirable in their prime and are miserably unhappy and even dislikable when they become old. Skill in the art of living in one stage is never sufficient for the succeeding one. We always need to learn new ways of life for new stages of experience. Thus, as there are many guides in the treasury of human wisdom for youthful living, and guides for the industrious activity of middle life, so there has been considerable writing from almost every civilization on the art of living in the later years. Great personalities, especially the Stoics such as Marcus Aurelius, have given serene and exalted counsel. But such noble advice is for the great and the exceptional. It would be better for us to observe also in this regard the latter years of the noble averaage man of Scripture, our father Jacob.

He had lived through his dynamic, active years. He had built up his family and created and accumulated rich possessions. But now that the active period of his life was beginning to slow down, he gathered his family and his flocks and his herds and his household of servants and began slowly making his way southward and westward from the land of the Chaldees to his family home in the land of Canaan. He was beginning the journey to prepare for his latter years.

Whether in the busy years in Chaldea he had thought much about his brother Esau, Scripture does not say. But now that he was approaching home, he thought of him vividly. He remembered now his brother's murderous rage and how in his anger, perhaps more at himself for selling the birthright than at Jacob for acquiring it, how Esau threatened to kill him and how his mother pleaded with Jacob to flee for his life from his bloodthirsty twin. Perhaps he could have coped with Esau in those early years, but he had obeyed his mother and departed. But now, returning home many years later, he was indeed blessed with family and with wealth but was, therefore, all the more vulnerable. Now he says, as Scripture records, "My brother Esau will attack and slay the women and children." So he prepares, if necessary, to defend himself, but primarily to allay the old anger of his brother, to win favor in his sight and to achieve reconciliation and peace.

Fortunately, our father Jacob did achieve his reconciliation with Esau. But suppose he had failed. What would his older years have been in the land of his fathers? An endless uncertainty, a living with fear, a bitterness between two families which would have been handed down as a vendetta from generation to generation. His later years would have been tragically miserable.

How human all this is. In our life perhaps there is no one who hated us as violently and as murderously as Esau hated his twin. But surely we all enter into the later years with recollections of former rivalries, of old competitions, of ancient jealousies and former dislikes. We do not think of them much in our active, busy years, but when we begin to arrive at the latter years, we know that we all now need what our father Jacob sought, the blessing of reconciliation and peace. What value is there in the old grudges and in the former rivalries? They are only destructive poisons in our heart. We cannot, or we should not, carry them any longer. What is more heartbreaking than to see a bitter old man or a mean old woman? How sad to see those who have been granted additional life, almost hate life itself. What we should regret, especially in the latter years, is our failure to do what Jacob did. How many old envies have we allowed to persist, how many old unreasonable dislikes have we continued to foster! The older people of every circle ought to be a source of calm, of patience and of serenity. It is a blessing to pray for but, more than that, it is a type of life to achieve. Consciously and patiently, as Jacob with Esau, we seek what we need most in our older years, the serenity of the heart, the restfulness of the mind, the calm tolerance with people's foibles, and the utter refusal to hate and to be bitter. May God grant us the power to achieve that calm sunset which He has intended for us all.

Benjamin Disraeli, Lord Beaconsfield, is still an honored name among English conservatives. But to attain his honored place, he had many obstacles to overcome, being a born Jew of dark Oriental type, restless as mercury, scintillating and brilliant among the slow-moving and often smug British. His very personality was an obstacle which only his brilliance could overcome. And as one might imagine, there were times in his long struggle when the whole effort and heartbreak did not seem worthwhile. It must have been from such a time of dejection that he wrote a famous statement which is of particular interest to us today, since it is the reverse image of all

232

that is to be learned from father of Jacob's life. Disraeli, in a moment of gloom, commenting on the stages of human life, said: "Youth is a blunder, manhood a burden, old age a regret." These are powerful words and true enough, often enough, to bring sorrow to the heart. But Scripture has a different summary of human life, since it is basically optimistic. Besides its oft-mentioned optimism about human society and its future, it has a profound optimism about individual human character. It believes, as we all are bound to believe and as this New Year's Day urges us to believe, that we can all be nobler than we are, that the nobility which we can attain is no miraculous gift, but a slow progress from stage to stage in our life. Each stage needs a different quality and each is revealed in the unpretentious embattled life of the ancestor for whom we all are named. We see how miserable life can be if youth is all wild energy, as Esau's youth was, if adult life is spent in half-idle futility and old age darkened by bitterness and rage. Jacob's life is a long journey but an upward one. Blessed are we if we share his simple, human virtues, to be sufficiently thoughtful in our youth, creative in our manhood, and calm and peaceable in our age. This is how noble we well can be. It is within our normal reach. May the New Year bring such a blessing to us all.

Amen.

XXII

JACOB'S DREAM
Every Man's Dream

The Bible is full of dreams. There may be a hundred of them recorded in Scripture. No one has made a systematic study of these Bible dreams, but the general impression they give is of great variety. They vary in the type of person who dreams the dreams, kings and servants, patriarchs and wanderers, heathens and prophets. The contents and mood of the dreams themselves are also in great variety. Some are happy dreams and some sad, some bright and some dark. The very richness of the dream material in the Bible should stir the imagination of modern people, for dreams and their analysis have become one of the great subjects of modern times.

In ancient times, also, dreams were a subject for study and analysis, for they were deemed to be very important. In fact, there seems to have been experts even in those days who specialized in the interpretation of dreams. Joseph, in Egypt, was considered to be an expert interpreter. When Pharaoh was puzzled by his own dream, he consulted Joseph. But generally speaking, the dreams were simple and the dreamer himself was satisfied that he understood them. The reason that the dream appeared to be simple was that the people in Biblical times had a theory by which they explained

Sermon delivered September 27, 1963

the purpose of the dream. They understood that dreams were a channel through which God spoke to them. Through the dream, God opened the gates of the future. Thus the dreams were revelations of what was to come. In other words, the dream was a prophecy.

Now this classic theory that the dream is a heaven-sent prophecy is still held to by many people. Millions believe that they were warned in a dream of some calamity which actually came. Yet the modern, scientific theory of dreams is entirely different from the theory held in the Biblical past. Dreams, say the modern psychologists, do not come down from above, but spring up from below. A dream is not a revelation from God to you, but a self-revelation from you to yourself. The dream, according to modern thinking, is a mixture of the visions and the aims and the desires which we human beings dare not express in the daytime. These aims and desires are hidden, therefore, deep in our subconscious self. They come to their expression in the dreams of the night. The dream reveals our real and our hidden character. So we might say that the old theory was that the dream is our destiny, and the new theory is that the dream is our true personality.

Like many new theories, this modern theory is generally an improvement, but in certain cases it creates new difficulties. It gives a better explanation of most of the Biblical dreams, yet it creates a new difficulty in explaining certain particular ones. For example, the most famous dream of the Bible seems to be explained better by the old theory of revelation than by the modern theory of suppression. This is the dream of our father Jacob, that struggling Everyman, the ancestor after whom we are named and whose life we have taken as our guide during this High Holy Day season. Now his dream is well known and is one of the classics, and we need only

235

mention its highlights. Jacob flees from the murderous wrath of his twin brother Esau, falls asleep in the desert and dreams. He sees a ladder reaching from earth to heaven, angels ascending and descending the ladder. Then God Himself speaks to him and blesses his future.

The old-fashioned explanation is simple. This dream is a revelation of God to our father Jacob. Yet the modern student would say the dream, like all dreams, is a suppression. But what is there here to suppress? There are no shameful desires here to hide and no cruel ambitions to disguise. Surely there is nothing for Jacob to conceal in the dream of seeing a radiant vision of God. He should be proud of it and openly avow it. Yet although the modern explanation thus adds difficulties, still it is intriguing and perhaps, also, profound. It goes deep into our subconscious and would actually imply that evil impulses are not the total contents of our subconscious. It is possible that sometimes goodness may also be suppressed and be relegated there. A man living in a race-hating environment may suppress his brotherliness. A man whose friends are all materialistic may be embarrassed to voice his spiritual ideals. There well may be a hidden subconscious store of nobility in us.

If that is so, then the oft-cited words, "O Lord, let us see ourselves as Thou seest us," may mean that we search our hearts not only for the evil in them, but also for the good, so that on this Day of Atonement we may reach a firm foundation upon which to build a nobler life.

The founder of psychoanalysis, Sigmund Freud, was a physician, and his interest in dreams was a medical one. When he started to record the various confused dreams of his patients, it was not out of literary curiosity,

236

but for the practical purpose of healing. So just as important as the dream itself, was the dreamer's reaction to the dream and how its revelation and interpretation would affect his daily life. Then it is noteworthy that the Bible gives us a description, not only of Jacob's vivid dream, but also of his waking reaction to it. The dream had disturbed him. It caused him to make certain statements which are of permanent spiritual value.

The first thing which Jacob said on awakening is really astonishing to us. He opened his eyes and, still under the influence of the dream, he said: "God is in this place and I knew it not." He seemed surprised to realize the presence of God around him. His surprise puzzles us. If he had been a heathen, who in a flash of enlightenment suddenly realized the folly of idol worship and suddenly realized the Omnipresence of the true God, then we would understand his statement, "God is here and I knew it not before." But this is no heathen, this is the grandson of Abraham and the son of Isaac, who taught with pride and conviction that the Eternal God is **everywhere**. Then how is it possible for the grandson of the world's first monotheistic home to say, "God is here and I knew it not"?

We can understand this puzzling statement only by the modern explanation. He had, indeed, been taught by his grandfather and his father of the presence of God, but the idea for some reason had become vague in his life. The reality of God had moved down out of his conscious life and become hidden in his subconscious. But the dream, then, released in him the knowledge that he always had, but had forgotten that he had.

His experience is typical and explains to us our own religious mood. We are children of the great and original monotheistic religion in the world, and we are taught of

237

God by all the Abrahams and Isaacs and Jacobs of our past. We know of Him, but we forget Him, and God becomes hidden in our subconscious. We do not think of God, but that does not mean that we have consciously rejected Him. It is not so much a question of believing or not believing in God, as it is a question of remembering God or forgetting Him. That is what Jacob's waking reaction meant. If he lived today, he would say, "I hid God away in my subconscious, but my dream reminds me that He lives and has always lived in my life."

This, then, is the healing purpose of this Day: to look more deeply into our hearts and discover that the basic faith has always been there. We had let God vanish from our daily thought, and certainly from our daily speech. He became for us what the Prophet Isaiah called "the hidden Divinity," and on this day we seek, as our father Jacob did, to bring the Divine back into our consciousness and to realize that He was in our life all the time.

The progress of Jacob's dream is not perfectly clear. It seems evident from the text that when he was aroused to the realization of the Divine presence, he relaxed and fell asleep again. Then he definitely awoke to continue his day's journey. Still being under the spell of the dream, he could not leave the place where he had slept and then forget about it. He therefore gathered the very stones upon which he had slept, built them into an altar, and he called the desert place "Beth El," which means "The House of God," and this remained its name forever, for it became one of the great sanctuaries.

Evidently the dream had made some radical changes in Jacob's life. He wanted never to forget it. He hoped that self-revelation of the Divine presence would remain permanently with him. Yet how could it become permanent? It came in a dream and might vanish like a dream. Jacob's instinct was to build an altar, a tabernacle, and thus to convert the passing inspiration into a permanent institution.

To make permanent our own noble moments, to preserve the flash of inspiration, is the basic motivation of all artistic endeavor. A man has a radiant idea. He fears it will be lost, so he is driven to put it into a poem or into a picture or into music. This is one of the profoundest instincts of man, to make permanent the fleeting radiances of life. Those of us who are not creative artists have that instinct too. We have these bright moments of religious feeling. We know that they will vanish as they came. How can they be made to endure? This explains the reason for our attachment to religious institutions. We know that they are devoted to keeping permanent that faith which in our own life is only fitfull. We know beforehand that generally when we come to worship, God remains hidden deep in our subsconscious. So the words of the prayers seem empty or, worse than that, addressed to emptiness. But it is sufficient for us that some day, at some part of the service, God's reality becomes clear again, and the words in the book begin to glow and burn like a fire upon a Temple altar. It is absurd to mock at people who come to Temple rarely or even twice a year. They should, of course, seek the Lord at all times and they do not. But in spite of the fact that their present need seems easily satisfied with a few sparse visits to the Temple, they still maintain the institution, knowing that it is the only way in which the inspiratiton can be made into a poem, the sound into a symphony, and the beauty into a permanent painting. We all share what we have inherited from our father Jacob, the desire to build in the desert of our lives an enduring altar to God, and

239

thus to convert a transient inspiration into an enduring faith.

On the New Year, we spoke of the fact that our father Jacob was subject to some scorn and contempt of certain non-Jewish theologians. Certain commentators, speaking of his dealings with his brother Esau over the birthright, called him too clever and too cunning. Now there is a part of his waking reaction here which, again, could be subject to rather scornful misunderstanding. Having become aware of God's presence in his life, and having built an altar to make that awareness permanent, he now enters into, or he proposes a sort of business contract with God the Eternal. How strangely practical—how almost commercial—his words seem! Scripture says that Jacob spoke as follows: "If God's will be with me and protect me on this road which I am traveling, and if He will give me bread to eat and a garment to wear, and if I return in peace to my father's house, then the Lord will be my God, and this stone altar which I have built here will be the House of the Lord, and from all that Thou, O God, wilt give me, I will give a tenth part unto Thee." What a contract! What a businesslike contract! How unspiritual it sounds and how easily mocked. Note what he seems to say, that if God will protect him and sustain him, then God will be his God. Are we to understand this to mean that if God will not protect him, if he, Jacob, falls into danger, if his twenty year career away from home ends in poverty and in failure, does he mean what his words seem to say, that he will then reject God?

We do not know what Jacob would have done if his life from that day onward would have been a failure. Fortunately his life was not a failure. He built up a family and an estate to protect them. God seems to have ful-

240

filled His part of the contract, and Jacob's gratitude to God became permanent in him and was transferred to his children, the twelve tribes of our ancestors. But had he suffered defeat in life, would he have abandoned the God Whom he rediscovered in the desert? We may safely assume that he would not, for Jacob lived for many years and many of the later years were dark and miserable. His beloved son Joseph was, he believed, slain by wild beasts. He was afraid that his son Benjamin, the last son of his unforgettable and beloved Rachel who had died so young, was also being taken from him, perhaps forever. Then, towards the very end of his life, he had to pack up all his belongings and become an alien in the land of Egypt. In his sorrow, he sometimes cried out to his sons, "You are bringing down my grey hairs in sorrow to the grave." But never once in all these years of terror, misery and pain did he cry out in indignation against God, and never once, in spite of the anguish in life, did he doubt that God was still protecting him.

No, this was no conditional contract in which his faith depended upon his prosperity. So with us his children, our relation to God never has depended upon our receiving continuous blessing. How often have the descendants of Jacob-Israel suffered disappointments, hatreds undeserved cruelties inhuman and exiles tragic! Amid the storms of their life they have cried out, as is only human, as King David cried out in a tragic moment, "Eli, Eli, my God, my God, why hast Thou forsaken me?" But they never really believed that God had forsaken them, or at least, they never believed it except in a transient moment of natural bitterness. Somehow they always managed at the deeper level of their awareness to hold on to their faith that God's purposes are mysterious and God's love is eternal. The Prophet Isaiah spoke for our millenial attachment to God in spite of misfortunes when

241

he said in God's name, "For a brief moment only have I turned My face away from thee in anger, but with great love will I now restore thee."

Then what is Jacob's ancient contract which we refuse to abandon? It always has had meaning for us on its positive side, that the gifts which life has given us are not to be looked upon as accidents of chance, but are undeserved blessings for which we ever return our gratitude.

This is a time to reflect on the positive side of our agreement with God, what we have received beyond what we ourselves have earned. We think of the mysterious healing power in this strangely complex body of ours. How many assaults of germs and virus we have thrown off without being aware of our successful defense. How many sicknesses the body has combatted, mobilizing its myriad forces and restoring us to health. How much friendship we have received which we could easily have lost by a careless word or a thoughtless action, and yet the bond of affection has remained unbroken. A man who believes that all the happiness and health that he has is entirely the result of his own merit, is either a heathen or a fool. We children of Jacob feel in a very profound sense the words of our father Jacob, "God has given us bread to eat and a garment to wear and has brought us safely home from many a dangerous journey." We know that our religion is never real unless we have an abiding sense of debt for unpaid kindness. We live in the spirit of our father Jacob when we say on this day, "Tell me what I can repay to the Lord for all His kindness to me."

The famous statement of Shakespeare, "To thine own self be true," goes on to a magnificent conclusion.

It says: "And it will follow as the night the day, that thou canst not be false to any man." In other words, if you are aware of your true self, it will lead you to a life of truth and justice to others. The process, then, is from self-study to human service.

This is, I believe, the fullness of the atonement idea. It all points to ethics and human responsibility, but it begins the ethical quest in an original way. In effect it says, "You cannot look outward unless you first look inward. You cannot be ethical unless, first, you are sincere. When you know yourself, you will begin to understand your fellow man." That is why our ethics is **religious** ethics. We begin by searching the heart. We find our weaknesses and can become tolerant of the weaknesses of others. We realize our own need for strength and so appreciate the help which others need. All of this quest from the subconscious to the social begins with the dream of the man for whom we are named, he who was surprised in finding God Who was already in his heart, he who built an altar to make that dream permanent, he who felt eternal gratitude for God's protection. We are guided by his dream. It tells us through all the generations that we have never lost God, but have just forgotten where He was. We will ever cherish the institutions devoted to Him and will ever find reason for gratitude to the Eternal. May God grant us many reasons to voice our thanks to Him through the coming year and for many years.

Amen.

XXIII
GROWTH
THROUGH STRUGGLE
The Young Joseph

There have been famous novelists in our times. There have also been some truly great ones. Who would be the greatest novelist of our era? Some would select the Frenchman, Marcel Proust; some would select the Irishman, James Joyce; and some would point to the Nobel Prize winner, the novelist, Thomas Mann. This much is certain, that Thomas Mann, besides being a great novelist was also a noble personality. He did not confine himself to the life of art but was profoundly concerned with the difficult art of living in the modern day. He was a Protestant, famous and honored in his native Germany. He could have received every reward from the newly risen Nazi government, but he preferred to protest against its evils, left Germany to live as a self-exile in the United States. So this great man considered his novels to be more than works of art, but proclamations of principle and guides to decent and worthy living in a troubled and corrupted time. Though he wrote on many themes, he finally decided on one central theme and wrote three novels exploring the life of a Biblical personality. He found what he needed to express and what he wished to proclaim to the world in the life of the young son of Jacob, Joseph, the beloved and the hated, the homebody and the exile.

Sermon delivered September 6, 1964

As for us, in our own sequence of themes for these High Holy Day preachments, we have come to the same theme. We had devoted one sequence to the pioneer Abraham, to that symbol of Everyman, our father Jacob, and now we too have come to the life of Jacob's beloved and suffering son, Joseph.

Necessarily our religious approach is quite different from that of Thomas Mann. He was an adherent of the famous psychoanalyst, Carl Jung. Jung believed that deep in our own mind there still live the thoughts of our father and mother; and that in **their** minds there still live the thoughts of their parents. As a result, in the subconscious mind of each of us the whole past still lives. So, being an adherent of this philosophy, Thomas Mann looked upon Joseph not as a separate person but as a summary of the life of his father Jacob and his grandfather Isaac and of his great-grandfather Abraham. Therefore the central problem of his novel-series was how to adjust the accumulating memories of the past to the bewildering problems of the present. This is a vital task and concerns historians and philosophers.

Our religious task is more practical. The old year is gone and a new year begins. Our thoughts start with the present and turn to the future. So we look upon Joseph not so much as a summary of the past but as he was at the beginning of the Biblical description, a young man with a character as yet unformed and often unpleasant but with a personality which had its potentiality to change, to grow, to improve. So we ask ourselves, what sort of people are we today and how well-equipped are we to face the future. This is a typical and a classical New Year question: What is there in our character which can be criticized and rejected, and what can be developed of our personality so that with greater understanding of life and with better ability to face it, we can confront with

245

hope and perhaps with joy the coming New Year of our life.

Joseph was a dreamer and his brothers mocked him for it. When they saw him approch from a distance, they said sarcastically, "Behold here cometh the dreamer." When he told them his dreams, they laughed him to scorn. But, says Scripture, Jacob their father uttered not a single word of rebuke. How could he have rebuked his dreamy son? Did not he himself dream at the same stage in his life, a generation ago when he fled before Esau, his brother? Yet he could well have rebuked him if he had had the heart to do so, for there was a vast difference between the dreams of the father years ago and that of Joseph that day. Jacob dreamed of angels climbing on a ladder to heaven and God standing by his side as he lay on the desert stone, reassuring him and promising him some day a safe return home. Joseph in his dream requires no encouragement at all. He has plenty of self-confidence. He dreams of himself as master and all his brothers bowing down to him in humility. God does not appear at all in Joseph's dream. Joseph himself is lord and master. If Joseph thinks of anyone as adored and worshiped it is himself.

Therein that self-centered young man is an uncomfortably true symbol of us all. As with him, in our dreams we admit that the center of our universe is generally ourselves. We picture our superiority, our success and grandeur. As Kipling put it, no matter how good we are at times, there is always "too much ego in our cosmos." If there is any struggle essential for our growth, it is our never-ending inner war against our personal self-worship We will always remain the most important person in the world to ourself, but if we find the right method, we can keep our sefl-worship within decent bounds.

246

That method was forced upon Joseph and he struggled with its use until he became a worthy personality. He who dreamed of himself as dominant was cast into a pit, was sold as a slave, brought to Egypt, thrown into prison and, in the solitary world of the stone walls had a new opportunity for true self-judgment. He learned to tell himself for the first time not what his glories would some day be, but what his weaknesses constantly are. He discovered the sharp weapon of self-judgment.

This is the central theme of the New Year's Day. It is called "Yom Ha-din," "the day of judgment," in which we say God judges and balances in the infinite scale our weaknesses against our strengths. Practically, since God is in our heart, God's judgment on the New Year means our self-judgment. Only a man who can look into his heart and know his own selfishness, who can look into his will and know his own weakness, who can remember crises and face his own cowardice, only that man has a chance to dethrone his own self-god and worship again on this Holy Day the true God of the universe. His foolish dreams may then become noble truths. So said King David: "O Lord, who shall ascend Thy holy mountain; he that speaketh the truth in his heart." It is for this self-judgment, if we are capable of it, that we are gathered on this New Year's Day.

In military life the ideal procedure is careful training of men in the disciplines and the techniques of the military profession, and only after the soldier is thoroughly trained is he brought into the ultimate test of actual combat. But often when a war drags out and the trained soldiers are used up, men are taken into the army and before they are half-trained or accustomed to discipline, they are thrown as raw recruits into the awesome shock of combat.

247

So it is in our life. We could be much happier and could manage our life much more successfully if we were given plenty of time for slow and gradual development, so that when we would meet the shocks of life, we would be well prepared for them. But, alas, it is not so. Often the experiences of life come to us as a shock and we engage in the combat without being ready for it. Sometimes we feel that we are never adequately trained because life brings its crises to us in explosive surprise. One such shock came very early to Joseph. He was suddenly cast into the shocking experience of hatred and hostility. In no way was he prepared for it. He was his father's darling child. He wore with confident pride his coat of many colors. He was sure that as he was beloved in his father's house, so he would be beloved everywhere. His father catered to him. The world would kowtow to him. Then he suddenly discovered that even his own brothers hated him with a murderous hatred. Here was a new bewildering struggle, perhaps harder than the struggle with his own self-worship. It was a struggle against the outer world with its meanness and its unreasoned hostility.

Thomas Mann took Joseph's shocking experience as symbolic of all mankind and of every youth who suddenly leaves the shelter of a loving home and finds himself in the battlefield of a hate-filled world. This is a correct symbol, indeed, but it is especially meaningful to us in a way which did not enter into the mind of the great German novelist. To us this is a specific symbol of the experience of the people of Israel. Exiled from the homeland, we were driven into the world and it was a world of prejudice and often blood-stained hate. The life of Jewry was a life of continuous struggle against hostility. In some way it is the experience of every young Jewish individual coming from a home in which the Jewishness was taken for granted as normal and entering into a world in which the shocked personality must face scorn and contempt and

248

unfair barriers. The struggle against hostility is a battle which every Jew has fought in various ways, sometimes as a mild discomfort, sometimes as a serious danger. What defense is there against unreasoning hatred?

Joseph, the beloved son, hated by his brothers, an alien in Egypt, found his own mode of defense. He did not defend himself with arguments because reason is usually useless against the unreasonable. He simply and quietly worked. He developed his abilities. He deepened his knowledge and in spite of all obstacles, ultimately reached the heights. The very men who hated him, seeing him in his attainment, now, if reluctantly, respected him. Work and achievement are not the only defense against the world's hostility but they have always been our favorite method. Thus have the children of Israel always defended themselves, by deeper learning, by harder work, by ceaseless energy, until many have learned to respect what at first they scorned. We never demanded respect and affection. We always worked to be worthy of it.

This mode of life, at least, brings us self-respect. The greatest harm of hostility is the danger of self-hatred; but those who honestly achieve through their own efforts at least can respect themselves and ultimately win some respect from others. If, then, we children of Israel and descendants of Joseph may presume to advise all the oppressed and the despised of this earth, we would say that more valuable than demanding is achievement. Study, grow, work; above all, do not judge yourself on any day of judgment by other people's hostile opinions; judge yourself by what you have attained. Joseph, the pampered darling, became Joseph the creative worker. So all who achieve can scorn the world's hostility and sometimes even overcome it. The word of the American poet in his psalm of life was really the experience of Joseph

249

and of all his spiritual descendants when faced with the world's hostility, "Learn to labor and to wait."

The Talmudic dictum reads, "The life of the father is repeated in the career of his son." As Jacob, the father, had dreamed, so Joseph had dreamed. As Jacob after his dream left his father's house and went to a strange land, so was Joseph, the son, after his dream taken away to the land of Egypt. But as the two dreams were different, one a dream of anxiety and the other a dream of self-assurance and superiority, so the two types of exile were different. Jacob, at least, went to the land of the Chaldees, to the home of his kinsmen, his cousins, who spoke the same language and had common memories. Joseph was taken down to Egypt to a people of a language strange to him. He came from the serene quietude of the shepherd life to the noisy, teeming cities, the hovels and the granite temples of the most urbanized civilization of ancient times. He came from the pure monotheism of his father's house into the lush and corrupt idolatry of that ancient land of corruption. Everything was strange to him. He was really an exile, absolutely alone.

This utter loneliness is a true symbol of the children of Israel in the long centuries of the past, as real an experience as that of hostility. The gentile prophet Balaam watching from his mountaintop in the hills of Moab, seeing the encampment of Israel around its little tabernacle and surrounded by the vast desert, said of them: "Behold, this is a people that dwelleth alone." This was the great psychological struggle of our people throughout the isolated centuries. They were in the world but apart from it, walled off and lonely, and they struggled against loneliness, for loneliness can be a poison. It can make a people feel exiled, scorned and rejected.

250

The health-weapon which they used was the weapon discovered by their ancestor Joseph. It is fascinating to notice how, when Joseph moved from the at-homeness of his father's encampment to his utter loneliness in Egypt, how his entire vocabulary changed. Never in his conversation to his father and to his brothers does he ever speak of God. God does not even appear in the imagination of his dreams. But now, in Egypt, surrounded by all the corruption of the idolatry of that confused world, God's presence seems to surround him like a halo. Right at the beginning, brought as a slave into Potiphar's house, we are told that "God gave this exile a special grace." When he was brought before Pharaoh, who was adored as a god himself, the son of Osiris and Isis, the name of the Eternal God comes unbidden to Joseph's lips, and he said to the idolatrous Pharaoh, "God will give to Pharaoh the answer of serenity." Joseph discovered in his exile what he took for granted at home, that God is in the world and when God is in the world, Joseph is never alone.

This was the healing faith of our people. The world may have isolated them but God had never rejected them. Wherever they wandered, on every lonely road, in every ghetto village, they were sure that they were not exiled from God's presence, but the whole world is "full of His glory."

The tragedy of people today is the lack of this faith of the Divine Presence. When a home finally breaks up and a man or woman is left alone and must face the bitter isolation of life, what have they today to sustain them? That is why we gather here today, not to argue theology, not to work out the details of philosophy and to prove by logic that God exists in the world, but to read the prayers and think of His Presence, until He Who is always there is rediscovered as near as our hearts and as close as our thoughts. There is no loneliness unless we exile ourselves

251

from the Divine Presence. A great Christian mystic said, "Homeless is the heart until it finds its home in Thee." And King David said it before him to all the lonely of the world: "Lord, Thou art our Dwelling-place in all the generations." To find our Eternal Father in the midst of our modern loneliness, we have gathered here this day.

In Thomas Mann's great trilogy, the first one is entitled **The Young Joseph**, and what we have considered on this New Year is likewise Joseph, the youth. But the meaning of his early life is not merely a message to youth, but to all of us of every stage of life, for in one way we are eternally youthful; not as we like to boast, youthful in our strength and in our love of play. More seriously and more relevant on this New Year, we are eternally youthful in our faults and our weaknesses. If when we outgrow our early years, we would all outgrow our early weaknesses, this would be a blessed life. But all our early weaknesses are only imperfectly overcome and we must continue the struggle for growth all through our life. In the very persistence of our weaknesses, we are chronically youthful.

Yet there is a virtue in it. As long as we believe in the struggle, as long as we have sufficient strength of heart and mind to look into our hearts and to grow stronger and better, in that way, too, we are young, blessedly young. So we are summoned on the New Year as people young enough to want to struggle, as people who have not yet given up the battle with themselves. On this day of self-judgment, Joseph's dynamic life leads us to our tasks. Our self-adoration needs the word of truth spoken in our hearts. The hostility of the world needs the building of the self-respect which only honest achievement can bring. And when the world turns into a lonely place, we must discover once more in God's sanctuary and in the world His Eternal Presence. Truly self-judged, strengthened by usefulness, blessed by God's Radiance, may we enter upon a year of growth, of happiness, and of joy.

Amen.

XXIV

MATURITY THROUGH
RECONCILIATION
Joseph in Egypt

A newborn infant is helpless. It must be carefully shielded and constantly served. Except for the joy of its presence, an infant contributes nothing. It only receives. But within two or three years the growing child must learn to fit into the world. It must be taught certain disciplines, certain self-control, in order to play its part in family life. But it is astonishing how often a child resists the necessary disciplines of the world. The child says, "No," and "I won't," to almost every command. Young parents are often shocked at their child's negativism. Yet it is natural. The child is concerned with itself and so gives an angry negative to the world around it.

Most of us grow away from this infantilism and to some extent become active participants in human society. But there are some grownup people who never have recovered from this childish negativism. They take no part in any social or public activity. They have no concern with the interests and the rights of others. They live defiantly for themselves alone. They still, like three year olds, angrily cry, "No," and "I will not" to the demands of the world. This negativism is passive. Those who are thus childish do nothing about it. They simply do not participate in any social effort. But there come times when

Sermon delivered September 15, 1964

this negativism becomes active and violent. At such times the world is in danger.

It is in such a period of active infantile rejection that we live today. Vast numbers of people, young and old, lazy and energetic, uncultured and cultured, declare that they cannot endure and cannot live in modern society. The very list of those who say "no" to the world has appallingly increased in the present age.

A large number of teen-agers in almost every society are rebels. They are brutally violent. They willfully destroy property. They cannot explain just why this childish violence persists in them but the reason is clear enough. City property, school property, trees planted on the streets by the community belong to the hostile grownup world and they reject it and are at war with it. It is not only in the wild years of youth that this rejection of society is found today. That widespread bohemian movement that we call "the beat" or "the beatnik" is really an infantile rejection of the world. The men wear beards in order to look different from the average man. The women dress in bizarre get-ups. The whole purpose or the whole motive is clearly expressed, for they are quite articulate. They say they reject organized society. In their language, a term of insult is the word "citizen." As for themselves, they say, they reject its manners, they scorn its ideals; in their own words, they are "not with it." This world-rejection has even claimed much profounder persons than these vagabonds. There are philosophers who reject the present world. They belong to the famous philosophic school of existentialists which numbers among its advocates some brilliant minds. The doctrine is that the world's ideals are false, that the world's standards are hypocritical, that the world's doctrines are hollow; all that a man can do is to live out his own existence by its own rules and say "no" to the world.

255

Philosophers, after all, are by temperament isolated, while novelists, on the other hand, must live in the world and reflect it in their books. Yet in the modern novel a new mood has arisen that has never been found in a novel before and that, too, is a mood of world contempt. Once a novel had a hero who indeed fought the world, but eventually came to his terms with it. Now the heroes do not seek to come to terms with the world but stand outside of it and laugh at it. They are not heroes any more; they are anti-heroes who flee the field of combat. The dominant mood in these modern novels of anti-heroes is described by the word "alienation." The people in it are "aliens," strangers to the world around them. So teenagers, beats, existential philosophers, novelists who describe alienated anti-heroes, all express the same attitude of the angry child: "No!" "I won't."

This widespread alienation in so many classes of society certainly indicates that there is something wrong and repulsive about modern life. Nevertheless, the total rebellion is childish. We have no other world but this in which to live. It is true that there are elements in the modern world that we must fight against, but we fight with the hope of success and world-betterment. Then there are elements in this modern world that are noble and beautiful in which we must gladly take part and share. A mark of maturity is to face the world, not with a general negative, but to distinguish that to which we are opposed from that of which we can wholeheartedly approve. The mature person, after his struggles, gives and takes and finally signs a treaty so he can live and work in the world in which he is placed.

In a sense this is a central theme of the Day of Atonement. Our English word "atonement" really means "at-one-ment." It means learning how to face the world, opposing its evils, and accepting its good and being at one with human society. The Biblical symbol of this reconciliation with the world is Joseph. He was catapulted into an alien world through no choice of his own, and his first reaction was the normal, childish "No," but he grew out of that immaturity and step by step learned to find a place in human society. The path to maturity through reconciliation with the world is the meaning of Joseph's development and an essential message of the Day of Atonement.

No student of surgery is required to submit to operations before he is permitted to operate on others. And yet something of this nature is required of those who are trained for psychoanalysis. No man may become an analyst until he himself is first thoroughly analyzed. When he has learned to understand his own subconscious and its complexes, it is only then that he can advance to healing the hurts in the subconsciousness of others. From this point of view, Joseph can be called the first psychoanalyst. He began with his own dreams, as did other Biblical characters before him. But he was the first Biblical personality who moved on from his own dreams to the study and interpretation of the dreams of others. Joseph came to Egypt with his own dreams of personal dominance, but no sooner was he there than he learned to listen and to interpret the dreams of others. Pharaoh's Court baker and Pharaoh's Court butler were in prison at the same time that Joseph was, and he noticed that they were unhappy and he inquired. They told him their dreams and he gave his interpretation of them. Then, growing famous as a man who understood the hearts of others, he was called from prison to Pharaoh's palace, for Pharaoh himself had dreamed a terrifying dream which Joseph interpreted and Pharaoh's heart was at peace.

It is the business of psychoanalysts to concern themselves with the inner life of others, but it is not the business, nor the practice, nor the interest, nor the competence of the average man. The average man is well aware of his own feelings, of his own fears and his own hopes, but that other people have fears and hopes and feelings is hardly a reality to him. In fact, Scripture considers that to understand the inner feelings of others is so difficult that only God Himself can do it. The Prophet Samuel says: "Man judges by the outer sight, but it is God Who reads the heart." We judge others by externals. We hear what people say, but their real motives we do not know. We approve or disapprove of what people do, but just why they do it, we only vaguely guess.

Nevertheless, to try to understand the deeper feelings of other people, difficult as it is, is the chief motive for Biblical ethics. Why is it that Scripture is the first literature in mankind's history to teach that we have an ethical obligation for the welfare of **all** people, alien, strangers, black and white? No one had ever taught such a doctrine before. What is the motive for such a new teaching of universal, moral obligation? Scripture answers the question clearly: "Thou shalt love the stranger, for thou knowest the heart of the stranger." Look into this alien person's heart. Learn to see that he shares your fears and your dreams and your hopes. The nearer you get to his inner thoughts, the more truly is he your fellow-man and the more is your world a united world.

There is no more emotionally self-centered profession than acting, and yet the great David Garrick, on retiring from the stage in the eighteenth century, said, "A fellow-feeling makes one wondrous kind." Now we do not expect to become, in Garrick's words, "wondrous kind," but we reasonably hope to become a little less unkind, a little less self-centered, with a little more awareness that round about us today are friends and neighbors full of worries and fear and uncertainties and hope. To grow away from childish, self-centered negativism there must be an emotional reconciliation, understanding of each other's hearts, shared griefs and joys in every Jewish congregation on the Day of Atonement. When Joseph began to read deeply the hearts of others, he was growing mature and was rejoining the world.

Jacob's family was a shepherd family and the pastoral life involved much work. The sheep had to be led from pasture to pasture and shorn. All this work in Jacob's old age was done by Jacob's sons, by all his sons except Joseph. Joseph was an elegant idler. The most he ever did was to visit his brothers at his father's behest. But in the actual work of the family, he took no part. And as long as he contributed nothing, he remained a child.

But in Egypt, with no brothers to work for him, he was compelled to grow up fast. His life changed drastically and all we read of him there is the work that he did; the household that he managed as steward of the priest Potiphar; even in prison, he took on his shoulder part of the management of the institution. Joseph became a worker and that obviously is one of the evidences of maturity. Men who do not work are never mature. When a man is rich so that he does not need to work, we do not call him a "play man" but a "play boy." Men who work but hate their work and are impatient for their retirement, all that can be said of them is that their hands are adult and their hearts infantile.

Yet Joseph's maturity through work moved on to a higher stage. At first he worked for his employer and therefore for his own benefit. But once he had interpreted Pharaoh's dream, the nature of his work changed. He now worked with hundreds of others through the years of plenty, gathering and storing the grain in preparation for the seven years of famine. He had reached the level of selfless, cooperative work.

To work thus with others ought to be easy, for do not even the bees and the ants work together in a perfectly organized colony? Why, then, should human organizations develop such difficulties as they always do? The answer lies in the fact that we are human. The bees and the ants cooperate by instinct; they cannot do otherwise. If we cooperate, it must be by conscious choice and by active intelligence. Therefore, if we work in some common cause, we must work with fellow humans, and in our common tasks, jealousy meets with jealousy. Energy is disgusted at laziness. Trustworthiness confronts indifference. Every common work must be, as the rabbis said, in the name of God, or we cannot keep it up. The free will social tasks in which we participate are our training in reconciliation, our step towards maturity. No man who works for himself alone, no matter how successful he is, is more than half a man. Only he who, like Joseph, finds some cause and works with his own weakness and strengths and with other people's faults and virtues, only such a person knows what it means to be reconciled to mankind. When Joseph read the hearts of others and worked with others, his maturity became real.

In the Middle Ages, Jewish scholars were forced by princes and kings into formal debates with Christian scholars. This habit of debating between the two religions still continues on an unorganized basis, but it rarely proves anything. We ought to say at the outset that a religion such as Christianity contains some noble truths, and Christians ought to say, without debate, that the daughter religion has inherited much from Judaism, the mother religion.

260

People often quote the great verse in the Gospel from the Lord's Prayer: "Forgive us our sins or our trespasses as we forgive those who trespass against us." It should not be surprising to a Jewish congregation to hear that this noble idea is an ancient, pre-Christian Yom Kippur theme. An ancient rabbi said that we cannot ask God to pardon our sins until our neighbor is willing to pardon the sins we have committed against him. It is classic teaching of the Day of Atonement that we cannot expect God to forgive us until we ask forgiveness and until we give forgiveness to our fellow man. Scripture puts the duty of our forgiveness to our fellow man in a classic sentence: "Thou shalt not hate thy brother in thy heart." He has offended me, he has done evil against me, I have defended myself, but the deed is done, and I must not continue to hate my brother in my heart.

The fact that Scripture uses the language of "man and his brother" raises the possibility that the writer of the Book of Leviticus, in which this statement is contained, thought exactly of some such case in which a brother, by all human standards, was justified in hating and yet, by a miracle of self-purification, refused to hate his brothers in his heart. Who would be more justified in hating his brothers than Joseph? They were about to murder him, and when dissuaded from that fratricide, they sold him as a slave. Now he was viceroy of Egypt and they had come before him begging for bread. What a long awaited opportunity for a real revenge! He would not have been human if such thoughts had not entered his mind. It must have been for such reasons of revenge that he purposely worried them, pretending to believe that they were thieves and spies. But he had actually outgrown all such bitterness. He no longer could hate his brothers in his heart. So he forgave them, was reconciled to them, and gave them a home in Egypt.

261

How real was his forgiveness could be seen after their father Jacob died. Now suddenly their old fears returned. Perhaps Joseph had forgiven them only for their father's sake and now that Jacob was dead, he would put them to death. But he assured them that whatever evil they did him was forgotten and that, in any case, God had turned it into a benefit to save the lives of millions. The fact is that Joseph did not forgive them for his father's sake, nor even for their sake. He forgave them for his **own** sake because he had become too mature to retain the poison of resentment in his heart. Of course he was a great man, a powerful man, and no one could hurt him any more. He could safely afford to be generous, but he also could have exacted an awesome vengeance. He chose and decided to be generous and he completely forgave.

We all come into the Day of Atonement bearing hurts that others have inflicted upon us. Some of them are old wounds. They should not be allowed to fester any longer. Partly for their sakes, more for our own sake that our heart be clean, but chiefly because of God's mandate should we resolve upon some purifying forgiveness and unite our own world with the world of those we have resented. Forgiveness is reconciliation, and reconciliation is maturity. The world is large and full of bitterness, but at least our little corner of it will be less bitter, less harsh, and more brotherly, more at one.

The English poet expressed his own bitter sense of separation from the world around him. He said it in words since then often quoted: "I am a stranger and afraid in a world I never made." We never created this world, nor as individuals are we responsible for its evils. But we are in it and often we feel like strangers, alienated and afraid. But the thought is expressed somewhat more deep-

262

ly in the Psalms, "I am a pilgrim," said King David, "and a stranger, as were my fathers." What the psalmist adds is that the same sense of feeling alone in a hostile world was also felt by earlier generations. In some eras, we are more comfortable and more at home than in others, but to some extent, in every age our childish negativism leads us to enlarge the gulf between us and the world. This day is the day in which we negotiate our bond with the world, decide what we cannot accept and what we can accept. We know the steps towards the unity. We learned them from an ancient Biblical hero, or a Biblical character who eventually became a hero. We know how to become mature. It is by reconciliation, by bridging the gulfs, by learning to read the hearts and appreciating the dreams of others besides ourselves, by finding selfless tasks in which we can work in mutual patience and tolerance side by side, and by cleansing from our hearts ancient hates and encrusted bitterness. We ask God to pardon us on this Day of Atonement as we try to pardon others and to rediscover our fellow man here and everywhere.

Amen.

XXV

MODERN ANXIETIES

Every tourist in Rome, certainly every guided tourist, is taken to see Michelangelo's great statue of Moses. The tourist's first impression is generally one of familiarity; he has seen it before. As a matter of fact, that statue has been reproduced innumerable times, in bronze, in plaster, or on picture postal cards. It is perhaps the best known product of the Italian Renaissance. Nevertheless, in spite of the familiarity which the visitor has as his first impression, there is hardly anyone so stolid that he is not moved by that tremendous image of magestic leadership. It is one of the grand statues of the world.

Naturally, legends and traditions have grown around that statue. One of these legends concerns our theme for this morning. The legend is that this statue has a flaw, a dent in the stone. This dent came, not as the result of careless handling during the centuries, but it came, actually, from the hand of the master artist himself.

According to the legend, when Michelangelo was finished, the statue overwhelmed him, even though he was its creator. It seemed to him to be alive, and he stood

Sermon delivered September 26, 1965

before it waiting for it to show signs of life. Then when the statue remained immobile, Michelangelo with his still remembered hot temper, raised his sculptor's hammer and struck the statue on the knee and cried out: "Speak! Speak!"

Which sensitive modern person, aware of the nagging problems of the present day and all the inner suffering which modern people have to endure, can fail to appreciate the feeling of Michelangelo and does not join in the wish that Moses, somehow, were alive and articulate? We refuse to believe that the great religion which Moses had founded is by now dumb; that it is so old and its writings so worn-out that there is no word left in it for modern perplexity. Because we prefer to believe that spiritual truths are eternal, we, too, echo the words of the sculptor and say to Moses, "Speak, O Prophet, speak!"

The urgency of our demand for Mosaic guidance springs from what is a unique situation in modern life. We moderns feel that we are more insecure than any preceding generation could have been. Everything upon which we relied has suddenly become unreliable. The mighty strength of our nation is threatened all around the world. The unity of our families, for which we have at last so well provided, seems shaky. And even the progress of science, in which past generations had trusted as a certain source of human happiness, has begun at times to bring new terror to us. We no longer can guess what the future will bring. So, especially at the New Year, the uncertainty of our tomorrows shakes the heart. Because it is a world of general insecurity, it has become a world of personal anxiety. If you do not realize that you are anxious, your doctor knows it. It is a time of wide-spread anxiety, and we seek from the best possible sources some sort of reassurance and strength.

265

The causes of general anxiety may change from historic age to historic age, but the emotion, the feeling, the inner disintegration is the same. Moses saw it developing in his people. They were, in a way, in a situation analogous to ours. In our modern life, just at the time of the great technological scientific advances, when we ought to be sure of the human future, we have suddenly become insecure and anxious; and it was the same sort of miserable surprise with the people whom Moses led. After forty years of living through the horrors of the desert, they finally were on the banks of the Jordan in the settled country and were about to enter into the Promised Land. Their sorrows should have been over now. But the scouts came back and said, "In that promised land there are ferocious giants. There are fortified cities. They are bitterly hostile people. Death and terror will await you when you cross the Jordan."

The people's hopes were dashed and they suddenly became insecure and anxious. In order to allay their anxiety, Moses spoke to them. In fact, the whole Book of Deuteronomy, the fifth Book of the Torah, is one long speech which Moses gave at the end of those forty years, at the banks of the Jordan, when the people were about to face the dangers on the other side.

The whole speech climaxes in a section that we, by tradition, read on the High Holy Days. In this sentence, in which Moses summed up what he felt should be the ground for their strength and hope, he said: "Ye are standing this day before the Lord your God, your elders, your young, to enter into a covenant with God."

As they listened, we listen too. On this New Year's Day in one of the most insecure and one of the most anxious periods in our life's experience, we do well to listen and to ponder the words of Moses, and to see what strength there may be in them for us.

266

For the last twenty years or so, writers and speakers have made use of the rather modern word, "togetherness." The word is about worn out now from over-use, but it still has had its meaning. It describes the sense of unity between parents and children playing together and working together. Then the thought extended perhaps to the whole country, to the various divisions, the various separations between races, between religions, between social classes. Perhaps some day these prejudices ought to give way to a feeling of "togetherness." Then the dream took wings and visualized the time when the hostile divisions of this dangerous world may suddenly discover their "togetherness." It is a grand word, really; a pity it has been over-used. Actually, it is the central theme in the statement of Moses. He said, "You are standing together, all of you."

Once a person develops the realization that he is not alone in the world, that he is not one person fighting the entire universe, that there are people by his side or people who will come to his side to help him in need—once a man has a sense of that potential, humane "togetherness," he begins to hope and to rediscover his strength.

In that "togetherness," Moses mentions specifically as the first element, "your elders." When we contemplate the words, "your elders," we realize that we have undergone a radical change in our attitude to older people. In the past, age was always deemed to be the repository of wisdom. The Roman "Senate" is from the word "senex," "the old." The Greek "Gerousia" is from the word meaning "the old," and so, too, the Hebrew "Zekenim." In our own time that universal attitude has changed. The aged are no longer considered a source of potential wisdom. We no longer believe that they have anything valuable to say to us. So we give them Golden Age amusements (which is, of course, good); we want them to be happy, but not to tell us anything.

But Moses wants to say firmly that in the togetherness of life, "your elders" have something precious to contribute. In every society the aged have a message, a unique message. This sentence of Moses which says that is only a summary of something earlier in his speech. He refers to the memories which live in the minds of the elders. In the earlier part of the speech, he reminds them of what happened to them in the desert. That whole lone and stressful experience began with the pursuing Egyptians thirsting for their blood, and then the sudden, raiding, murderous attack of the Amalekites. There was danger after danger. The old people remember it all. Moses says, in effect, "You young people, you think that this danger that you are about to face when you cross the Jordan in the Promised Land is the first such danger we have had to face. Your elders can tell you we have faced many dangers and we outlived those dangers."

The old people represent the memory of miseries overcome, of troubles outlived. That is their precious gift in every generation. And is it not a valuable gift in our personal life? How many times in our lives have we had griefs that we thought we never could endure and we **did** endure them! We had burdens put on our shoulders that we thought would crush us to earth, and we somehow stood up and carried them. The memory of past endurance is the reassurance of future strength, and that is in the memory and is the message of the old.

In our day such memories of strength are still significant. It is true that past generations could know nothing of the horror of the atomic danger; but there is no use talking about that. If, God forbid, that world-explosion comes, then all our problems will be solved in the silence of death. So that immense danger does not really exist as an active source of daily anxiety—it is simply too final. Our anxieties spring from other and more chronic sources, yet are related to that danger. We are anxious because we are subject to a constant bombardment of hatred all over the world. All the self-sacrifice of the American people, all the generosity, all the millions of tons of grain that have kept millions from starving day after day in Asia, are met with riots at the first opportunity. We are subject to an unremitting attack of bitterness, and it is hard to get used to it. That is one of the sources, perhaps the basic source of our anxiety.

Let us remember the past: As far as those hatreds are concerned, there have been many in the past and the world has lived through them, and we will live through them. We can only believe that we can conquer that anxiety if we remember what we have conquered in days gone by. So the message of the elders is that the memory of past victories is the resassurance of future strength. What old people tell us, what Moses meant for the old to say, is what Tennyson put in the mouth of the aged Ulysses: "We are not now," said the old warrior, "the strength that once we were. But what we are, we are: Strong in will, to seek, to find, and not to yield."

That is the contribution of the aged to the healing of modern anxieties.

We could more easily endure the unremitting dislike directed against our country if only we were united at home. Since we are a land that is comparatively new, built up of various elements, and in which many different traditions hostile to each other in the old world came together in the new, we always have been to some extent a divided country: the bitterness between Catholic and Protestant that sometimes came to bloodshed, the bitterness between the farm and the growing cities, between Labor and Capital. Fortunately, many of those divisions have been mitigated in our country.

But a new one of which our ancestors did not know has arisen and grown, and is the source of deep anxiety, namely, the division between two generations in the human family. Never was youth so separate from the adult working generation. For about thirty, forty years, we have been accustomed to speaking about the revolt of youth, that youth no longer listens to its elders. We grew accustomed to reading of youthful slum gangs, but we believed they could be cured by a little sociology and some clever psychology. But who could have dreamed that young people from good homes, well-nurtured, would every holiday descend like a plague of locusts on some vacation resort and leave nothing but destruction and filth after them! Who could have predicted that in a great university there would be a whole year of constant war against the university authorities! To keep up a whole year of rebellion, violent rebellion, bespeaks a degree of bitterness between student and teacher which would be unbelievable in the past. It seems that the young generation has broken away from us. It does not believe in our old standards. How much moral looseness there actually is, who can tell! The statistics of illegitimacy, of loathsome disease, are appalling. There is a wide gulf now—two worlds, mutually hostile and irreconcilable. That is a source of deep anxiety in the modern heart.

Yet as we speak of it, we know that there is an exaggeration involved here. We are unable to say just why. It is not that all these facts are not true. But we get them from the public prints and from other news media, and it is the purpose and the duty of news media to print what is new, not what is well known. Therefore what appears in the newspaper is the startling, the exceptional. We know that these horrors are facts, but they are not necessarily typical facts; that just as there is wild youth, so there is disciplined youth, and just as there is rebellious youth, so there is youth united in heart and in love with

270

their parents. The error seems to be one of proportion. It is the wildness which is always put before our eyes and not the self-discipline and the decency. We know that.

And Moses knew it well. He must have had wild youth in that vast mass. What about the boys who grew up in the slums and in the slave barracks of Egypt? There were plenty of them. But Moses implies more than that we must keep a sense of proportion; he says something much more positive. In the sentence, when he speaks of those who unite in covenant, he refers not only to the aged who have memory of troubles overcome in the past, but also he says, "The young are present." There are youth present to take part in a great covenant. That is something positive which becomes understandable in the light of what occurred, again earlier in his address. Earlier in his great oration, he tells how he pleaded with God. This is one of the most pathetic passages in Scripture. The old man says, speaking to his people, "I pleaded with God and I said, 'O God, let me cross the Jordan. Let me just look at the Promised Land.'"

Which old person does not wish in his heart that he would be privileged to "cross the Jordan" of the coming years and see a blessed, promised future? But God said to Moses, "Stop; not another word. Do not speak of this again. Be consoled, Joshua your disciple will lead the people across the Jordan and will give them their inheritance."

This is what Moses means when he says that youth is standing in the covenant group. Joshua is the symbol of youth, the youth of high standards, the youth of leadership. When we think of the young people of our time, let us think of the Joshuas among them, the many young men and women toiling in the fetid jungles of Africa and Asia to alleviate the lot of strangers. Thousands of young

271

people have been volunteering for the Peace Corps! And what of the thousands of young boys and girls who have risked safety and gone South to take part in marches and in protests and in sit-ins? It is immaterial whether any particular sit-in was valuable or not. It was an outpouring of idealism, of self-sacrifiing idealism. We have learned to our joy that there is a glorious Joshua-spirit, a spirit of selfless leadership awakened in the youth of our time. So we can endure the anxiety of the mad youth and be proud of the self-sacrificing youth of this generation. They are the ones who will "lead the people across the Jordan" to its rightful inheritance.

Sociology is a social study, dealing with human beings, and human beings are hard to classify. Nevertheless the sociologists like to believe that their study is also an exact science. That is why they like to be mathematical. They love to move away from the individual human being who is complex and deal with figures which can be manipulated. So sociologists love to send out questionnaires. Those questionnaires are their last direct contact with living people, because when the questionnaires come into their hands, it is the figures which are recorded. The figures are then put on a chart or they are fed into an IBM machine, and the sociologist comes up with conclusions which are then taken to mean a description of the realities of human life.

A group of sociologists made such a study of young Jewish men and women in the city of Washington, young people working for the government. These are young people not living at home, out of contact with their traditions and their people. The sociologists discovered the percentage of intermarriage and neglect of any contact with Judaism among this group. Then they added to those statistics the statistics taken in a small town in Iowa and

272

put the two facts together and came up with the conclusion that Judaism is fading away in the United States. Then some national pictorial magazine excited the country with the title: "The Vanishing American Jew."

Whether or not these statistical conclusions are to be taken at their face value, the fact remains that added to our anxieties is this one also. Besides our fear of the world's hatred, besides our worry about youth, there has grown up an anxiety that our ancient faith, after swimming through so many tempestuous seas and arriving at last at this blessed land, is here beginning to fade away and will not long endure.

Moses said in his grand sentence, "You are standing together, your elders, your youth, and you are making a covenant and taking an oath to the Lord your God." That closing part of the statement is again a shorthand reference to something that he said previously. Earlier he said, "Ye who are loyal to God are the ones who are alive today." He meant that not all of those who came out of Egypt or even their descendants have reached the banks of the Jordan to cross over into the Promised Land. Six hundred thousand men of fighting age had come out of Egypt. There were therefore millions of Israelites and "a mixed multitude" also among them. What became of them all? Some died in the desert, some fled away at the time of the raids and the dangers. They dropped away. They disappeared. Only those who remained loyal to God, he said, are the ones who have lived and are now at the banks of the Jordan.

In that Moses gave a prophetic view of what happened to us in our history. In all our long march through the "desert" of the centuries, we have always lost the laggards. Groups always broke away from the marching column and disappeared in the desert of oblivion. When

273

we speak of the survival of our people, we might recall what we have lost. How many Jews disappeared in the Babylonian captivity? Of the twelve, ten whole tribes! In the Roman Diaspora, how many Jews were lost in the general population? In the bitter Middle Ages, how many were lost? We have always lost, but we have always remained. Those who went were gone and forgotten. Those who were loyal to their faith were the ones who remained and maintained.

The trouble with those statistics is that though they are correct enough, they describe only the crumbling periphery, not the solid heart which nothing in history has yet shaken, nor will the future shake. We must know beforehand and without needing statistics that we will lose many, but we have always lost many. As for those who leave us, let them go! They do not count. It is we who come and stand firm who enter into the covenant and maintain the future.

Of course we have problems these modern days. It is natural to have problems. To live means to have problems. Without problems we would not exercise our minds and without them we would not mobilize our will. We should be grateful for the problems of life which make us strong.

But there are certain problems that make us weak. Those problems which break down the strength of the personality are those which seem to us to be insoluble, those perplexities before which we feel helpless. They are the ones that create our inner anxieties.

Fortunately for us, it is not a marble statue but a living prophet who speaks out of the past. Is our anxiety due to the hostilities of the world? The elders remember

274

for us what we have lived through without being crushed. Is it the division between the generations that causes anxiety? Think of the Joshuas, the devoted ones, who bless and who ennoble all of modern youth. Is it that we fear that laggards, stragglers, break away from the march? They go — let them go. We continue onward. We are stronger than we think.

So let us take a step towards the conquest of anxieties, then a second step towards increasing strength, and voice a prayer that we may continue to walk into a series of New Years of greater happiness.

Amen.

XXVI

MODERN

FRUSTRATIONS

There is a strange legend in Jewish lore about the creation of the world. The legend tells that this world is not the first one which ever existed. There were others before it. What the Midrash actually says is that before God created this present world, He had created others and was discontented with them and so destroyed them. In other words, God the great Creator was also God the great Experimenter. He destroyed His first experiments until He finally made a world of which He could say, "Behold, it is good."

This old Jewish idea of breaking down the universe and remaking it somehow found its way into Persian folklore and came to expression in the **Rubaiyat of Omar Khayyam.** There the brilliant and pessimistic Persian poet said:

> "Ah, love, could you and I with Him conspire
> To grasp this sorry scheme of things entire,
> Would we not shatter it to bits—and then
> Remold it nearer to the heart's desire."

Sermon delivered October 5, 1965

What the Persian adds to the ancient Jewish folklorist is a wish that we were able to do what God, according to the legend, did do: Being dissatisfied with the world, take it apart, and then remold it nearer to our heart's desire. Surely such a dream wish lurks in the heart of many a thinking person these days. There is so much that has gone wrong in God's world and in ours. There is so much bitterness, so much destructiveness, so much corruption and, oh, so much unnecessary pain and suffering. We sometimes wish that we could imitate the Creator and take this world apart and substitute a better one for it. But, of course, that is only a day-dream. This old world is hard to change. For example, the disarmament conference has been meeting in Geneva for over three years. Yet in spite of real atomic danger, nothing at all has been accomplished. The United Nations is more necessary than ever before; yet it seems to be getting more confused and futile, year by year. Yes, this wicked old world seems to resist all improvement, and just now its evil seems to have flared up and all its follies and its clumsiness and its violence are rampant. Not even the greatest statesmen are able to cope with it, nor the most powerful nations do more than just endure it.

This sense of hopelessness spreads through the entire world. It is really a wonder that being helpless as we are in a violent age, we have not all become pessimists and cynics. In fact, modern character is breaking down under world pressure. The general situation is affecting us all. Things seem hopeless and we know we are helpless. When we count up the inner stresses of our life today, add to the modern anxieties of which we spoke on the New Year, the modern frustration, the pathetic sense of futility.

This is an unendurable mood and we must find a way of emerging from it. From long ago, from the first of the prophets, from Moses our teacher, comes a suggestion as to how to face an evil world, to keep from inner surrender, to overcome the sense of frustration, to achieve a faith in our own usefulness, and thus a degree of personal dignity. He spoke to his people just when they were facing the seemingly insurmountable dangers of the hostile land of Canaan which they were about to enter. And he gave them this advice: "What I command you this day is not too difficult for you. It is not beyond your reach. It is not up in heaven and not overseas. Your duty is in your heart and on your lips that you may achieve it."

We notice at once that his words indicate a shift of attention from the universe to the human spirit, from the international world to the island within, from politics to psychology. He seems to say that the world can yet be improved and its evil overcome, but you must know where to begin. Study first what the world is doing to you as a person. Cope with the mood of frustration. And to us it means that our immediate problem is not in Geneva, not in the United Nations, but in our own hearts.

It is as if he warns us that there are certain great ideals by which we have hitherto lived and which now have been weakened. Certain nobilities have now been besmirched. So we must understand frankly what is happening to us. Then, facing the new changes within us, we can strengthen ourselves and perhaps make a real beginning towards rebuilding the world from within. This is what confession and repentance should mean in the bewildering moods of a modern Day of Atonement.

The great German economist of the last generation, Max Weber, was also a philosopher. He was concerned with the relationship of the spiritual life and its subtleties in connection with the material life and its realities. In a

278

merger of his religious interests and his economic specialty, he created a new idea in modern economic thought. He coined the phrase, "The Protestant Ethic." What he meant was that the historical progress out of medieval economy into modern industrial society developed first in the Protestant lands; that, for example, the teachings of Benjamin Franklin, advocating careful thrift and hard, devoted labor, somehow was connected with a Protestant idea that the acquisition of wealth was almost a religious duty, certainly a stewardship and an opportunity for service. To waste money, to waste time was actually a sin. That is why it was this branch of Christianity which urged people to work hard, to save their money, to accumulate capital, and thus to build the modern, industrial society. This is what he meant by "The Protestant Ethic."

Like all creative ideas, this one is open to objection, but there is a great deal of truth in it. What might be added perhaps is an explanation as to why this gospel of hard work and of thrift should have come from the Protestant branch of Christendom rather than from the Catholic. One difference between the Protestant and the Catholic was the devoted reading of the Bible. The Puritan branches of Protestantism were virtually "Old Testament people," and the spirit of the Old Testament is dynamic and activist. It is a Jewish Biblical idea that work is a commandment. God Himself is described as working and we are described as His fellow-workers. God is the great Employer and we, conscientious or indolent, work in His enterprises. This concept of the duty of work might be considered as the great mental hygiene of the people of Israel throughout their history. They needed no Rudyard Kipling to tell them that when their world was broken, they should stoop and gather the pieces and build it up again. The opportunity to work, the pleasure, also, of mental work, the joy of growth in skill of hand and mind, began with the Bible and has kept us alive and sane all through the ages.

From this viewpoint, we can see what has gone wrong spiritually in our world. This Biblical ideal, spread by a branch of Christianity into the wider world, this gospel and glory of work for its own sake, has faded from the modern world. People no longer love work for its own sake. Even the revolutionary regimes in Russia and in China who mobilize their people like soldiers, even they have to cope with indolence, indifference and negligence. And in our free world it is no better. Workmen and industrialists, people in every walk of life do less than they should, hope to do less still, look forward to idleness earlier than they should. Who ever heard before our day of children, in spite of the urgings of their parents, regularly dropping out of school, unwilling to face the duties of school work? It is not the fault of these drop-outs, nor of their parents, nor of the slums in which they live. It is the fault of a new mood of the world. Since the world is at a standstill, since progress seems stalled, it is natural that personal work should seem futile. So people no longer believe in the nobility of toil. They believe in the excitements of pleasure. They believe in buying for their whims, whether they can afford it or not, whether they have worked for it or not. No one speaks of **earning** the right to pleasure and enjoyment. They believe, and they are told, that they are **entitled** to it. The fading of the old faith in the nobility of work is to be counted as one of the great inner changes of the modern world.

To rebuild our world, we must rebuild ourselves. There is no self-respect unless a man knows that he is doing something useful. It makes no difference how productive the machine is. A man **needs** work for his spiritual health. That is what Moses means. God's commandment is in your hands, that you should do it. Idleness should never be elevated to an ideal. It is a futility, a frustration of our nature. It is a rusting away of the character. If we would repent on this Day of Atonement, we should regret the lazy hours frittered away in indolence. We should realize that every useless day weakens the inner world, and we should hope that the coming year will give opportunity for achievement, physical and mental, for a chance to be what Judaism always wants a man to be, a fellow-worker with God the Creator.

Early in this twentieth century a remarkable Polish Jew died and for a while it seemed that he had earned a lasting place in history. Now, unfortunately, that is doubtful. The man's name was Ivan Bloch. He was an engineer, a great railway builder for the Russian empire, and a writer on economics. Among his considerable writings was a five-volume work proving that modern economy has so greatly developed over the world that modern wars would be more destructive than any in the past and even victory would be an economic defeat. Therefore world peace is logical and therefore world peace is inevitable. His idea that in the modern industrial era world peace is inescapable, influenced Czar Nicholas II to call the first attempt at international cooperation for peace and summon the Hague Disarmament Convention in 1899.

Now, of course, it is doubtful whether Ivan Bloch's name will ever find a permanent place in the history of human idealism. Lucky is the man whose name is connected with an idea that lives. Unfortunate is he whose name is associated with an idea that has faded. It is a regrettable fact that the general belief in world peace is one of the faded ideas of our modern spiritual life. There was a time when the world could accept this engineer's dream as practical and even as inevitable. But since his time, World War I came, and hardly had the wounds healed from that world destruction, when World War II came, to say nothing of the many smaller wars that our great peace organizations do not find the power to extinguish. The fact

281

is that this whole faith has gone largely from the hearts of men, and if we, as we should, struggle to maintain and strengthen the United Nations and such organizations, it is because it is better if they exist than if they would vanish. But no one can say that the hearts of most of the people of the world have any strong confidence in this ideal. Once people believed that peace is on the way, that all nations desire it. Now they are no longer sure of that. They do not quite know what hinders it, what spoils every disarmament conference. They only know, as did Jeremiah, that we cry "peace, peace," and there is no peace.

This constant failure is one of the frustrations of the modern age. It is a world situation which has a psychological effect in every life. Therefore the words of Moses take on an unexpected meaning. He says the duty is not overseas, but in your heart. His words lead us to think of the problem from the inner point of view; not the struggles and the maneuverings of diplomats, important as they may be, but the effect in the hearts of men of the vanishing of the faith in world peace. You cannot lose a great ideal without the heart growing empty through its absence. The effect of its fading can be traced. It is certainly not merely the battles between hitherto peaceable nations, or the use of force and the threat of force in every continent, but count it as a contributing element in the increase of violence within a country and within a city and between types of people. For when peace fades as a world ideal, it weakens as a personal ideal. So there is greater violence in our own land than ever before, an increase in crime, a spread of rioting, of civil disobedience. Violence everywhere is a new and growing danger of our age, for people no longer believe in being peaceable. The frustration with world peace has led to a contempt for law and order and a scorn for peaceable living. Thus the words of Moses have a meaning and mandate on this day. When he says that the problem is not overseas, but in your hearts, he is translating it from the international to the spiritual. What of the violence in your own heart? You cannot change the world of international struggle; but you can change your own relation with the people around you. This is a classic message on the Day of Atonement. Build peace. Cease quarreling. Abandon gruges. Forget resentments. Ask forgiveness for whatever you have done to increase the bitterness and the words of hate between you and your dear ones and your friends and whomever you meet and know. The problem of world peace may, please God, some day be solved in the world, but we must never allow the eclipse of the idea to turn our own life into a battlefield. Let our prayer be on this Day of Atonement that God Who createth peace in the universe, build serenity into our hearts, that we may live in brotherliness as He has intended.

There are certain new phrases which cultured people pick up from each other and use as an evidence that they are in touch with modern thought. One of these new culture-phrases that we read and hear frequently nowadays is the term: "the theatre of the absurd." Obviously the phrase is descriptive of a certain new mood in the American theatre, a new type of play which emphasizes the miserable, the futile, the defeated and the mutually hateful. Such scenes of misery have been depicted on the stage in past generations, but for an entirely different purpose than today. When the great Henrik Ibsen depicted social evil, it was in order to arouse us to social reform. This is not the motive of the new "theatre of the absurd." These miseries are now depicted as an evidence that all of life is always miserable and all of life is meaningless. So the plays begin nowhere and end nowhere. They merely describe life as mean and miserable and without sense. The theatre claims to hold a mirror up to nature and therefore the theatre of the absurd means that the world is absurd. There is no sense and no logic in world affairs, in family life, or in personal destiny. This theatre of the absurd, the picture of a world of absurdity, is the dramatic child of the post-war philosophy of existentialism or, at least, of its negative foundations. This gloomy doctrine stated in philosophic terms what the theatre now states in dramatic terms, that there is no logic to life, no doctrines to follow, no philosophy to trust. Life is essentially meaningless.

Of couse it is clear on the face of it that this is an anti-religious philosophy. The Talmud describes the Godless man as one who declares that there is no law in the universe and there is no Law-giver. In other words, the Godless man believes that the world is not a government, it is an anarchy. It has no rules, no law, no logic—it is meaningless and absurd. One cannot say that avowed atheists have increased in number—who could prove that one way or the other? What seems to have happened is that the intensity of religious faith in the average life has somehow been weakened. One may count, therefore, among the frustrations of modern times, not only that work seems pointless, that peace is an unreality, but that life itself is absurd and there is no ruler who governs it. There has subsided in the human heart a strong sense of trust in God Almighty. People are not atheists. They are not even agnostics. It is simply that their religion half-faded away.

How is it to be restored? Here there is evident a divergence of method between Judaism and Christianity. The need of intensifying faith in God is approached by each of these in a different way and it is pointless to say that one is right and one is wrong. There are two different psychologies involved. Christianity would have its people become religious again by conversion, by a grand acceptance, by a dramatic decision. This is not the Jewish way: No drama, no grand assertions. God returns to our hearts in a way that Moses indicated. He said, "It is not in heaven as it is not overseas, but in thy mouth and in thy heart." To us religion returns, when it does return, in a simple, undramatic way. We simply try to keep God in our thoughts and in our speech. We attend worship, read prayers, address Him in our devotions, and thus keep Him near to us. In this regard there is a telling phrase in Scripture and it is repeated often of certain deeply devout men. It is used of Noah, it is used of Abraham, it is used of the good King Hezekiah. Of all of them it is said in simple human terms, "He walked with God." Think of the word "walk," step by step in the company of the Divine. That is why Scripture says, "These words shall be on thy heart when thou walkest by the way." It is not the spirit of Judaism to be dramatic about God's Presence, but to be natural every day. "In all thy paths, know Him." One may well repent on the Day of Atonement for the hours and the days and the weeks and the months that we have allowed to slip away without one thought of God and without one awareness of His Presence. So simply by walking, simply by thinking of God, simply by coming into His house, without avowals, without declarations, faith returns and God is real again, and one of the great modern frustrations is gradually overcome.

Legend does not speculate as to how many worlds the great Experimenter destroyed before He decided that this was the one that would endure. But sometimes in gloomy moments we believe that this world, too, should have gone into the oblivion of chaos and the Creator put a better one in its place. But God was satisfied with it, and at every day of this world's creation He said, "It is good." But what is there good about this world? To him apparently this was a good world because He created in it the seed of its own betterment, He put man in it to be a perpetual creator and recreator. That is why it is a good world; not because of what it is, but because of what we are privileged to make it be. We know that our world today is more a chaos than a noble creation. We know that the world's chaos reflects itself in one's heart in a feeling of futility and frustration. To face this is our process of confession.

So on the Day of Atonement we see now that the ideal of work has faded; the blessing of work must be rediscovered. The faith in peace has vanished; but peaceful brotherliness can be the seed of its reconstruction. The faith in God has faded; in our simple thought of Him day by day, He may return. The Lord is near unto all who call upon Him in truth. We cannot begin by changing the world. We must begin by keeping the world from corroding us. The way we rebuild the world is to rebuild ourselves. We will live by the words of Moses: Not in heaven, not overseas, but in our hearts, and on our lips, shall live and grow the creative word of the Living God.

XXVII

THE EARTH
IS THE LORD'S

Not every great man is a famous man. There is many a genius who is hardly well known. In English literature, everyone knows the name Shakespeare or Milton, but not enough people know the name and the career of the English artist and poet, William Blake. William Blake was born in London in 1757 and died there seventy years later. To most people the name is unknown, but every now and then students of art and literature return in admiration to his career. They do well to admire him. He was a many-sided genius. Born in humble circumstances, he became an engraver, then an etcher, then a poet, and we may truthfully add, finally a prophet. What stirred him to prophetic social idealism was the evil state of English life in the eighteenth century. It was the early days of the industrial revolution. The beautiful English landscape was already scarred with sterile, smoking slag heaps, its blue skies blackened with belching factory smoke; and in the factories, children of eight, nine and ten lost the springtime of their lives in the cruel child labor of those days. No wonder he spoke of "the dark, satanic mills." He turned from the existing horrors to dream of a nobler, happier England, and he declared his devotion to that distant vision and said:

> "I will not cease from mental fight,
> Nor shall my sword sleep in my hand
> Till we have built Jerusalem
> In England's green and pleasant land."

Sermon delivered September 14, 1966

287

In this powerful stanza William Blake speaks like a true Biblical prophet. His vision of the future which he calls "Jerusalem" can only come after what he calls a "mental fight." In other words, the ideal is indeed attainable, but only through inner personal struggle. No schemes, no doctrines, no blueprints will in themselves create the future unless the heart and the mind of man prepare themselves to work for it.

These two moods, personal and social, are basic in Judaism, namely, that the individual must be purified in thought and heart before society can be cleansed of violence and evil. This dual emphasis, the social and the personal, may be considered to be also the essence of the message of the New Year. The lesson of Rosh Hashonah begins as personal. We are called upon to judge ourselves in the light of God's standards and to purify our hearts. But the message is also social: The prayers speak of the birthday of the world, therefore the rebirth of a better world; and we are described as partners with God, co-workers in the building of a better society.

So on this day, each person must judge himself in a special way. He must earnestly ask himself, not merely, "How righteous am I," but, "How useful am I? Of what value am I as a person in human society? Am I just self-centered in my corner of life? Or am I, in some degree at least, useful, trustworthy and creative in the sector in which I have been placed?"

Such a private yet public concern can be found by clear implication in the Psalm which we have chosen to be our guide in this year's High Holy Day season. It may well be that it was this very Psalm which stirred the mind of William Blake to write his poem, for it concerns Jerusalem, the old Jerusalem, the Palestinian Jerusalem, that pagan city which became the Holy City and the radiant, golden symbol for the ideal society on earth. Psalm Twenty-four was written by King David when he conquered this city from the pagan Jebusites and decided to bring into it the Ark of God, so that by that symbolic presence the city might become forever the Holy City. Hence the words with which the Psalm comes to a triumphant close:

"Lift up your heads, O ye gates. . .
That the King of glory may come in."

This grand processional Psalm begins with majestic words which will be our specific text on this New Year's Day. It opens as follows:

"The earth is the Lord's, and the fullness thereof;
The world, and they that dwell therein.
For He hath founded it upon the seas,
And established it upon the floods."

As we go into the thought behind those words and read the minstrel king's philosophy in them, we will see what Blake means by "the mental fight" which all of us must wage within ourselves before the ideal future can be dreamed of and each successive year becomes a better New Year.

There were two genius nations in ancient times, the Greeks and the Israelites. Both created treasures of the mind which still enrich us. One gave us Sophocles, Socrates and Plato, the other, Moses, David and Isaiah. Though both were original and creative, it is remarkable how they differed from each other. The Greeks were a sunlit, happy people. The Israelites were serious and concerned. Yet the happy, life-loving Greeks were basically pessimistic about the future of mankind. They believed that history was a continuing degeneration and that the story cf man would end in darkness. But the Hebrews were the first to have an optimistic view of the human future. Their Prophets originated the vision of a warless and a brotherly world. The Greeks were playful about the present and gloomy about the future. The Jews were worried about the present but confident about the future. Both moods about the future were deep-felt and creative. Greek pessimism produced the greatest of stage tragedies ever written. Jewish optimism produced the vision of Isaiah and the other prophets.

There is no need to explain the Greek pessimism because that was virtually identical with the pessimism of most of the peoples of the ancient world. But the Biblical optimism was a radiant exception, a lightning flash of light in the darkness, and it needs to be explained. Really it is no mystery: The Jewish optimism sprang from their special idea of God. The Psalmist said, "The earth is the Lord's and He has established it." Therefore it would bo unbelievable to them that God created the world out of chaos only to let it run down into chaos again. So the Prophet Isaiah states it clearly (45:18): "Thus sayeth the Lord, the Creator of the earth, 'I did not create it to become a wilderness, but to be a habitation for the children of men.'" So it was a natural conclusion for them to come to that earthly evils will some day be overcome, that swords will be beaten into plowshares, and that in some future generation a brotherly world will finally be established.

This optimistic view of the human future remained hidden in the Bible and did not influence the world for many centuries because Christianity, which spread the bible through the world, was not interested in this earthly life at all, but only in the life hereafter. Therefore the gloomy view of the ancient Greeks darkened the thoughts cf men for endless centuries. Then as the dominance of the Church began to fade in modern times and men's minds were inspired by the progress of science, the old Biblical optimism, by what physicians call a "delayed reaction," struck the hearts of men like a new revelation, and a century ago the shofar-call of optimism was heard from European poets, novelists and speakers. Typical of them was Victor Hugo. He was optimistic enough to see the glorious future almost right at hand and said, "In the twentieth century crime will be dead, prisons will be dead, the scaffold will be dead, wars will be dead, and man will begin to live."

Alas, poor Victor Hugo! Alas, all the hopeful Victorian poets and orators! Alas, for human optimism! What has died in our twentieth century are not the old evils, but the new hope. We have reverted to Dark Ages of despair. The reasons for our modern-day hopelessness are known to all, but the effects of that hopelessness have not yet been assessed. Because people no longer believe in the future, they do not prepare for the future. Therefore thrift and prudence have faded out. Because people do not believe in the future, they do not believe in controlling present pleasure for the sake of future happiness, and so morality is sick and dying; and as nations cease to believe in the possibility of a cooperative world, they may turn to those desperate measures and to those reckless attitudes which may bring us all to destruction.

It is clear that the modern despair is sterile. It has achieved nothing. Hopelessness is spiritual suicide. Only hope, even if it is merely a dream hope, can inspire man to planning and action. We had better begin without delay our battle against despair. It must be fought, not only in the chancellories and in the parliaments of the world, but in the hearts of average men and women. It must be what William Blake called "a mental fight" that shall never cease. With us at the New Year, confidence in the future

291

is more than practical wisdom. It is a religious duty. We Children of Israel who have seen so much and have outlived so much have always resisted the poison of bitterness and hopelessness. Whatever good it may do or not do, we join all who trust in the future, for we are standing in the presence of Him Who created the world. We proclaim our stubborn faith that there will be a New Year and another New Year and many, many others.

Notre Dame University, which has a large Law School, has been conducting a number of annual institutes on what the Catholic Church calls "Natural Law." The first two annual institutes were conducted by Catholic law professors and judges. The later "Natural Law" institutes were led by non-Catholics in order to demonstrate the idea that all great spiritual traditions share the belief in "Natural Law."

What Notre Dame University and the Catholic Church mean by "Natural Law" is that the laws which govern society are based not only upon social custom and conscious legislation, but go beyond that. The idea of law is inherent in the very nature of man and in the universe itself. This concept that law and order are inherent in the very universe itself is a Biblical idea and is the strong implication of the Psalm which we are now considering. The Psalm, when it says, "The earth is the Lord's, He created it," means that the entire universe, being the creation of the Eternal Mind, is governed by His thoughts and by His intention. The universe follows the laws inherent in it from the beginning. This means two things, the laws of nature which is science and the laws of society which is morality and law. That is why Judaism became uniquely a religion of law. Almost every step of daily life was in accordance with what came to be considered as God's Law. It is true, as always happens, that certain specific laws become "dead letters," and Jews may therefore dis-agree today whether this item or that item is truly God's Law, but the principle is common to all Children of Israel that worship of God means obedience to His Law. This is the basic mood of our faith.

To be religious means to be law-abiding. Every-body accepts that, or at least **did** accept that a generation ago. But, alas, how the world has changed in one gener-ation! We are living today in one of the most disorderly, riotous, violent eras of many centuries. Our age may be described as an age of anti-law, a time of willful anarchy.

There are many causes for present-day scorn for law, some of them of outright evil and some of mistaken idealism. One cause is certainly the world Communist movement, which seeks everywhere to overthrow non-Communist societies, using subversion, rioting and teach-ing the arts of violence as the road to revolution. Perhaps present disorder is also due to the breakup of the great empires. This struggle for independence taught millions of people of various races that the way to liberty is through rebellion, fire and murder. This mood of illegal violence, whatever be its source, affects all of our so-ciety, and even our noblest causes are now besmirched by them. The struggle of our Negro fellow citizens for liberty and justice began as it should have begun with non-violence and with the reliance upon the passage of new laws; but even that noble movement has degenerated at times into riots, arson, looting. As always happens with violence, it begets counter-violence. So now we are seeing in many of our cities the dread specter of group fighting against group with missiles, with shooting and civic anarchy. In good causes and in bad causes, in every country in the world and, alas, in ours too, the respect for law and order has dropped alarmingly.

This modern scorn for law is not only a contempt for man-made law, but a defiance of the mandate of the Divine Law-giver. Children of Israel, molded by the longest legal tradition in the world, must have a clear attitude in these riotous days. We will support no cause, no matter how noble its ultimate aim may be declared to be, if it advocates civil violence. Certainly we ourselves will not participate in any tearing apart of the fabric of the law. More than that, we must help to rebuild the respect for law, not only through enforcement of it, but through a restored orderliness in the hearts of men. Men must be convinced again that there is no social progress if faith in law is destroyed and anarchic violence takes its place. The New Year is a good time to resolve to obey all laws, to be doubly scrupulous in conforming to them. For us to be law abiding is part of our religion. Isaiah put it for us: "The Lord is our Judge, the Lord is our Lawgiver, He will deliver us."

The Hebrew Union College Library publishes a quarterly magazine entitled "Studies in Bibliography." As its name indicates, the journal is devoted to the study of Jewish books, book collections and libraries. I have been planning an article for "Studies in Bibliography" to be entitled "The Pilgrimage of a Book." The article would be based merely on the title page and the fly leaf of a Hebrew law book in my library which was published in Venice in the sixteenth century. On the fly leaf there is the faded name of an owner who lived in Padua, Italy. Then in somewhat blacker ink, the next owner who lived in Amsterdam. Then in the city of Cracow it was given as a gift to a young learned bridegroom and that is recorded. Then it wandered West again and bore the stamp of the library of an endowed study circle in Mannheim. Over this was the cancelling stamp of the Nazi government which confiscated the book and stored it in a warehouse in Offenbach outside of Frankfurt. Then General Patton's army captured Offenbach and the book found its way to the United States and into my library. So this book wandered from Italy over the Alps, north to Holland, east again to Poland, west again to the Rhineland, over the ocean to Pittsburgh. Where, then, does the book belong? Who, then, is its owner? The fact is no one owns it. A succession of scholars have had a lease on it for a few years, have studied from it for a few years, and then it passes on to other scholars, perhaps in other lands.

This pilgrimage of a book is symbolic of the pilgrimage of all human possessions. There was an article in a recent copy of the "National Geographic" on Gold. It spoke of gold as an indestructible metal which is melted and remelted and put into different shapes, and a woman today may own a ring which contains the actual gold that was in an ornament owned by Helen of Troy. This concept that we are only temporary owners of books, of ornaments, of houses, of securities, which have passed to us from other hands and after us pass on to still others, is a basic concept in the Jewish religion and springs from the doctrine clearly implied in this Psalm. The words, "The earth is the Lord's," mean that only He is its permanent owner, and we are in temporary possession, being transient inhabitants of God's earth. That is what the Psalmist meant (Psalm 39:13): "I am a pilgrim and a stranger with Thee, O God, as were my fathers before me."

From this realization that we have only a brief tenure of our possessions, two opposite conclusions may be drawn, the one described in Scripture as wicked and the other as worthy. The wicked is in the words spoken by the evil ones in Isaiah, "Let us carouse and drink, for tomorrow we die." This very conclusion is drawn by many in this world of ours in which, because of the threatening dangers, everything seems impermanent. And so there is an increase of wildness, slovenliness, carelessness, since nothing is going to last anyhow. But there is an opposite conclusion possible, and the one that Scripture considers to be the duty of man: Precisely because it is not our world but belongs to God, we have no right to despoil it, to waste its resources, to befoul its rivers, to erode its soil, to turn God's Garden of Eden into a sterile desert. More positively, our duties on earth become urgent precisely because we will possess that Book of Life only a short time. We must use it well and try to understand its meaning, and perhaps if we are lucky, add a commentary to it that will make the meaning of the Book of Life clearer for our successors. As a whole year of our life has vanished, it for us to ask: What have we achieved with these possessions? What have we done in the short time we have to improve even our restricted corner of the world? This question was asked of himself by the Quaker missionary Etienne de Grellet. His answer made use of the Biblical concept that we all are strangers and sojourners here on earth. He said:

"I shall pass through this world but once.
If, therefore, there is any kindness I can
show, or any good thing I can do, let me
not defer it or neglect it, for I shall
not pass this way again."

It was over a hundred years ago that the English artist-poet William Blake spoke of fighting "a mental fight" before a better world, "Jerusalem" as he called it, could be built on earth. He was a prophet but still he could not have dreamed how stressful "a mental fight" we need to fight today, almost a hundred and fifty years after his time. We have bitter moods to combat of which he could not dream. We have moved into a world which has

296

lost the Biblical hope of a brotherly future. We have come to a time where even good causes make use of violence and lawlessness and an age in which the sense of insecurity and impermance often corrodes the foundations of character. At such a time when our New Year begins, we turn to the words of King David and hear his grand assertion and firm faith that no matter how shaky the world may seem, it is God's world, created by His infinite mind. He still intends it to have a future. His Law is the basis of its order and a mandate to us. His eternity, contrasted with our transience, spurs us to the urgency of our work. So we ask God's guidance to recover hope, to re-achieve lawful discipline, to be responsible workers in the world, so that in this way our life proclaims our faith that the world is His and we are His co-partners. In this mood, we hope for a New Year, a better and a more blessed year.

XXVIII

WHO SHALL ASCEND?

Everyone daydreams, for daydreaming is a natural, human impulse. Whatever we wish for in life but fail to get, we daydream it into imaginative reality. Daydreaming is the dramatization of our frustrated desires.

King David, whose Twenty-fourth Psalm is our guide this Holyday season, had many wishes which were not fulfilled. Though he had risen from shepherd boy to King of Israel, though he had defeated the enemies of his people and had established a powerful kingdom, there was nevertheless one ardent wish that he was not destined to attain. That wish concerns this very Twenty-fourth Psalm. The Psalm was written after the Ark was recaptured from the Philistines, who had taken it when they defeated King Saul. After regaining the Ark, David captured the city of Jerusalem from the pagan Jebusites and now had brought the Ark into Jerusalem, which henceforth was to be the Holy City for a third of all mankind. He had placed the Ark into an ornate tent within the city walls and then said to Nathan the Prophet, "It is not proper that I should live in a palace panelled in cedar and the Ark of God should remain in a tent. I shall build a Temple on Mount Moriah in the center of Jerusalem." But the Prophet said to him, "You will not be permitted to build the Temple, for you are a warrior; you have slain thousands of people. Not you, the man of war, will build it; but your son Solomon,

Sermon delivered September 23, 1966

whose name means 'peace' will build God's Temple on the holy mountain."

David bowed to the verdict of the Prophet Nathan but, being human, could not help daydreaming that his dear wish to build the Temple was somehow fulfilled. So we can easily imagine how he must have stood on Mount Moriah where the Temple would some day be, and on the stage of his daydream, he saw the gleaming Sanctuary as if it were already in existence. He looked into the distance from the imaginary steps of the imaginary Temple and saw the people streaming in pilgrimage to the Sanctuary on the great festivals. From north and south and west and east they came, and generation after generation. They thronged the roads, those pilgrims of the future. And he must have asked himself in his daydream, "Why are these people of the future worthy of seeing the Temple, and not I?" This thought voiced itself in the line of the Psalm which he wrote: "Who are those who shall ascend the mountain of the Lord, and who shall stand in His Holy Temple?"

We might well believe, since the wings of dreams are tireless, that the king also foresaw the days when the Temple would be destroyed and vanished into history, but that in its place synagogues would rise all over the world and to them, also on the great religious occasions, the distant descendants of David's people would likewise throng in pilgrimage to the holy place, as we do today. In such a vision, the question that David put in the Psalm is addressed to us. He asks, "Who shall ascend?" He answers his own question and says, "He that hath clean hands and a pure heart."

These words of his in their clear simplicity indicate the basic difference between the mood of the New Year and that of this Day of Atonement. On the New Year we spoke of our attitude to the world, our confidence in its future, our resolve that it be established on law and order. But the Day of Atonement is much more personal. It concerns not our world philosophy but rather our inner life. So we ask ourselves what David asked: Who are we who have come today to the House of the Lord? What makes us worthy to come? Which qualities of heart or mind should we look for in ourselves or which elements of personal integrity do we hope somehow to acquire, as today we "ascend" to the Sanctuary of the Lord?

Thomas Carlyle described the difference between animals and human beings as follows: "Man is indeed part of the animal kingdom. But man is a tool-using animal." That is to say: Man is the only animal that can make complicated tools and instruments to aid him and thus to create a civilization. The reason man alone could become a tool-using animal was not only mental but also physical. It was the evolution of the human hand, the fingers and the opposite thumb, which enabled him to grasp a stick and turn it and bend it. The flexible human hand is one of the prime physical evidences of our being human.

No wonder, then, that the hand of man has become one of the great symbols in literature and in religion. If one would study a listing of all the words in the Bible, he would be surprised at how many different ways the hand is used as a spiritual or ethical symbol. The closed hand, the fist, is a symbol of violence and war. The open hand is a symbol of generosity and friendship. The hands raised upward are a symbol of prayer, and the hands forward with the palms down are the protective symbol of affection and blessing.

So when King David speaks of those who are worthy to come to the Sanctuary and asks, "Who shall ascend," he answers simply, "He that hath clean hands." We know at once what those words meant to the king himself who uttered them. He knew why he was not permitted to build and stand in a Temple. His hands were not clean but were stained with blood. Violence stains the hands and makes them unworthy to be raised in prayer. So the Prophet Isaiah, denouncing his people for their hostility to each other, tells them that because of this, God will not listen to their prayers. He puts it in words of unforgettable vividness. He has God saying to these violent people: "When you lift up your hands in prayer, I will close Mine eyes, for your hands are stained with blood."

This primary meaning of bloodshed which stains the hands and makes them unworthy to be lifted in worship is, of course, understandable, but surely to us decent, average people it is inapplicable. We have taken no life; we have, most of us, never struck a human being in anger. Then what can it mean to speak to us of hands bloodstained? The applicable meaning to all of us refers to a special kind of violence of which at one time or another we all are guilty. The Talmud says, "Who is a shedder of blood? He who speaks evil of his neighbor." So in Talmudic parlance, slander is called bloodshed. In fact, David meant that too, as can be seen from his Fifteenth Psalm which is parallel to this one. Here, too, he asks, "Who shall dwell in God's habitation?" And he answers, "Who hath no slander upon his tongue and taketh not up reproach against his neighbor." If slander and gossip were considered bloodshed, then we all have committed violence. Who has not secret joy at being able to whisper some evil against some other human being? Who does not indulge at times in the cruel pleasure of gossip? It is this sin of verbal violence which stains the hands of prayer. The reverse symbol is the open hand of generos-

301

ity, to be kindly when we judge people, to be generous, not only with what we may give, but what we think about others; to see their merits, to appreciate their good intentions—all these turn the fist of violence to the open hand of ethical benevolence.

This explains why the ancient law declares that the sins which we might commit against God directly, God forgives willingly; but the sins that we commit against our fellow man can never be forgiven unless we appease him whom we have injured. The ancient symbol of the hand that strikes and hurts has, then, a definite meaning on the Day of Atonement. None can truly pray unless he strives for this special sort of ethical discipline: never to find joy in other people's sorrows, or delight at their mistakes, or satisfaction at their shame. Once we decide, having come to the House of the Lord to seek in this special sense for clean hands, then the clenched fist of our violence opens into the generous hand of friendship and may even turn over to become the sheltering hand of gracious benediction.

The entire human body is still somewhat a mystery. Although it has been studied by anatomists and physiologists through many centuries, there are still parts of it the precise function of which is not entirely understood. So we must not feel too superior to the people of ancient times that they had mistaken notions about the function and purpose of certain parts of the human body. For example, the people of the past had an entirely wrong idea of the function of the human heart. To us moderns, the heart is a machine whose function is to regulate the movement of the blood through the body. People in ancient times, not knowing of the circulation of the blood, had a completely different idea about the heart. They considered it to be the source of thought and of emotion—in fact to them the heart was the central seat of the entire personality. The many functions that we today would assign to the brain and to certain glands, they assigned them all to the heart. The heart was the sanctuary of the soul, the temple of the personality.

This exalted spiritual function of the heart is referred to in all ancient literature and especially in the Bible. Of a brave man Scripture says, "His heart is firm." Of a truly intelligent man, "He has wisdom of the heart." Of a kindly man, "He knows the heart of the stranger." And deep religious devotion is expressed in the mandate, "Thou shalt love the Lord thy God with all thy heart."

So it is to be expected that when David sought to define religious worthiness, after saying that he who would ascend the mountain of the Lord should have hands cleansed of violence, he adds "and a pure heart." These are simple words; that is to say, the words "a pure heart" would be accepted at once by our fathers as a clear and self-evident ideal. But, strangely enough, this simple ideal has become difficult and unreal to us, their modern descendants. Nowadays we have all been convinced of the truth of Sigmund Freud's doctrine that there is no such thing as a pure heart. He has taught modern mankind that the human subconscious, or as we might say, our heart of hearts, is constantly obsessed by animal appetites and selfish brutality. The idea of a pure heart is out-of-date. It does not exist. It is not even human, and certainly is unattainable.

Yet Freud himself tells us that the natural wildness of human emotions are generally controlled by the influence and discipline of society. Scripture says that too, but somewhat differently: that the evil which certainly exists in our hearts is controlled and disciplined by our religious ideals. So there is the constant prayer in Scripture: "Create in me a clean heart, O God."

303

What needs to be cleansed in the heart is suggested by Freud's great pupil, Alfred Adler. In his judgment the chief source of our emotional storms is what he calls the inferiority-superiority complex. Our greatest misery is the fear that we are treated as inferiors, that our true worth is not appreciated. We hate those whose superiority or whose pretensions of superiority make us feel inferior. This touchiness about our personal importance is natural, but it has become considerably exaggerated in modern times. Every advertisement panders to our sense of superiority. It tells us of our status and our right to the very best products which, of course, means theirs.

This mood of boastful superiority may be a necessity in a competitive world, but it is far from being a religious virture. So for this day when we come out of the boastful world into the Sanctuary, we quit talking of status and of self-importance. Here, at least, we may realize our unimportance, our weaknesses and our many failures. We need not speak of them to others; it is not safe to let other people know our weakness. But at least we can whisper to God and say, "Lord, my heart is not haughty." So to us the Day of Atonement in the Sanctuary is one time and one place in the world when we do not need to put on a bold front, we do not need to advertise our superiority, but can afford to be modest, quiet and humble. Rudyard Kipling, he who was so often Biblical, put it vividly. When all the glories and the boastings melt away:

"Still stands Thine ancient sacrifice,
An humble and a contrite heart."

Only with bowed head may we ascend the mountain of the Lord.

Every legal system requires an oath on the part of

every man who testifies. The oath is an invocation of God to strengthen the claim that what is spoken is the truth. It says, in effect, God is my witness. The ancient Jewish legal system also made use of oaths, but in a way that might seem strange to modern lawyers. It avoided using an oath as much as possible; and if a man was suspected of previous perjury, he was not even permitted to take an oath. It was feared that his oath would be a false one and he would thus commit the sin mentioned in the Ten Commandments of "taking the Name of the Lord in vain."

This protection against the contagious danger of a false oath is mentioned here by King David in his description of the personal religious ideals. After speaking of him "who hath clean hands and a pure heart," he adds as a climax, "who hath not taken My name in vain and hath not sworn deceitfully." Now why should David have considered this legal caution so very important as to include it in his list of cardinal virtues? Clearly he is expressing an idea classic in Judaism that when a man profanes the Name of God, his act affects everybody else and diminishes the holiness of human life. God represents a sacredness that must not be profaned, and to maintain the sense of holiness must be the constant effort of true religion. This feeling is more than Jewish, it is universal. One may truthfully say that there is no religion, no matter how primitive, which does not make a clear distinction between the profane and the holy. In fact, a great European philosopher insists that the sense of holiness is the core of religion and has been so always. There can be no religion without it. If we do not feel that there is something in the world which we revere, something that we must not profane, if we have no sense of sanctity at all, then we have not the slightest scintilla of religious feeling.

Our people in the past understood that well and tried to preserve this sense of sacred reverence. The word

"Kodesh" ("holy") is used hundreds of times in Scripture. The Temple was called "Migdash," "a place of holiness." The Sabbath was called "Shabbas Kodesh," the day for sacred thoughts. The festivals were called "Mikra Kodesh," "the holy convocation," and God was called "Kedosh Isroel," "The Holy One of Israel." They needed no philosopher to tell them what was the central mood of religion. They understood that a life without reverence is a life without decency, without nobility, and without the hallmark of humanity.

That which our fathers understood easily, we who are wiser in many ways than they find it now hard to grasp. Everything in our modern life fights against reverence. No sooner does a great and honored leader die than a biography like an ugly weed leaps out of the mud to besmirch his memory. We are not reverential today. We prefer to be sophisticated, as we call it, too smart to trust anybody or to respect anything. Because of the modern mood of irreverence, we suffer more than we realize. There is no public servant whom we really trust, no leader we honor, no institution which we deeply revere. There is nothing higher than we ourselves, and nothing beyond our cynical contempt. It is, of course, true that many things that were revered in the past do not deserve respect, and we have gained by tearing down certain idols from their pedestal; but there must be something left in our life which we consider too pure to be besmirched, too noble to be scorned. That is the meaning of David's declaration, "Take not the Name of the Lord our God in vain." God in our life represents the inner and sacred sanctuary of our existence. Him we revere. His is the Final Sanctity from which is derived our respect for all of life.

This is the climactic mood of the Day of Atonement, which is the Sabbath of Sabbaths, the Holy of the Holies in our religious calendar. Here we understand that our religion is our inner sanctuary; that it must never be cheapened, but will be maintained in the unspoiled splendor of it. For everything we revere in life springs from this central, breathless reverence. Holy is the Lord of Hosts. The whole world is filled with His glory.

The founders of the State of Israel, many of whom were not particularly religious, found nevertheless a special inspiration in this Twenty-fourth Psalm. Just as in David's daydream, when he saw the pilgrims of the future streaming to the mountain of the Lord and asked, "Who shall ascend," so the founders of the modern state saw Jews from every land streaming to establish a new commonwealtth; and they, too, used David's term and called the pilgrimage of new settlers a climbing up to the homeland, an ascent. For this world-wide immigration they used David's term and called it "Aliyah." Thus we might say that that new state is a part of David's daydream, as we all are part of it, whatever be the land of our habitation. The word which David used, an ascent, an Aliyah, reveals the essence of our faith. Our religious life is a constant uphill journey, never ended. We do not believe that anybody has ever reached the religious goal, that he is forever saved; nor that he is forever lost on the way, that he is eternally doomed. Whoever falls on the road can rise again and continue his march to the Sanctuary. We know when we are on the right road. There are landmarks along the way. There is the marker which reads "clean hands," that we rise above verbal cruelty and be merciful in judgment and action. There is the further marker called "pure heart," which means that we brush aside pretenses of self-importance and attain some humility in thought. And right at the gates of the Holy City, a monument marked "reverence for the Name of God the Eternal." On this road marked out by the ancient king, we journey this year and, with God's goodness, for many more years on this Holy Day unto His Holy mountain.

307